WHAT OTHERS ARE SAYING ABOUT *CASTING QS*

"This is a peculiar business and the process of getting work can be a frustrating one. While many actors arrive in Los Angeles with a good knowledge of their craft, they have no understanding of the business and can wind up discouraged and jaded. Bonnie's book does a tremendous job of demystifying the *other side* and can shave years off the learning curve. A very valuable resource."

—Bob Clendenin, SAG/AFTRA/AEA

"Every casting director is different, and each one has strong opinions on what is expected of an actor at an audition. Knowing ahead of time what that particular casting person likes and hates can be extremely helpful to the performer. Bonnie's book is an invaluable source for this information, and should become a part of every actor's preparation."

—Michael Donovan, CSA/CCDA

"When you're involved in an industry as complex and complicated as casting, it's essential to know the ins and outs without ever getting lost in the shuffle. Bonnie's writing is always clear, to the point, purposeful and thoroughly readable. She delves deep into her subject matter and breaks it down to the basics so that her writing is at once simple yet inspiring and always insightful. Her entertaining style engages readers from the get-go and she doesn't let go until you walk away with a clear understanding of her topic. Whether you're a beginner in the industry or a polished professional, her writings are informative, fun-to-read gems everyone—at any level in the industry—can appreciate."

—Carla Lewis & Angela Bertolino, Hollywood OS

"When it comes to the business of acting, we actors like to put our heads in the sand so we can concentrate on our art. Bonnie Gillespie expertly reminds us that, by doing a little homework, we can have more control over our careers than we think. Reading Bonnie's book is like having a personal manager who not only can guide you through the general audition process, but who also can prepare you specifically for auditions in sitcoms, dramas, soaps, commercials, films, and theatre. As a former actor, she asks the questions we need answered. Bonnie captures the personalities of each casting director and therefore humanizes that necessary evil we call The Audition Process."

—Faith Salie, SAG/AEA

"Bonnie is the only one who has the most up-to-date casting director information."

—Judy Kerr, actor/author/coach

For my mother,
whose spirit writes with mine.

TABLE OF CONTENTS

8–Casting Qs

FOREWORD

Like all industries, the entertainment industry is composed of people doing their jobs, and of applicants seeking jobs. But similarities to most other industries end there. In what other big business is the work as transient, as job-to-job, as it is in showbiz? Even in our age of full-time work-at-home freelancers, Hollywood still has the market cornered on turnover; every project is like a new small business for which a new team of workers must be assembled, then disbanded, and then the next one assembled, disbanded, and so on, ad nauseam, in an endless continuum that stretches from yellowed back issues of the trades to casting breakdowns yet to be released.

Add to this ceaseless upheaval the fact that there's a huge imbalance of supply and demand—literally hundreds of thousands of actors, and just hundreds of available roles each year. Small wonder, then, that in Hollywood not only the task of seeking work has become professionalized—with agents and managers out pounding the pavement for their clients' next gigs—but the task of hiring has become a full-time professional post, as well. Casting directors for films are either hired film to film, on a freelance basis along with the caterers and editors and the actors, though some toil regularly on contract at big film studios; casting directors for television, like most everyone else on that golden teat, tend to have staff jobs. But even for the salaried casting folks, the secret at the heart of their job is that they're the most actor-oriented workers on any project; they are the closest to the potentials and pitfalls of the acting craft; they are often the only ones on the production payroll who are in the actors' corner; most of them are former actors themselves, and/or have paid dues in that crucible of all narrative arts, the theatre. And the best of them are craftspeople as skilled and as essential to the aesthetic quality of a Hollywood product as the cinematographer or the composer; the Emmys recognize this each year, while the Oscars have been notoriously intransigent about adding a "casting" category. Certain myths die hard—and the myth of the director or producer who "discovers" the Next Big Thing is one of the hardiest.

Savvy actors, among whom I count the readers of *Back Stage West*, know better. They know that behind every actor introduced in the popular media as an "overnight success" are years of hard work, training, striving, and dedication. And while smart actors certainly don't shun connections with directors, producers, and the town's miscellaneous mucky-mucks, it is casting directors they most sincerely want to impress, casting directors whom they crave as fans, casting directors who give them some semblance of an appreciative, attuned audience, and who strive to create some space for the acting process, in this town of pitch meetings over conference calls.

If their gatekeeper status perhaps confers an inflated or intimidating sense of power on casting directors, that is where a column like Bonnie Gillespie's probing, informative, practical-minded "Casting Qs" comes in handy: to remind the actor-readers of *Back Stage West* that these are people, after all, just doing their jobs. And it's my hope that readers will not only gain a touchy-feely new level of understanding of the people across the table or on the mailing label, but that this information will in fact be useful in getting them work and preparing them for auditions. As much as the bookstore shelves are clogged with "inspirational" self-help tomes, is there anything more inspirational than information that fairly cries out to be used?

In short, I hope that Bonnie's new book, culled from "Casting Qs" columns that previously appeared in *Back Stage West*, is one that you'll keep wanting to put down—just so you can immediately act on its advice, now—but which won't let you go 'til it's done.

That's what actors do, after all: take in the text, then make it live on its feet. Prepare, then let 'er rip.

Read, then act.

—Rob Kendt
Editor-in-Chief/Associate Publisher
Back Stage West

INTRODUCTION

Most people understand that a film is first a script. Next, a producer agrees to see the script through the process of becoming a film. A director is attached to the project, bringing to the table ideas of ways in which the script can best take shape in becoming a successful feature film. Then, filming begins.

Wait... not so fast. Before the first reel of film is loaded into a camera, there must be a cast. Time to hire your film's casting director.

The job of casting director is a behind-the-scenes one. The casting director is typically hired very early on in the pre-production period of filmmaking. A casting director prescreens hundreds, sometimes thousands of actors for the dozens of roles in each film. The roles are summarized by the casting director, who reads the script and creates role descriptions, called character breakdowns. The casting director then begins pouring over headshots (8x10 black-and-white photographs of actors) and resumés, auditioning actors using short scenes from the film (called sides), and, often, working with the actors in order to bring out their best performance prior to bringing selected actors to the attention of the film's producers and director. Once a film is populated with its cast (selected by the producers and director, after having been recommended by the casting director), the casting director typically moves on to her next project, usually changing production offices, assistant staffs, and, frequently, style or genre of projects... drastically. Casting directors are required to know what actors are "out there" and which actors might be capable of playing what types of roles. This expertise is what the producers and director count on, when hiring a casting director for their projects.

There is no official training program for casting directors. Most casting directors in Los Angeles have a background in theatre, are former actors, have worked as agents, or simply knew from an early age that the job of casting director was their destiny. Working up from casting intern to casting assistant, getting promoted to associate casting director and then starting to win jobs as the primary casting director is a typical course of action for the casting director-to-be. This process can take anywhere from three to ten years.

Most casting directors enjoy their behind-the-scenes status, as their glory comes in assembling a strong cast, contributing to the overall process of producing an excellent end-product. There is no Oscar for Best Casting Director, although there is an Emmy for Best Television Casting. The Casting Society of America awards several of its members an Artios Award each year for excellence in casting. Most casting directors find joy in the journey of taking words in print and helping turn them into living words, delivered by actors who allow consumers to get lost in the world of the creation.

* * *

For years, I felt as though my edge over many actors in my category came not necessarily through talent, but through my ability to work a room, to target my self-promotion, and to maintain contacts. Many actors, at industry events, will gravitate toward the celebrity they recognize, hoping that schmoozing that person will get them closer to a job. The business-minded actor has an eye on the casting director in the room, knowing that a well-timed conversation with that person could be far more beneficial.

In addition to being a valuable resource for specific casting director interview content, this book includes compiled overviews of information that actors so desperately crave, when trying to demystify the casting director relationship. I have interviewed a broad cross-section of the casting community and the information I've gathered is quantifiable. The presentation of this information can only further assist the actor on her journey.

I have long believed that the more information an actor has, the more prepared, the more professional, and the more skilled she has the opportunity to be. The focus on the art becomes much clearer, once the business end is mastered. Actors who write to me have questions about the total environment of casting. I have perspective on this that benefits the acting population.

My goal in interviewing casting directors is to have the reader feel as if she were sitting right there in the room with me, getting to know the casting director. I have chosen not to include contact information on these casting directors (with the exception of the occasional website or hotline number) due to the fact that casting tends to be a nomadic profession, wherein casting directors will move from one production office to another several times throughout one year. What I recommend readers do is purchase the Breakdown Services *CD Directory*, published several times per year, in order to find current mailing addresses for submissions.

Additionally, the credits within each interview are by no means comprehensive. I recommend a visit to IMDB.com for a more complete list of casting credits. The information I have provided is merely a snapshot of the casting directors' resumés.

This book is intended to be a reference guide. I suggest that you pull it from the shelf before an audition with any of the casting directors I've interviewed. If you read this book cover-to-cover, you may be frustrated with the conflicting advice or bored by the repetition of specific words of wisdom. For an overview of information, I have set aside an analysis of the most commonly-asked questions about how an actor may put her best foot forward. Note that any specific mention of a company within these pages is simply that: a mention. I have not been paid to represent any company or service in good favor and no assumption as to the reputation of such companies and service should be made by the reader. Additionally, the information provided herein does not represent, on the part of the author or publishing company, a recipe for success, a guarantee of a job, or even a promise of increased confidence in audition situations.

Finally, please note that I have chosen to refer to casting directors using the female pronoun in my non-interview chapters. This is not due to some feminist agenda, but due to the fact that casting is one of the only female-dominated segments of the entertainment industry.

Please enjoy *Casting Qs*. If you have borrowed this book from a friend and would like one of your own, please flip to the back of the book for an order form or visit CricketFeet.com.

ACKNOWLEDGMENTS

Not one page of this book would exist were it not for the generous spirit and open office doors of every casting director I've met. Actors live a courageous life... and I have learned that casting directors do too. Thank you, casting professionals, for your enthusiastic candor.

Thank you to the tireless and talented staff at *Back Stage West* including Lori Talley, Jamie Painter Young, Scott Proudfit, Dany Margolies, Pamela Bock, Laura Weinert, and Tracy Miller. Rob Kendt contributed not only the foreword, but also guidance in my process as a writer. Thank you for bringing me on board as a columnist, and thank you for being in my corner at all times. I appreciate the secret weapon of all good things at *Back Stage West*, Rosa Fernandez. Your help—and, most of all, your friendship—means the world to me.

Whether they will ever know it or not, I need to express gratitude for the guidance provided by Deborah Jacobson (whose excellent book, *Survival Jobs* changed my life) and Dan Poynter (whose excellent book, *The Self-Publishing Manual* would change it again). I can only hope to bring such guiding light to my readers.

Thank you to my family and friends, too numerous to name one-by-one. Your excitement over my process has kept me going more than you may ever know. Specifically, my online friends at Wolfesden.net, The Actor's Bone, BackStage.com's Career Chat, and my heroes at Yahoo! group Somesuch-

Whatnot inspire me constantly. Additionally, I am grateful to Roxbury Publishing Company and the family it has created for me in Los Angeles. A very special shoutout goes to Rose Auerbach, whose influence is felt in my life every day.

Of course, I must thank my many, many actor friends who have requested specific interviews, suggested topics that interest them, and forced me to refine my work when it needed that. Also, thank you to every casting assistant and associate casting director who helped me woo an interview out of some shy casting director in your office.

Finally, I humbly admit that I owe so much to my partner and publisher, Keith Johnson. His faith in me has resulted in far more than this book, and for all of the bounty, I am forever grateful.

THE FIRST THING AN ACTOR SHOULD DO

Those of us who live in Los Angeles may take for granted the fact that actors coming to Los Angeles have already trained, saved money for living expenses, gotten great headshots, and auditioned for an amazing play. Not so fast. Those who come to Los Angeles need to prioritize and that's where a few busy casting directors can help.

What's the First Thing an Actor Should Do Upon Arrival in Los Angeles? *I asked that one question of casting directors, hoping their answers could help actors understand the fundamental ingredients to a successful Los Angeles experience.*

Participating Casting Directors

Judy Belshé, commercials, films
Terry Berland, CCDA, commercials
Victoria Burrows, films
Craig Campobasso, CSA, films, television, former actor
Mike Fenton, CSA, films
Elisa Goodman, CSA, films, MOWs, television, former actor
Marc Hirschfeld, CSA, Executive VP of Talent & Casting, NBC Television

Melissa Martin, CCDA, commercials, former actor
Mark Paladini, CSA, films, television
Linda Phillips-Palo, CSA, films, MOWs
Kevin Scott, CSA, Warner Bros. Television
Tina Seiler, films, television
Caprisha Smyles, All Smyles Casting, Inc., films
Pamela Starks, commercials
Mark Teschner, CSA, ABC Television, former actor

Motivation

There are people of all walks of life that arrive in Los Angeles every day to become actors. Have you defined what will make you different? Do you have an internal goal? This goal is not the one you talk and grumble about. It's the one inside that you truly believe about yourself. —Belshé

Truly examine your motivation for becoming an actor. Be honest with yourself and don't settle for the easy answers like, "I just want to work," or "I just want to be respected." Figure out your personal mission, and hopefully, it's more resonant than showing up Marcie Schwartz back home who beat you out for Marian the Librarian in the high school play. —Paladini

Have the passion, desire, and commitment to your craft. Come to Los Angeles believing in yourself, having complete confidence in your ability. This business is too competitive and cruel for the weak. —Smyles

Preparation

Buy a car! This is the very first thing an actor should do. Then go buy [an] agency [guide] book, get a list of acting classes, and *Back Stage West* and read up on what is [going on] around town. —Burrows

When you arrive in Los Angeles, you should create an orientation month, just like colleges do. Itemize your needs: housing, car, insurance, day or night job, union card (a must talk to other actors and find out how they got theirs). —Phillips-Palo

The first thing you should do upon arrival is get a *Thomas Bros. Guide* and drive around to all the different studios and networks. This will help ease the anxiety of not knowing where your next audition may be and how long it may take you to get where you are going. —Scott

Go to Samuel French [bookstore] and buy agency and casting director guides. Circle the agents you think you would like to be with. Circle the casting directors you want to target based on what specific shows or types of casting they do. — Martin

Training

Invest time and effort in the activity of training. Classes can help you advance in your craft as well as give you the chance to interact and learn with other actors. —Smyles

Audit a number of classes. This gives you the opportunity to get a feel for the different sensibilities in this town and, just as importantly, puts you in contact with other actors. That energy opens up ideas to other classes, photographers, theatre companies, etc. The only way an actor who is new to town is going to get a feel for what is going on is by connecting with other actors. —Teschner

Classes help actors blend into the community and help [when selecting] agents and managers. Stay away from packaging groups that want to set you up with pictures, agents, classes, etc. They charge too much for stuff you can do on your own for a fraction of the cost. —Burrows

Get into a strong acting class for six months. Then take an audition class. Get on–set training by being an extra. When you're ready, go out on audition calls from *Back Stage West* to iron out any flaws in your audition techniques before you start meeting agents and CSA casting directors. — Campobasso

Actors who come from regional areas usually do not have the proper edge that is needed to compete in Los Angeles.

Being in class will give you the time to adjust and gather information about the new arena you are competing in. — Berland

If you are a very new actor, you must, of course, get yourself into acting classes. There are many types of studies and methodologies. Hopefully, if you are coming to Los Angeles to act, you have done your homework so that you are not a green actor, just agentless. If you can come to Los Angeles with your SAG card from another city, all the better. —Martin

Getting into a good acting class is the priority, but I also recommend classes that deal with the practical aspects of the job, which most colleges are loath to provide. —Paladini

As a talent, you don't work every week, but when you are in class, you are working and validating why you are here. Shop around and learn from different teachers. The business is not made up of just one personality and neither should your experience. Glean from each class what helped you. —Belshé

Find a good class if you need one. It helps ease anxiety of being alone. You might hear about projects being cast you might be right for. It keeps your mind and instrument flexible. —Goodman

Headshots

Headshots are important. Be in control of your own look and style for the headshots. Interview numerous photographers. —Burrows

Get some good headshots. —Seiler

Start by getting recommendations from people who know, and look at examples of the photographer's work and meet the photographer. A photo from a regional area will not fly in Los Angeles. —Berland

Put together your postcard or headshot and resumé with a teeny–tiny cover letter that says you're new in town and seeking representation, or to casting directors saying, "Please feel free to call me directly at this number." Be brief. [We] already know what you want. Use your circled names from the guide you bought at Samuel French to do your mailers. If you are overwhelmed and not normally a good businessperson, do ten mailers a day. —Martin

Get a good headshot that looks like you. Although when you do land an agent, they may want you to get them re–shot if they want to sell you a particular way. —Goodman

Obtain a photograph that really looks like you and represents the sense one would get from you in person. So many people misrepresent themselves in their photos, which usually doesn't get them much but disappointed. The photo doesn't have to be a professional one. A casual, clean headshot just taken by a friend can sometimes tell a casting director so much more than the specially made-up and lit so-called professional photo. —Starks

Invest in a good theatrical and commercial headshot that looks exactly like you look *now*. Too often, actors submit headshots that look nothing like [them]. —Smyles

Survival Job

It's not a simple job. At the end of the week, there is no paycheck for auditioning. How are you going to support yourself? Nothing makes a person more depressed or makes you feel off base like *no money*. This business does take money, even if it's buying shoe leather to walk to the next audition. — Belshé

From a very realistic point-of-view, an actor should get a flexible day job. You will definitely need it until the acting work hopefully starts rolling in. —Starks

Find a job that supports your time constraints. — Goodman

Theatre

Do some local theatre. —Seiler

Theatre companies are great places to work on your craft. —Burrows

If you want to get into a play, pick up *Back Stage West* for possible leads. If the play is too far out of town, people may not come to see you. Make sure the commitment-level of those involved is high. Most people in this town do a play for the exposure instead of committing to do the material. That is why most plays are so uneven and the agents and casting directors have been burned going to see so much bad theatre. If you are going to do a play, serve the material first, yourself second. Otherwise, it will not turn out well. —Goodman

Join a good theatre company and start networking with other actors. Don't do mass mailings unless you've got a good tape to show or you're in a piece of theatre you're proud of. —Hirschfeld

Representation

Get a good—notice I said *good*—agent. —Fenton

Seek and secure representation, whether it is an agent at a large or small agency or even a personal manager. Most important is that whomever agrees to represent you is really interested in you, your abilities and appearance, and actively wants to seek work for you. A lot of agents will take an actor on and then do absolutely nothing to advance that actor's career other than sending out the actor's headshot along with several hundred others. —Starks

Find a good agent that can commit to the representation of you and your career. A commercial agent is usually the easiest to find. Finding a good theatrical agent can be a hard task (especially if you are new to the game and have no credits on your resumé), but keep searching and don't get discouraged. —Smyles

Mail submissions to agents and managers only if you feel they are open to your style and type of character. Learn that through the agency books. Agents and managers are great for careers. They are supposed to collect ten to 20% from talent depending on what deal you strike up. It is not customary for talent to pay for representation. —Burrows

Networking

Network, network, network. Don't be afraid to ask questions and get advice. —Phillips-Palo

It's actually a very small town and there is always a connection from one person to another who knows someone who might help you. —Goodman

Once you are sure of your goal and you've settled on your income, it's time to network. I will always believe in acting classes. This is where you meet others like yourself. People that are having the same experience and drive as you. That is very comforting in this business. Network, make friends, be a friend. Then pray you get on a show that is the next *Friends*. —Belshé

Try to go to some of the commercial casting offices that are in town. You can drive your headshots around to the offices that have multiple casting companies in them. Put your headshot in the bin of each casting director. Do it once a week. It will help alleviate any intimidation you might have when you become familiar with each space and see fellow actors inside. Also, if the casting director happens to be casting a project that you are right for at that moment, you have as much a chance as anyone else to be considered and selected. Make sure your phone number is on *everything*. Casting directors do not always keep headshots on file, so keep making the rounds. You will feel proactive and professional. Hard work and talent always pay off. Success is nothing but hard work [recognized]. —Martin

HOW TO CONTACT A CASTING DIRECTOR

So, you're in Los Angeles, you've trained, perhaps you've secured representation, you have amazing photographs and a decent resumé. Now, how do you make contact with casting directors? When? And what are the rules of engagement?

According to Jeff Gerrard, there are no rules. "You must feel it out for yourself. There is no right or wrong," he said. "Do what you need to do to get seen without imposing."

With that in mind, read on for the guidelines as spelled out by several busy casting directors, keeping in mind that, as always, the number one priority for all casting directors is that you approach them with professionalism. Everything else is secondary, although still vitally important.

Participating Casting Directors

Judy Belshé, commercials, films
Terry Berland, CCDA, commercials
Jackie Briskey, CSA, television
Lori Cobe-Ross, films, television
Eddie Foy III, television
Jeff Gerrard, CCDA, commercials, former actor
Cathy Kalmenson, Kalmenson & Kalmenson Casting, voiceovers

Donna Morong, CSA, VP Casting, Disney Touchstone Pictures
Stuart Stone, CCDA, commercials
Katy Wallin, CSA, films, television

How To Contact a Casting Director

Send a headshot and resumé to the address specified in the Breakdowns. For guidelines specific to me, visit the Ask Judy section at www.showbizkid.com. —Belshé

The best way to contact me is with a postcard. —Stone

The very best way to meet a casting director is to know someone who knows the casting director and who may set up a meeting. Other than that, send an 8x10 with a short note and follow up about every three months with a photo postcard and note. —Berland

In theory, actors should not contact casting directors but should have their agent or manager do so. —Cobe-Ross

Send a photo and resumé, stapled together, along with a short cover letter that has your own unique personality coming through. Make sure that the photograph represents you and the way you're going to walk through my door on your best day or your crappiest day. Actors are getting aware of the fact that the *real* actor is who we want to see, especially in commercials. —Gerrard

Use the mail. It's not a good idea to call a casting office. —Wallin

Send your photo and resumé with a note letting me know you've just come to town. Without a cover letter, your picture gets lost in the shuffle. There's just not as much of an impression without a letter. Postcards are good to notify me of your TV appearances, plays, changes in your representation. —Morong

In voiceover casting, it doesn't matter what the heck you look like. It's all based on what you can communicate with that God-given instrument commonly known as your voice. Ours is an endeavor to develop or uncover talent that has not been used before in our voiceover community. So, you should submit your demo tape (under two minutes) via your agent, come to me via performance showcases (flyers and postcards are welcome), or via education (we conduct eight classes a week). —Kalmenson

Send your photo and resumé with your height and age range noted. —Briskey

By phone or mail. I answer my own phone. —Foy

When To Contact a Casting Director

A representative should submit an actor only when the actor is appropriate for a specific role. —Cobe-Ross

Submit when you hear we're working on an actual project (via *Back Stage West*, Breakdown Service's Actor Access). The information is open to everyone. Not everyone has an agent (less than 25% of Los Angeles actors, according to my independent research). My job is to service the producer by finding the best talent. I want to give everyone a chance to audition. I utilize every online service to get the word out about my auditions. It's not privileged information. It's public! —Belshé

Contact me to let me know when you're on TV or in a play. —Briskey

I prefer agent submissions, but also accept manager and unsolicited submissions based on the breakdowns I have out at the time. I love postcards to know when you're doing a play, have a new agent, have a spot on TV, are doing an independent film. I get hundreds of postcards a week. It lets me know you're working. It's a great marketing tool. Market your own business. Be very specific and have a great headshot, since it is your calling card. —Wallin

I respect the actor's desire to tell me what they feel is appropriate, so they can contact me whenever they want to. —Stone

Submit your photo and resumé when you have an update, a new picture, a new look. Always stay current and send a postcard or 8x10 every three months or so, as that's how often we rotate out our crops of photos. Let us know, with a flyer postcard, when you're doing a show or appearing on TV. —Gerrard

Call during the workday to let me know you want a job. —Foy

I don't think there's ever any one right time to submit. When we're doing work that you think you may be right for, get your photo and resumé to us. Be smart, target who you're sending to, and know why you're contacting me. Do your homework so that you know what the casting director is casting. Check the trades, and when you see that a movie I'm supervising is in the casting stage, that's the ideal time to contact me. —Morong

Absolute No-No's for Casting Director Contact

You should never, never, never audition for a casting director until you are ready. Study, study, and then study some more. You'll know it's time to contact a casting director when your inner self, your confidence, says so; when your acting coaches say so; and when you are sought out in your workshops and classes as an actor others want to pair up with. Everyone gravitates toward good actors. Once that's you, send me your stuff. —Gerrard

No drop-ins, but a drop-*off* of your voiceover tape is okay. —Kalmenson

Phone calls are never appropriate. Don't crash my audition. Let me decide who I want to see. I'm already pretty open, so please don't crash. —Belshé

With a phone call, you could be bothering me during a bad time. A postcard is better. —Stone

If an actor does not have representation, the actor should contact a casting director by sending a photo and resumé by mail only. We are swamped with calls. —Cobe-Ross

Calling is not such a great idea. Also, no unsolicited tape, for my office. Beyond that, I don't respond to gimmicks. An actor once sent me a piece of gum every week. I never brought him in. Chewed the gum, though! It just cheapens you. You have to trust that you're enough. —Morong

A lot of new actors do outlandish things to get my attention. I was once sent a box with bloodstains on the outside. We opened it, and inside was a bloody foot. I was sent a bloody, severed foot! The note attached read, "I just want to get a foot in the door somehow." Please don't go to that extent! Let your headshot and resumé be your marketing tool. That should be enough. —Wallin

No phone calls, except from agents and managers. No unsolicited tapes, photo and resumé only. —Briskey

Do not call me to ask who I am, what I do, what's my address, what I'm working on. If you don't know who, what, why, and where you're calling, I respectfully suggest you find another occupation. It shows me you haven't done your homework. An actor can't participate if he isn't trained and prepared. I believe if an actor is careless on introduction, then he will be careless in his work. —Foy

I was once on a shuttle at LAX with an actor who [had] just arrived to pursue his career. He found out I was a commercial casting director and said that he wasn't interested in commercials, as he was a theatre actor pursuing a career in film. I mentioned it was unusual and interesting not to want to pursue all venues. A year later, I was greeted in the reception area of my office with, "Remember me? I shared a shuttle with you a year ago." I said, "Oh, yes. What are you doing here?" He answered, "Commercials." I laughed to myself at that point. —Berland

The moral of the story? Keep in mind that the first impression lasts, even when it occurs outside of the casting director's office. Be ready. Always.

CASTING DIRECTOR STATISTICS

Casting directors have shared with me their preferences for actor contact, their tolerance for various pet peeves, and their interest in attending theatre or using online casting methods. Rather than asking you, the reader, to sift through the interviews to quantify that information, I've put together the statistics here, with the hopes that you will be able to choose how to best spend your money. Should you invest in the purchase of props for your auditions? No. Should you spend money getting your headshot and resumé on a website? Not just yet. Should you pay a small membership fee to a theatre company? Possibly.

Those decisions, of course, are up to you. Here are the numbers, based on the over-100 casting director interviews I've conducted.

Casting Directors' Top Pet Peeves

57%   **Unpreparedness** (actors who haven't picked up sides well in advance of their audition, actors who haven't made solid choices with their character portrayal, actors who don't know whether the show for which they're auditioning is a sitcom or a dramatic episodic)

25%   **Tardiness/No-Shows** (actors who come in anything less than *early* for their audition, actors who have booked auditions and then do not show up or call to cancel)

18%   **Props/Manhandling the Reader** (actors who use props in their audition, actors who follow physical directions in the script to the extent that they handle the casting director— kissing, hugging, hitting, grabbing, etc.)

17%   **Misleading Headshots** (actors who submit headshots that are overly-glamorous, that are older than a year or two, that were taken at a lower or higher weight than the actor is now, that were taken when an actor had more or less hair than she does now, that misrepresent the person who will ultimately walk through the door for the audition)

Non-traditional Casting Methods

57%   **Attend Theatre Regularly** (especially plays with large casts, good reviews, and at theatres with easily-accessed parking and facilities)

54%   **Will Consider Using Online Casting Methods** (mainly for specific—and unusual—needs not met by more traditional casting methods, additionally used for checking actors' representation or credits much more than for seeking talent—the percentage of casting directors that prefer online casting methods to traditional methods is closer to 3%)

Remember, most casting directors are pleased to receive postcards with updates about your theatrical performances, appearance on TV shows, screenings of films you've worked on, changes in representation, and general, "Hi... I'm still here," notes. Phone calls are not ever encouraged.

The most frequently-mentioned "wise use" of the actor's dollar is a listing in the *Academy Player's Directory*. When casting directors do go online, they usually go to the online version of this directory. Every casting director I have spoken with still prefers to sit on the floor of her office, surrounded by stacks of headshots. The casting director is working to assemble a puzzle. That is a hands-on activity.

DOING THEATRE

Casting directors always advise actors, "Do theatre. Get involved in theatre. Do a play. Period." Actors write me to ask, "Does that really work?" So, I posed a few questions to several busy casting directors, in an attempt to find out precisely why they so strongly recommend working in theatre.

Participating Casting Directors

Judy Belshé, commercials, films
Terry Berland, CCDA, commercials
Kate Brinegar, CSA, films
Danny Goldman, CCDA, commercials, former actor
Michael Greer, CSA, films
Richard Hicks, CSA, films, television, former actor
Harvey Kalmenson, Kalmenson & Kalmenson, voiceovers
Dino Ladki, films, television
Melissa Martin, CCDA, commercials, former actor
Cathy Reinking, CSA, films, television
Stephen Snyder, films
Katy Wallin, CSA, films, television

Why Los Angeles Actors Should Do Theatre

Doing theatre develops a whole separate set of muscles, which only enhance your work in TV and movies. —Hicks

Having come from a theatre background, I am a gigantic believer in stage work. My biggest beef with watching some of the theatre in Los Angeles is that the evening is used primarily as a tool to get an agent. The bio will even suggest to the audience that [an actor] is in need of one. I've seen some pretty sloppy work with half-hearted commitment and generally very green acting skills. Theatre is a worthy medium and should be treated as such. —Martin

Theatre does a lot of things for people that actors don't even realize. Take out of the equation whether you're going to be seen. Ask yourself, "Am I an actor?" If the answer is yes, then theatre needs to be included in your life. It lets you feel entertaining and it means you're being faithful to the part of you that says you're an entertainer. —Belshé

The theatre scene in Los Angeles is growing. Anything that an actor can do to fuel their soul and work out as an actor is important. It allows people to see their work and allows them to continue to exercise their acting muscles and rejuvenate their own self. I feel like theatre is growing in Los Angeles. I have found so much undiscovered talent in theatre. I really respect actors that are involved in the theatre community. They're working. They're taking a proactive role in their career. The theatre scene needs to be more acknowledged here. It is so key to keeping people balanced, being in a community to support your creative work. —Wallin

It's very important for actors to always keep working. I give preference to theatre actors at commercial auditions. If you think about it, commercial auditions are really just face scans. We have to go to theatre to see who's improvisational and who can work on their feet. —Goldman

The most important tool facilitating the actor's strength and growth is and always will be live theatre! The stage generates and represents a never-ending educational stimulus for actors in all stages of their career. —Kalmenson

Actors should do theatre because it is the ultimate workout in their craft. It is good to have strong theatre on a resumé. It shows tenacity and is also a good way to possibly be seen. An actor should not do theatre for the sole purpose of being seen. They should do it because they enjoy digging their chops into a piece. —Berland

Doing theatre is valuable to learn your craft and get exposure! —Snyder

Acting is a profession you can't do from home. Unless acting is as important as eating and breathing, you should do something else. But, if this is what you want to do, you need to perform in front of an audience as often as possible. It's good practice (most of us get better at something we do often), it's good discipline (all those rehearsals, matinees, shows, late nights), and there is the opportunity to be seen by people who could help you get bigger, better projects (no one's going to notice you sitting by the phone or waiting tables). I can't imagine an actor not wanting to do theatre. Performing in front of an audience is so immediately gratifying. [There is] nothing like applause, nothing like a standing ovation to make you love what you do. It encourages and energizes. —Greer

Theatre is an outlet for actors to keep themselves warmed up, supple, pliable. As a former actor, I think theatre frees your soul. It's the most wonderful exercise an actor can have. —Brinegar

Actors should do theatre for the love of it, not because they want to be seen. Sometimes, even if the play is not very good, there are good people in the play. We remember them. —Reinking

Their Opinion on Actively Attending Theatre

Our staff of ten casting directors attends theatre on a weekly basis. Finding new talent is an absolute must. Attending theatre also allows us to experience a broader scope of actors than we otherwise would be exposed to. —Kalmenson

I actively attend theatre. Unfortunately, I only end up going a couple of times a month. —Berland

I attend theatre very, very regularly, about once or twice a week. I see a lot of theatre, from equity waiver to regional. —Reinking

I attend at least four to six plays a month and three to four showcases a month. I guest in about 12 different casting director workshops a year. —Snyder

I go at least once a week or more. —Goldman

For me, Los Angeles theatre is a 100-mile round trip, so I don't always get to theatre. It's an event, when I do. —Belshé

How often I go goes in waves. Generally, I attend theatre two to three times a month. —Hicks

I do actively attend theatre. How often I go is dependent on the type of project I am casting and what sort of deadline I am looking at. When casting for sketch performers and/or hosts, I make the rounds of plays, one-person shows, showcases, and comedy clubs several times a week and often bring my producer with me. It is not unlikely that I attend a show because a friend of a friend is in something or an agent I am fond of has asked me to attend their client's performance. I attend theatre whether I am actively casting a project or not, because I enjoy it. —Ladki

I do attend theater. It depends on how busy I am. I probably go [to plays] five or six times a year. I also regularly see the Groundlings and showcases at USC and UCLA. —Greer

Calling Actors in After a Show

I do it often. I pull people in from plays, showcases, whatever. —Brinegar

I do bring people in from theatre. I brought my eight-week-old baby to a play because I was casting for a pilot. I had to leave at intermission because he decided to start babbling. Even so, I found an actor at that show that went all the way down to the final callback for the pilot. —Wallin

I call in actors I've seen in plays all the time. I'm more impressed by a long list of plays an actor has appeared in than a dozen TV or indie credits. —Greer

I have called in countless comedian/actors after seeing them perform on stage at local comedy clubs. For example, after seeing the one-act play *An Evening with Price, Nash, and Blieden* at the HBO Workspace, I called in all three performers (Matt, Jason, and Michael, respectively). The trio is currently developing a sitcom with Warner Bros. TV, NBC, and HBO based on this one-act play. —Ladki

I have seen actors on stage and brought them in for a session. By the time a play is over, I'm in love with one or two of the actors and I will call them in. —Belshé

Not only have I brought actors in, but I've found them agents. I'll call an actor in here based on a theatre performance and then get an agent on the phone and work something out. I do that regularly, when I see someone I really believe in. Theatre allows me to do that. —Goldman

On average, I bring in about 20% of all actors I've seen in plays or showcases, as well as rediscover actors who I may have lost touch with or have temporarily forgotten to call in. —Snyder

I have looked for actors at theatre. A good casting director will always make a mental note of interesting talent. —Martin

I have called actors in who I have seen on stage. One of the best shows I have seen in Los Angeles is *Cider House Rules*. I saw the play in two parts with a week in between. All week long I got to feel the characters and the situation and got to be with the story and the characters the following week. I called people in for commercial auditions from that show who did not have commercial agents at the time. Now they do. It's fun to bring people in even before they have that agent representation. —Berland

Best Way To Promote the Show

I'm a big fan of email. Email apitbull@prodigy.net to let me know about your show. Mailings are good and faxing is okay too. —Snyder

Send us postcards and theatre bills. Tell us in person when you come in to audition. Have your agent contact us with the information. Advertising is important. Even the best play with the best cast and production value requires the proper promotion. —Kalmenson

Invite me by sending flyers, postcards, and faxes. — Berland

I really appreciate actors sending me their invitations and flyers for shows. —Wallin

Be in a good play. I read the papers. I know what's getting a good review. If you're in a good play, you'll get seen. Believe me. —Hicks

I see the plays I want to see, productions with friends in them, ones I've heard good things about. It's really random, but postcards are still the best way to get a casting director to come see you in a play. —Reinking

Postcards are the very best way. —Belshé

The best way for actors to invite casting directors to see them perform is probably through distributing flyers and postcards via the mail and fax. —Ladki

Unless it's a great show, don't go touting it. You'll have used up your good reputation if you promote a lousy play. — Goldman

Theatres Casting Directors Frequent

This list is by no means comprehensive, but casting directors have mentioned theatres to me by name, in interview after interview. These are the ones that came to the top of the list in Los Angeles, again and again.

ACME Comedy Theatre
Actor's Gang
Area 51
ASK Reading Series
Beverly Hills Playhouse
Black Dahlia Theatre
The Blank Theatre Co.
Cal Arts Disney Space
CBS Comedy on the Lot
Circle X
The Coast Playhouse
The Colony Theatre
Company of Angels
The Complex
Coronet Studio Theatre
Fountain Theatre
The Groundlings
HBO Workspace
Highways
The Hudson Theatre Guild

The Improv
Improv Olympic
Interact
Lillian Theatre
Los Angeles TheatreSports
Mark Taper Forum
Matrix
The MET Theatre
Music Center
A Noise Within
The Odyssey Theatre
Pacific Residence Ensemble
PS-NBC
Reprise! UCLA
Rubiat Ride
Second City
Tamarind Theatre
Tiffany Theatre
Victory Theatre

JINGLE SINGING

Some actors—many actors—sing. So, I decided to interview a casting director who casts jingle singers for advertising spots. That turned out to be a more difficult task than I'd anticipated. Turns out, producers do not call casting directors to find vocal talent for their clients' ads. Instead, they rely on the heads of recording studios to offer up the best vocalists in town.

I spoke with two such studio-heads in an attempt to demystify the process singers must go through in order to join the talent pool from which jingle singers are cast.

There Are No Jingles Casting Directors

"It is funny," said Dain Blair, creative director for Groove Addicts. "In New York, there are a couple of companies that specialize in casting vocalists. That's just not the case in Los Angeles."

Getting on the Radar Screen

Blair summarized, "People get to us using many different approaches. Most singers will send in their demo CD or tape and discography and sometimes will include a photo."

"It doesn't matter to me whether there's a picture or not," said Marc Cashman, president of Cashman Commercials.

"However, if the resumé is specific, listing jingles you've done, I'd hold onto that. If the resumé is about the musical you did in '89, that's no good to anyone," he commented. Cashman prefers that the jingle singer provide a list of clients and production companies with whom they've worked. "That way, the producer can call up a rival company and get information on how the singer did with the phone patch or with people in the booth, etc. With that information, we can get a good vision of what the person is able to do and how they perform," Cashman said.

Jingle singers send unsolicited submissions directly to recording studios, according to Blair. "It's generally pretty easy for people to find out who to get their tapes to, when it comes to the major music houses. If a singer goes through a directory like *LA411*, he or she usually can find the top music houses on the west coast," he explained. "Somehow, they find us," Blair joked.

Frequently, the way singers find the studios is by referral. Blair explained, "We'll be using some vocalists or musicians on a project who will refer somebody. When that demo comes in with a note that the singer has been referred by someone we've already worked with, their demo goes closer to top of the pile. No one is going to refer someone who isn't talented, so that helps with our screening process."

Cashman concurred. "We find jingle singers primarily through referral by another producer who says, 'I just used this singer and they were great, you'll love them, they were easy to work with.'"

Whether sent by referral or unsolicited submission, Blair and Cashman both indicated that demos they receive will be heard. "We listen to everything receive," Blair promised. "And that's a lot of material. I have a straw basket here behind my desk filled with demos. Any time we have a break in the action, we go to the basket and start listening to demos. We are always looking for a new voice or a unique voice. Of course, we have to have a need for that person's type of voice. If I hear a good voice but the style is a duplicate of the style of people we already work with, I may not hang on to that demo."

What To Include on a Jingle Demo

According to Cashman, ideally the demo should consist of "jingle snippets from work they've already done." However, neither Cashman nor Blair indicated that jingle singing is closed to newcomers.

Blair stated, "People don't have to have done commercials before in order to get hired by us. Singers should be sending in something representative of their vocal style, what they're good at. I'd prefer not to hear whole songs. Sixty to 90 seconds of their voice (a verse and a chorus) is fine, and then that should fade out and go into the next thing. The number of selections should be anywhere from three to 12 selections. I usually know within the first two pieces whether the person has the talent or style we're looking for."

Cashman indicated a preference for a full range of genres represented on a demo. "With your demo, you need to put together a spectrum of different styles you can do: uptempo, ballad, rock, jazz, pop, hip hop, country; whatever's in your repertoire."

Blair, however, suggested specialization. "On your demo, don't try to be all things. You are not a chameleon, so just do what you are best at. Go with your strengths," he summarized.

Important to both Blair and Cashman was the separation of selections on the demo. "Individualize the tracks so that I can hop from one track to another," said Cashman. "A medley shows me a range, but not a performer's ability to go from A to Z. I only hear them going from A to B."

Blair added, "Make sure that you don't oversing. Know when to sing under control and know when to open it up and show us your chops."

Important Details for Demo Production

"There is a very specific way of singing a jingle that is very different than singing on an album," noted Cashman.

"Singers submit songs and many times, it's difficult for a producer to make the leap on whether the singer can do a jingle. Jingle singing is a completely different animal."

Blair concurred. "A demo with musical stage work on it is not going to get a singer a lot of work with us. We need chorus and verse that is recorded decently with decent equipment. We've gotten demos that were done all at the home of the singers, all themselves, singing, playing the guitar, having programmed the percussion. If the equipment is decent, a home recording is a fine demo," Blair insisted.

"The hardest thing for singers who are trying to break into jingles," said Cashman, "is putting the demo together. They don't have access to jingle tracks. That takes some doing. I think there are a couple of places in Texas where you can secure jingle tracks that you can put vocals to. Singers may want to check on the Internet for resources to jingle tracks."

Additionally, according to Cashman, "Singers can call the biggest jingle houses in the country (there are at least 20 monstrous jingle houses in Los Angeles, New York, Chicago, San Francisco, Boston, Dallas, and Atlanta, just for starters) and say, 'I'm a professional singer, I sight-read, I work well with people, I perform well under pressure, and I want to put a jingles demo together.' Those jingle houses might be able to help you put that together. Some music libraries have prerecorded 60s and 30s that you may be able to put vocals against. These resources make it relatively easy to produce a demo and at a reasonable cost," Cashman assured.

One caution from Cashman involved packaging. "The mistake made by the majority of newcomers to the jingle singing industry, and it's real critical, is sending demos out with no spine printing, no tray card, no cover. All that expense [to record the demo] and there's no spine information. Without that, on the shelf, they're invisible. I throw them out. I'm not going to take the time to make a tray card to put on your CD. You spent all the time and expense and you didn't think about how I'd be storing your CD," Cashman warned.

Studio In-House Demos Are Different

"Our demos are the time to experiment with people of different styles," said Blair. "We just finished a project for Burger King. The client was not sure what they wanted, vocally. On our demo presentation to the client, we had five different composers working on it. We experimented with someone new as a vocalist, just to try it out at that point. Sometimes something we've tried out ends up being what the client wants, as was the case with Burger King. The client heard the vocalists on our demo and immediately gravitated toward a certain voice. That's the one we ended up using," Blair said.

Jingle Sessions Require Specific Skills

"Recording a jingle is more like recording a voiceover than recording a song for an album," said Cashman. "The client is there physically or on the phone, listening. There is time pressure, and you're asked to do multiple parts, many passes. There is a lot of pressure for the singer. You're under the gun to produce for the ad agency, the producer, and the client."

Cashman continued, "In advertising, you may need the singer tomorrow, you may need them in years. Years ago, a girl sent in a demo. I thought she was fantastic. She was killer. I really wanted to use her, but I didn't have anything going on that she was right for at the time. I called her and told her I was looking forward to the opportunity to get her in the studio. She said, 'Great. But I may be on the road by the time you call.' Sure enough, by the time I called, she was on the road doing back up. This was Sheryl Crow. She was fantastic and she was just someone shopping her jingle demo just like everybody else."

INDIE FILM CASTING

Casting is casting is casting. The process, for the casting director, involves reading the script, creating the character breakdowns, scouting for new talent, reading actors for specific roles, and presenting actors to the directors. No matter how high the budget or the profile of the film, casting is done—for the most part—the same way. Where indie film casting differs from mainstream film casting is in the collaborative element. While many directors, of projects with any budgeted amount, prefer collaboration with their casting directors, indie filmmakers seem to depend on it. The indie filmmaker-casting director relationship is vital to the success of their project and to the careers of every actor involved.

For this piece, I interviewed three casting directors with recent indie film hits to their credit. Their experiences, their candor, and their willingness to reveal unknown actors make them true collaborators in the indie filmmaking process.

Participating Casting Directors

Susan Shopmaker, CSA, Series 7: The Contenders, Hedwig and the Angry Inch, Hurricane Streets, Trick
Adrienne Stern, The Believer, Never Again, 13 Conversations About One Thing, Girls Town, Knots, The Toll Booth, Falling Off the Verge, My Girlfriend's Boyfriend, Girls Town
Wendy Weidman, Blue Car, The Invisibles, The Cooler, Rituals

Indie Casting vs. Mainstream Casting

"What's different about casting an independent film is the creativity that goes into casting the film," Stern began. "You're working with the director who may have also written and may also be producing the film. The director is counting on your expertise as a producer somewhat. For me," Stern explained, "when I become a team player, casting tends to become a really wonderful experience."

Weidman noted about her experience in casting *Blue Car*, "I found, in working with a first time director [Karen Moncrieff], she was going on looks, for the most part. Karen was going through the pictures with me and picking actors based on their looks. From my experience, you can't just cast from a picture. You get them in the room and see their work. Luckily, Karen was very open and willing to try anything. I had had Agnes [Bruckner] audition for me in the past, so I was aware of her work and knew we needed to bring her in for Karen."

Moncrieff's appreciation for Weidman's persistence is clear. "Wendy was wonderful. I really, really enjoyed collaborating with her on this. She showed me Agnes' picture and I didn't know her at all. I said no initially, just based on her picture. [It] made her look very glamorous and older. Luckily, Wendy didn't listen to me and brought [Agnes] in anyway. When [she] came in, she had an immediate connection to the material and was very emotionally accessible. That was really important to me."

Weidman indicated that most indie filmmakers are open to a collaborative relationship with the casting director. "I find that true of most people I've worked with, in any position. Creative people have very open minds to see someone new. Sometimes I'll feel very strongly about [an actor] and the director will disagree. In those cases, I'll do my best to get the actor in front of the director. I don't always win when I work to get someone in, but most of the time we succeed because indie filmmakers are just open to [casting directors]."

Shopmaker, who works exclusively with independent filmmakers, speculated on the differences between studio films and the casting work she has done. "I would guess there are more people to answer to with the more mainstream pictures. The bigger budgets dictate that casting directors go for movie stars. However, more and more, indie films are casting big stars. So, what's the difference? I don't know. How would I know, really? I have nothing to base it on other than my experiences," she concluded.

How Indie Casting Directors See Actors

Stern, who tapped Ryan Gosling for *The Believer*, explained, "Each film takes on a life of its own. So, what I look for in an actor has to do with timing. If it's smack in the middle of pilot season my chances of attracting talent are more limited. Even if I'm not working on a pilot, actors are busy. If you have a wonderful project like *The Believer*, you have many people wanting to be a part of that project. So, those are the projects you want to work on."

For Shopmaker, her method of bringing actors in involves, "a little bit of everything. It really depends on the movie. As with most casting directors, I try to know everybody who walks in the door. I attend theatre about two times per week. Some New York casting directors go three and four times, but we just don't have time. Still, we scout talent there."

Stern, who began casting theatre before taking on film work, added, "I do like attending theatre, but a general meeting with a young actor is the best way for me to see what [the actor] can do. I'll attend a screening of a little film rather than a play, most nights." And, regarding submissions, Stern commented, "in the dozen years I've been casting, I do tend to trust my relationships with agents and managers." That said, Stern did encourage unsolicited submissions of headshots and resumés. "A headshot may catch my eye now and then. An older character actor probably isn't going to catch my eye, just because I've seen them already. But actor submissions really do help in finding new, fresh young talent." One caveat Stern included involves demo reels. "I am happy to see a reel if I've requested it, but I get so many tapes, I never watch the unsolicited ones."

"I don't know that there is one best way to get in front of me," Shopmaker said. "It just depends. I don't know how easy or how difficult it is to get in front of me, honestly." Shopmaker conceded that her current project has her seeing more new talent than usual. "We're prescreening 20 new people every day right now. I put an ad in *Back Stage* and I haven't done that in ten years! It just depends on the project. A movie we did last year needed a certain type of person and we had to do a search. I was calling all the schools and all the people we knew, trying to get this project cast."

Another Shopmaker project provided a very specific challenge. "*Party Monster* [from directors Fenton Bailey and Randy Barbato] was a feature based on the documentary. These people actually exist. While we were not looking for lookalikes, we did try to cast with a physical proximity. It poses a problem, doing that. I needed a girl, age 20, weighing 200 pounds." Of course, Shopmaker prefers to cast trained actors, but with time running out, she said, "I'm at the point where I'm going to call Weight Watchers."

Their Biggest Indie Casting Challenge

Shopmaker joked, "Whatever I'm doing at the moment is my biggest challenge." She then added, "No matter what the challenge may be, I've worked with directors who have real vision. I've been taken along for that ride and have been asked to be a part of the creative process. That is what makes me remember why I wanted to do [casting] in the first place."

Stern would like to see indie films receive the "green light money" that studio pictures get. "I'd like being hired with every film financed completely. That would be the clincher, honestly, having money to play with when working on projects of indie caliber," Stern concluded.

Live your dreams.
If you don't, someone else will.

SANDE ALESSI

Hanging out at The Casting Couch *is like being in a sorority house between classes. Sande Alessi, Jennifer Alessi, and Kristan Berona each have their own office, but only retreat there when it becomes too busy to gather in the central office, fielding phone calls and faxes between sips of coffee and riotous outbursts of laughter. The pace of the Coffee Talk is as rapid as the filling of jobs for countless extras (on films such as* Austin Powers in Goldmember, Minority Report, The Truman Show, *and* Fear and Loathing in Las Vegas.

Sande Alessi, involved in every element of her company's operation, is a vibrant mix of energy, know-how, and chutzpah. Without a doubt, her goal of focusing even more on principal casting in the future should be easily met.

Road to This Position

Alessi came from the recording industry. "I was in the music business in the '80s. Big hair, good times!" she recalled. "I did some non-union extra work, and then worked as a SAG extra, did stand-in work, and then became a set coordinator," Alessi continued. "I liked being a wrangler for the extras," she said of her position as set coordinator. "I was a waitress on *Seinfeld* but I was too shy. I preferred casting. It's creative, like shopping."

Before starting her own company in 1996, Alessi worked as an intern for Bill Dance. "In order to see if I had an eye for it, he gave me some tiny films. Bill taught me how to create a palate of actors, sit on the floor with headshots all over and know when there were too many blondes, that sort of thing."

Coolest Casting Gig

The feature *AI.* "We needed exotic amputees. We did a huge search. Most of the folks we found were from out of state and had no acting experience. We got to give a crash course on acting. I worked with Avy Kaufman to do that. It was a major thrill. These are strong, amazing people." For her work on *AI,* Alessi was awarded the Stan Winston Award of Excellence. "I'd like to see more minority representation [in casting] of all kinds," she shared.

Key Things She Looks for in an Actor

Accountability. "When you go in for your photo, show up in wardrobe. Know your look and go with it. Dress up-to-date. We need more upscale people than not, so dress up, and we'll let you know when to wear a t-shirt," Alessi laughed.

Her Take on Extras Casting

"The principal casting director moves on to the next job before shooting begins, and I'm still on duty, finding extras. That means I sometimes cast [last-minute] principals too. I remember who [as an extra] is reliable and easy to work with, and will bring them in for auditions."

Advice for Actors

"Don't join SAG and *then* learn how to act," Alessi advised. "Do your learning first. Work out with other actors."

Further advice from Alessi included staying in acting class, studying improv, and working in student films. "Work for free. That work will lead to other work. Too many actors get their vouchers, get an agent, and still don't know how to audition," Alessi commented. "We'll always remember if you're a bad actor. You have one shot. Make sure you're ready for it."

To that end: "Read the entire breakdown before your audition so you know the characters. Staple your headshot to your resumé and please just bring one headshot. Don't make me choose the look for you. You should have one picked out, stapled, and ready to go, when you come in."

Regarding acting itself, Alessi advised, "Make a choice that's deeper than what's on the paper. Be ready to take direction."

Pet Peeves

"No shows, lateness, saying you have certain wardrobe and showing up to set without it, and random calls to the office to say you're looking for work," Alessi listed. "We know you're looking for work. We're looking [for the work] for you!"

If an actor encounters a problem on the set, Alessi hopes the actor will call her first. "I'm a SAG member, so I understand wanting to let them know that something's not right, but there's no need to make calls so that, four months later, I'm getting a call from SAG that the head of a studio is mad for having to deal with this issue. Call me, and I can get you that $12 for a fitting," Alessi concluded simply.

An audition-level pet peeve for Alessi centers on lack of common sense-behavior. "Don't look over my shoulder to see my notes. Don't leave something behind so that you can come back into the room to get it. Don't add a monologue of your own to the sides you've been given. Don't bring your gun, your knife, your buddy, a selection of hats to your audition. Really."

Alessi's opinion on headshots: "8x10s should come with an expiration date," Alessi stated. "People are using ten-year-old pictures and it's just not right. I'd rather have a recent color photo."

Her Favorite Extra Tale

Alessi had cast a gentleman based on the clothing requirement: upscale elegant suits. The actor showed up to the set wearing sweats and carrying a gym bag. "When the AD asked him about the suit, he pulled this rumpled coat and tie out of the bag. They hung it up, steamed it, tried to make it work. When I called the guy to find out what happened, he said, 'The strangest thing happened. I was driving down the 405 and my suits flew out the window!' The worst part," Alessi continued, "was that he'd pulled the same stunt on another set [booked through another casting director] just the week before. I was like, 'Man! Get a new excuse!'"

How To Register

"Hollywood OS is where registration happens," Alessi summarized. A $15 one-time fee puts you in the fully-searchable online database that Alessi and her staff use to populate the worlds of every project they cast from feature films to music videos and from TV shows to commercials. Once registered, actors submit their availability on jobs listed on the Casting Couch hotline. "By submitting when you know you're right and when you know you're available, you're not going to show up and not fit the part," Alessi explained.

Best Way To Get Seen by Her

Send your headshot and resumé. "I'd prefer a small color photo, though," she emphasized. Alessi lists casting notices in *Back Stage West* and attends theatre, especially in the Valley. "Submit your photo, send a flyer, send a postcard with your photo on it, let me know about your improv group," she said. "I'll see you."

Her Opinion on Alternative Submission Methods

"I use online services. I love 'em," she quipped. "It eliminates [the task of] opening headshots for hours. We use the Extras Casting Guild website, do a search for what we need, email the sides out to the actors, and basically are saved the work of the first audition."

Highlight of Her Week

"Late night wine runs to Trader Joe's," she said with a laugh.

Most Gratifying Part of Her Job

"To see the work I did on the big screen. Calling people to tell them they got the job. It's such a competitive business, that part is really nice. Also, I hired my best friend and my sister. We have fun all day here."

Registration Line: 818.623.7040

JULIE ASHTON

Julie Ashton stresses the word "director" in "casting director." "I'll always ask the producer after an actor reads, 'Do you want to give the actor notes?'" If the producer's answer is, "No," you can count on Ashton to step in with notes of her own. "There are benefits to reading with me because I'm going to help you nail it," she said, during our interview in the new offices of Julie Ashton Casting in the Miracle Mile.

Ashton, who has cast several of the Olsen twins' films, The Rerun Show, The Wayne Brady Show, *and* MadTV, *has much to be proud of in her new venture, including the fact that the two pilots she cast earlier this year have been picked up. After unpacking, she took a vacation just long enough to allow her to relax before getting back to work. Lucky for the community of actors, this is work for which Ashton has a passion.*

First Casting Job

With casting director Caro Jones. "I was one of her readers. Reading with the actors was my first experience in a casting office on a day-to-day basis. Working in Caro's office just clicked for me. She is an amazing person," Ashton recalled.

"I'd been an actress for about five-and-a-half minutes," she joked. "I was smart enough to know that I was not very good at it. Working as a reader opened my eyes to the fact that I was better-suited to casting."

Road to This Position

Ashton moved on to assist Mike Fenton and Judy Taylor in 1989. By 1992, she worked as associate casting director for the feature film *Bad Girls* and continued on with Fenton & Associates until 1996. "I got a call from Saban Entertainment [producers of the *Power Rangers* series]. They were creating a talent and casting department and that allowed me to build a path there. It was really instrumental in my being able to open my own business. I got to create the department from scratch," she explained.

When Saban merged into Fox Family Channel, Ashton became the head of casting there. "I worked so hard. We cast 54 projects in the first year. My group of casting directors was so amazing. We didn't farm out anything. In 1999, I became non-exclusive, which was the gift of a lifetime. My contract with [the new] ABC Family Channel permitted me to cast other things, which allowed me to be on my feet by the end of last year, when my contract ended. That's how I was able to get my own business set up. I would've never expected this is where my job with Saban would lead," Ashton marveled.

Coolest Casting Gig

"There is no one coolest gig. I love all my projects. I love it all," Ashton exclaimed.

Key Things She Looks for in an Actor

Preparation. "If you haven't prepared, how do you make choices about your acting? How can you hear notes from the director and make changes? It's so obvious, but you'd be surprised how many actors come in without having prepared. You should know the material really well. In TV, we try to get you the material 24 hours ahead. But you need to be able to hear the director say, 'You're not right for this role, but would you read this one,' and be ready to make choices. If you need time to look over the material, ask to go out and come back in. I respect that. But you should be able to learn the material quickly. Take a class in cold reading," Ashton advised.

Pet Peeves

Tardy actors. "It drives me nuts," she stated. What bothers Ashton is not that actors arrive late, but that arriving late affects the performance they deliver. "Being late makes you scattered. Call me or have your agent call me if you're going to be late and let's push the meeting back. Don't come in here saying you just got the material. Kids do it cold. Kids are amazing in their ability to memorize something so quickly. Adults don't seem to tap into it as easily, but we can. That's an important skill to develop. It's all about you in that room. Just remember that producers don't ask the scattered actor back. Without exception, I find it's the well-prepared actor who gets the part."

Another issue that bugs Ashton is the increase in the number of actors who will not preread. "An agent will call and say that the actor will only come in if he or she can go straight to producers. I can't take the risk that we'll waste the producers' time with a poor fit. They could be brilliant actors, but not right for that particular role," she said, noting that the very nature of her job is to handle prescreening prior to bringing actors to the producers.

"I trust agents to send me the best actors. Producers trust me to weed through them and bring the best of the best to them. Actors, do yourselves a favor and tell your agent, 'I'll preread for anything,' to make sure you're not being kept away from me," Ashton advised.

Advice for Actors

Ashton explained the importance of focusing on the business side of acting. "Be sensible. Treat acting like a business. Study the business end of it while you perfect your craft. Get a game plan in place and set goals. I equate the study of acting with becoming a lawyer, a teacher, a doctor, any of those professions. You do have to study and pay your dues and pound the pavement in order to succeed. Ultimately, acting is a job. A lot of it is fate, but your chances as an actor are much better if you have done the work required of you. You can't rely on fate alone," Ashton clarified.

Her advice on choosing material for generals was simple, but powerful. "Figure out what you're good at. Pick material that you're close to, that you're good at, that you relate to. It's just the easiest thing to do. Be sensible. If you are a comedic actor, don't pick *The Bell Jar* for your monologue. I'm not trying to pigeonhole actors, I'm hoping to make a tough job easier for an actor by suggesting that," she said.

Specific Advice on Improv Acting

"Get in an improv class. Be around other funny people. Learn what it is that really works in comedy," she listed.

Ashton has seen hundreds of actors for sketch shows, and the auditions usually include an element of improvisation. One limitation Ashton has observed in these auditions is that actors do not tend to know their strengths. "Even Meryl Streep is better at one thing than another," she said. "Figure out what you're good at. Learn your strengths by being in a class and testing things out early on in your career. Find your forte. Hopefully, you will do everything you want, fulfill your dreams, and feel challenged on a daily basis. It is important to know what suits you. Acting is tough. Knowing your strengths will make it easier. I find nine out of ten actors don't know what their strengths are."

Best Way To Get Seen by Her

Agency referrals. "I do open every envelope and sometimes bring someone in who's just graduated from a great college or had amazing theatre experiences," Ashton added.

She regularly attends showcases ("I even go during pilot season," Ashton claimed) at locations such as Area 51, the Improv, ACME, Improv Olympic, and the Groundlings. "You name it, I go to all of those shows. I've cast five sketch shows. I need to find new faces. The only way I'm going to do that is to be out. I can't rely on agents to have all the best people. Sometimes great people just aren't represented. I have to find them. So, be in something, and I'll see you," she insisted.

Her Opinion on Alternative Submission Methods

"I don't do [Internet casting]. I'm old fashioned that way. I can take a tape to a producer easier than I can get a producer to pull your reel up on a computer."

Most Gratifying Part of Her Job

"Working with an actor on a preread, having that actor go to producers with my notes in mind, seeing that actor get to network and then book the gig. To see that process through from A to Z and have the actor come up to me and say thanks; that's what I find to be the most gratifying."

PATRICK BACA, CSA

Patrick Baca, one half of a partnership [with Robin Nassif] in Nassif Baca Casting has cast many MOWs, feature films, and pilots (including Halloween: Resurrection, Gentle Ben, Strip Mall, *and* Hell House*). The following information came from his appearance on a casting panel hosted by the Talent Managers Association at Los Angeles City College.*

Key Things He Looks for in an Actor

Preparedness. "It's not always what you do with a line. It's the wonderful stuff between the lines that writers can't write but actors can bring to it, the quiet background work. It's unforgivable if you come in unprepared, winging it. That's not going to get you the job."

"Make a strong choice. I'm more apt to direct you if you go with a good, thought-out choice, than if you play it safe and stay right down the middle," Baca explained.

Advice for Actors

"Include your service number [on your resumé]. If I kept your headshot from a play I saw you in three years ago, you may not be with that agent anymore, but your service number could help me find you. And you wouldn't know to let me know you've changed representation if you don't even know I'm a fan of yours.

Also, stay in contact with the agency departments at SAG, AFTRA, and AEA. When I think of you and can't remember who you're represented by, that's where I can go to get that information. Be findable. The agency department is a resource I use every day."

Baca made it clear that he is happy to see non-union and non-represented actors. What he is *not* happy to see is the high-maintenance actor. If you're going to be a lot of work for him in the audition, he knows you'll be a lot of work for the cast and crew on the set. "I've had to discourage the hiring of high-maintenance actors," he said.

Pet Peeves

In addition to having a low tolerance for actors who show up unprepared and without headshots and resumés in hand, Baca mentioned disdain for crossing-the-line audition tactics. "I've been slapped," he exclaimed. "I'm totally there for the actors, but if you're going to slap me, get my permission first!"

His Opinion on Alternative Submission Methods

"Online casting is the wave of the future. I regularly use IMDB and the *Academy Players Directory* online. I think the tech-friendly younger casting directors will cause it to take off," Baca speculated. He added that the current climate has influenced the move toward high-tech casting. "Especially today, in the Anthrax world, that's the case. Casting directors at Sony aren't opening unsolicited mail right now. That's a strong push for online submissions."

Baca is a fan of seeing work on demo reels, but he has a qualifier. "Put your best stuff at the beginning of the reel. And keep the whole thing under three minutes."

In addition to seeing a demo reel, Baca may see you at a workshop. "I do workshops because I love to teach, to give something back," he explained.

What He Would Change About the Casting Process

Timing. "When I was casting an MTV pilot, I had to see the whole town. We had six to eight weeks to cast, and saw 30 to 40 people a day every day. A MOW is limited. We'll get maybe three weeks to cast it."

Trends He Has Noticed in the Casting Process

Diversity. "I'll sit with the director to find his vision for the roles and what his parameters are, how flexible they are with the way writers have written the roles. I try to go in and add color. I make that a part of my process before we even go to Breakdowns," he explained.

"People will submit ethnicities that aren't mentioned in the breakdown and I think it's great. Terrific."

His Opinion on Agency Relationships

"I like the small, boutique agencies. They're more efficient, more creative, and more willing to help. The biggest godsend when a big agency is involved is learning that a personal manager is also involved. Talking to the manager is like talking to an actor's wife. It's personal."

How does the name on the envelope influence Baca? "As for submissions, it goes: agency, manager, individual actor submissions. I open envelopes in that order."

And once he's opened that envelope? "Your credits, your photograph, and your representation: that's why I'll bring you in." And training? "Training doesn't make that decision [to call an actor in] for me."

JEANIE BACHARACH

Jeanie Bacharach knows actors. She was one. Her husband is one. She spent years in theatre before making the move to episodic television casting (for which she has cast Judging Amy, Ally McBeal, *and* The Guardian*). In fact, she and her husband fantasize about opening a theatre company in Maine someday.*

Because of her connection to the world of the actor, Bacharach understands the struggle that culminates in a visit to her office. She'll give you feedback, so that you'll realize why you're not being cast, and, if you are being cast, you'll be a part of a team. Despite the fact that Bacharach doesn't currently cast theatre, she aspires to the level of teamwork in her current projects that she enjoyed in New York theatre.

First Casting Job

"I did an internship for Playwright's Horizon, an Off-Broadway theatre company," Bacharach said. She came to the business as an actor from Louisville, Kentucky, having worked in the Actor's Theatre of Louisville's apprentice program. During the theatre's Humana Weekend, she met Daniel Sweed, Playwright's Horizon's casting director. During the writer's strike of 1988, Bacharach studied the business side of acting via a casting internship under Sweed and decided her days as a performer were over.

Road to This Position

Bacharach was hired by Brian Chavanne who was then Julie Mossberg's partner. "They did a lot of regional theatre and some television, and I was with them for a couple of months. Then I worked at ABC primetime as a casting assistant," she said. Bacharach freelanced in New York for a few years and, after starting a family, decided Los Angeles was filled with more opportunity. "I'd worked in theatre in Florida and went to Lincoln Center before coming to Los Angeles in 1994," Bacharach said. She hasn't done any theatre casting since coming to Los Angeles, although she misses the community that theatre provides. "I did help out a friend on a Naked Angels production when I first came out here," but having a paying gig, in Los Angeles casting, typically means doing TV and film, rather than theatre.

Coolest Casting Gig

The first two seasons of *Ally McBeal*. "It was the first series I ever did," Bacharach revealed. "I totally lucked out, thanks to the fact that executive producer Jeffrey Kramer took a chance on me. Judith Weiner had done the pilot and my husband had tested for one of the roles, so I'd met Jeffrey. I was very excited to come on for the series casting. No one really knew what [the series] was going to be," she continued. "I knew most of the cast from New York. It was as if I had a fantasy list of actors and was able to choose a few off of that list." Bacharach specifically enjoyed the fact that the show was unlike anything else on television. "Some of the rules went out the window."

Key Things She Looks for in an Actor

A sense of humor. "It's always amazing to me what other people find funny," Bacharach revealed. Additionally, the actor should be intelligent. "I want to see someone who has an understanding of the text, who is good with the language, who has made strong choices—whether they be right or wrong—but someone who has thought it all out."

Her Favorite Audition Tale

"I can't name who the actor is, but I was doing a play in New York and it was a young, innocent part, and this guy was neither," she recalled. "He came in for the preread and was lovely, but not right for the role. Now, I try to let the actor know why they're not getting a callback before they leave my office. You leave there thinking you did well and you don't understand why, but being married to an actor and having been on the other side of it myself, I want to let you know. This actor wanted to argue with me and convince me that he was right for the role. He was trying to negotiate. I felt intimidated by his intensity." Bacharach understands that actors crave that information from the casting director, those notes that could help them improve their auditions in the future. Did this actor's aggression stop Bacharach from providing such feedback? "No. It didn't change my doing it, but it did get intense. He got quite angry."

Pet Peeves

Actors who talk their way out of the job. "These actors who make apologies before auditioning prevent themselves from being cast. Just make it work! Not making choices, winging it in an audition, these things show a lack of respect for me, for yourself, for your agent," she revealed. "If you don't like the material, don't accept the audition. Don't come in and make excuses." And if you are asked whether you have any questions, don't ask her what choices you should've made, in the read you just finished. "If you're intelligent, you can make the adjustment, if I give one to you. And in episodic, there's not a lot of time on the set to make changes, so I need to see that you can adapt. But don't ask me to make your choice for you."

Be yourself. "There is no way for you to know what I am looking for," Bacharach continued. "*They* don't even know sometimes! Just try to tell the story in those few lines or that physicality you posses. A lot of times it's not about the work. Make choices that show you can commit. You can set up a whole world with a look." If you get a callback, according to Bacharach, you've done the work. "That's an indication of your talent. Be glad. You have to keep your own center and realize that getting a callback is an accomplishment."

Advice for Actors

"Stick it out as best as you can. It's a tough business. It's enormous. Every time I work on a pilot, I get thousands of envelopes. Piles and piles and piles! It blows my mind," Bacharach said. Do those envelopes get opened? "We try to open them all, but there's only a certain amount of time with episodics. On pilots, we have more time."

"Network and stay proactive," Bacharach advised. To that end, she recommended studying. "Not just in on-camera classes. Yes, it's different than theatre, but it's also the same. Stay creative. Have an outlet so you're not just waiting for the phone to ring. Trust your instincts. Life is too short and there is so little joy. You need to find balance so each job doesn't become everything to you. You need to study so you're not rusty. An audition shouldn't be your only opportunity to act. Class gets you up every week."

Once you're in Bacharach's office, own the experience. "The audition is your time," she explained. "Don't feel rushed. Make the most of your time in front of me."

A valuable experience, in Bacharach's opinion, is being a reader. "You see how the audition process works while building a relationship with the casting director. The reader is a very important part of the audition. If you're reliable, you know the work, and you give enough without stealing the scene, check into being a reader. If you have any type of a relationship with a casting director, ask about being a reader."

Best Way To Get Seen by Her

"It's hard when you're unrepresented, but in that case, workshops are a good idea. I have mixed feelings about it, but my associates attend workshops and they absolutely bring people in from those." The key to success when choosing workshops, according to Bacharach, is examining the show on which the casting director works. "Are you appropriate for it? Don't spend money showcasing for a casting director whose show you'll never get on."

What about postcards? "I brought in two people from unsolicited postcards last week," she revealed. "They said, 'Oh my God, it worked!' Sure. Sometimes. Let me know when you're in a play. I do try to attend plays. My staff will go if I cannot."

As for unsolicited headshots and resumés, not only does Bacharach try to open them all, but she hangs on to them for quite some time. "There's a joke around this office: how many calls is it going to take to find this actor? Those contact numbers are sometimes so out of date, they're calling all over to try and find the actor from the headshot I've kept." Bacharach doesn't do generals too often, since she prefers to see people reading for roles she is actually casting at the time.

Her Opinion on Alternative Submission Methods

"I'm not the most technical person," she admitted. Like most casting directors, Bacharach enjoys the hands-on review of headshots and resumés. "Demo reels are okay, but I prefer to see the live performance."

Trends She Has Observed in the Casting Process

"Unfortunately, it's all about perception. It's frustrating that, until someone makes a decision about somebody, people are unwilling to take a chance. It's all about what agent you're with or what you just did and trying to cash in on that," she lamented. "You hear, in pilot situations, that there's not enough talent to fit the need. I have a very difficult time with that [perception]. I think it's that people are unwilling to take a chance. There's more than enough talent to fit the needs. You can't even get an opportunity if you're not with one of six agencies." Bacharach asked, "How can the statement, 'There's no talent,' be made if you're only seeing a fraction of what's out there?"

What She Would Change About the Casting Process

"In television, the whole testing process seems somewhat antiquated. It really comes down to a one-shot deal. It's brutal," Bacharach exposed. "There's the negotiating and deals aren't closed, there's pressure on the actor, there's posturing, there's money, and it's just hard on the actor." Bacharach admitted having no solution for this counterproductive system, and summarized, "auditioning is just such a different process from the actual job."

Highlight of Her Week

Bacharach indicated that she feels fortunate that every day she's working on quality projects with talented people. It's great to cast an episode and see it all come together. I like to sit and talk after sessions to steer the look of some roles. We're open to diversity and our concept meetings are a collaborative effort."

Most Gratifying Part of Her Job

"Getting someone to see an actor in a new way, to think of a role in a new way. The angle of the story changes with risks we take in casting and that's nice. We try not to go the obvious way with every role. Having been an actor, I enjoy the creative process and building relationships."

DEBORAH BARYLSKI, CSA

*Deborah Barylski is known for "finding good kids."
Whether it was spotting Jonathan Taylor Thomas when he was
seven or putting Haley Joel Osment on the TV show* Thunder
Alley *when he was five, Barylski knew that their natural ability
came through because they were "extremely bright."*

*When asked about her "best" discovery, Barylski was
quick to explain the nature of the job by saying, "[Casting
directors] go to bat for someone every day." In over 20 years
(casting projects such as the feature film* Neowolfe *and the
television series* Just Shoot Me, Home Improvement, *and* Life
with Bonnie*), that's a lot of times at-bat, and Barylski is still—
enthusiastically—at the plate.*

First Casting Job

As an assistant with MTM Television. Barylski assisted
producers on shows such as *Lou Grant, St. Elsewhere, The
Bob Newhart Show*, and *Remington Steele*.

"My background was in theatre. I had been teaching
as well as doing theatre management and directing on the
side. I was deciding between going through an AD/director
training program and casting, and casting just seemed more

immediate," Barylski explained about her choice to become a casting director. With an MFA in Directing and Theatre Management from Illinois State University, Barylski has also worked as an instructor at Cal State Long Beach.

Road to This Position

"In this business, we all count on the kindness of those we meet along the way," she revealed. After MTM, Barylski worked as Lori Openden's associate and then Simon Ayer hired her for her first job as a casting director, at Stephen Cannell Productions. After a year at Cannell, she was hired to do a Viacom pilot for executive producer Hugh Wilson. "It was never my intention to be a freelance contractor as early as I was," she said. "I thought I'd work in one place, build up my contacts, and then go out on my own. Instead, I was very quickly thrown in the water and I went with the flow."

That flow included casting programs such as *Frank's Place*, *The Famous Teddy Z*, *Home Improvement* (the pilot and eight years of episodic casting), *Just Shoot Me* (pilot, plus three years), and AMC's *The Lot*, just to name a few.

Coolest Casting Gig

"Coolest really has to do with people more than the script sometimes, and then sometimes it's the script, more than the people," Barylski explained. She notes that *Doctor, Doctor*, a show she cast with Cami Patton, was a favorite project. "We had fun with the actors. The producers saw the script as the starting point, and the actors got to play, to improvise. The only thing was, every actor felt that they nailed it, because the sessions were so fun." That project also marked the beginning of a long association with Wind Dancer Productions, right up through *Home Improvement*.

Key Things She Looks for in an Actor

"It depends on the project," Barylski said. For example, the Midwestern look was important to *Home Improvement*, whereas *Just Shoot Me* required a more sophisticated, cosmopolitan look. "For *The Lot*, I was able to use of actors I hadn't been able to use before, because they had that '30s film look. I used a lot of theatre people for that show."

Always important to Barylski is an actor's experience in theatre. Her theatre background translates to a knowledge of the work and discipline involved. "A sitcom really is just a 22-minute play."

Pet Peeves

"Actors who aren't prepared." In Barylski's opinion, being prepared encompasses more than simply making choices. "It's getting sides, being on time, not coming in hung-over," she continued. "Have you compared the directions [you were given] to your *Thomas Bros. Guide*? Have you driven the route? At that time of day?"

Further preparedness comes from doing your homework. "Know the style of the show, the network it's on, other things the producers have done. Know when you're walking in what kind of show you're coming in for. Next to making specific choices, tone is everything," she summarized.

Advice for Actors

"When you're preparing for an audition, have two or three ways of doing the role in your back pocket. The producers don't always know what they want, so they may just ask you to try something else. Have something else ready."

Many times, according to Barylski, good audition technique is more important than being a good actor. "The auditioning process is a different craft from acting. Become a good auditioner and you will book more work," she said. And how does an actor do that? "It's a science. Develop a strategy for what happens in the room. Improv helps, in that it keeps you in the moment, but most of the time in television, they don't want you to deviate from the script."

Barylski noted that the business is very self-involved, by its nature. "Partly, you have to be, or you don't get anywhere. You have to be able to self-assess and set goals. I suggest to people that they have to do something on a regular basis that gets them out of themselves. Your sense of community is important, and such a source of satisfaction. Whether it's a retirement home or a children's hospital or anything, get out there, perform, or just touch people so that you can get through any frustration, anxiety, depression. Once a week, go somewhere that gets you outside of you."

Further advice from Barylski, "Keep training. You should never, ever stop acting. Even if it's just ten friends getting together and working scenes once a week for four weeks, there is no excuse for not working out."

And finally, if you are not yet a member of SAG, according to Barylski, "becoming SAG is your ultimate and only responsibility. Get that card."

Her Opinion on Alternative Submission Methods

"Internet casting is the way of the future, but it's not there yet," she said. Barylski showed me her most commonly used links, to the *Academy Players Directory* online, IMDB, Variety.com, and WhoRepresents.com. "Until every casting director and agent is online, it won't be universal. But you should follow the guidance of your agent. If your agent does a lot of work online, you should do it," she advised.

Bottom line, "Make sure you're in the *Academy Players Directory* and keep your listing updated," Barylski said. "I don't know a single casting director who doesn't use this tool. Do it, do it, do it."

Best Way To Get Seen by Her

"With network TV, I don't do a lot of Breakdowns because so many of our scripts come in on the fly," Barylski explained, noting that she calls about 20 agents to gather actors. "I attend showcases and plays two to three times a month, so send a flyer," she advised.

How about unsolicited headshots? "I look at every single piece of mail that comes in," she insisted. "Not always in a timely manner, but I do look. I love postcards, though. They're easier to file and keep. I keep photos of actors who are the types I need for the show as well as the ones that have, 'Meet Me!' bounc[ing] out of the picture at me. Then, when I have time, I'll hold generals."

Her Biggest Casting Challenge

Nine years ago, Barylski struggled to cast the role of the mom in *Thunder Alley*. "We had three different actresses in the role. We just couldn't seem to get the right combination of actress and role. This was before *Gilmore Girls* and actresses didn't want to make that leap to playing mom roles too early because they felt they could never turn back. I was pretty much trying to cast that role for a year," she said. Barylski's solution was to, "cast the net again," until availability and interest combined with talent and the right look.

Highlight of Her Week

"Sometimes, it's the table read. It's like opening night, when all of the guest stars and series regulars come together," Barylski said. "And some weeks, it's that somebody we really liked on tape came in and we liked him just as much in person."

"This job is about finding pieces of a puzzle that will work together, work with the project, and work with the producer. It's great seeing the puzzle take shape."

Most Gratifying Part of Her Job

"Working with the actors. Actors are my currency. I enjoy playing with them through the prereads, because that's where I'm most like a theatre director and that process is fun for me. To finally get the job for someone I believe in, seeing them get the work, that is very satisfying."

TAMMARA BILLIK, CSA

Casting can be a very personal job, especially when you work on projects that you know are important—to you and to the world. Tammara Billik knew, when casting Ellen, *that she was a part of something that would make television history. In her nearly 20 years in casting, Billik has worked on the films* ET, Brewster's Millions, *and* Streets of Fire, *as well as the series* Married... with Children, Unhappily Ever After, *and, of course,* Ellen. *She stays grounded by focusing on what's really important: real life.*

First Casting Job

Billik began as an intern with Mike Fenton and Jane Feinberg while she was an undergrad at UCLA. Between answering phones and opening mail, she became involved in the casting of *Raiders of the Lost Ark*.

Road to This Position

After graduation, Billik began working in the office of Judith Holstra and Marcia Ross as a casting assistant. It was at Embassy Television, "where I got my first break, which was casting *Married... with Children*." She was the casting associate on the pilot and the first 12 episodes and then became the casting director for the show, a position she held for seven years. "I like the pace of TV casting. There's some longevity to it, being a part of a series. It's like a family. You really connect with people." That was certainly the case with Ellen DeGeneres, who brought Billik on to cast her show, and who hired her again in 2000, to cast the pilot for the star's variety show. She also cast *Nikki* and that was due to a relationship with Nikki Cox created in doing *Unhappily Ever After.*

Coolest Casting Gig

"By far, the best thing I ever did was working on the *Ellen* show. I thought it was an amazing experience. In half-hour we don't generally get an opportunity to do things that are important or emotional. I got to be part of something that was important to me personally and professionally, and something that was important to the world, I think. That was, by far, the highlight of my casting career; working on the coming out episode and the subsequent episodes, it was really just amazing how it all came together. It was this team of people working together in secret, basically because there was so much talk going on. It was very, very exciting and personally fulfilling. It was a remarkable time. I'm very connected within the gay and lesbian community and I felt the build, I felt the shift, and it was important. We knew exactly what we were doing."

Key Things She Looks for in an Actor

Billik believes that training indicates a seriousness about one's career. "It's about the business of acting and not just wanting to be a star." She also looks for that intangible spark we hear so much about. "You just see it when an actor comes in the door." Also important to Billik are commitment and preparation, as well as a sense of humor. "This is a tough business for an actor and I think actors have to be balanced." This sense of balance, Billik indicated, is how actors can have enthusiasm for the work, rather than desperation for it.

Her Favorite Audition Tale

When Billik cast an episode of *Married... with Children* set in a Chippendale's Bar, she auditioned actors with a specific look, rather than looking for extensive training. An auditioning actor spoke his lines, as well as the stage directions. "He was talking to Peggy Bundy and said, 'Yes, Mrs. Bundy, I do work here at Chippendale's. He turns to her and smiles.' I pulled the actor aside and said, 'Y'know, the stage directions are to be read silently.'" When the actor began again, he made an adjustment: he whispered. "No one in the room would make eye contact because we knew we were going to burst out laughing."

Pet Peeves

The usual: unprepared actors. This includes being unprepared with sides and not knowing anything about the show for which the actor is auditioning. "There's nothing worse than an actor coming in, particularly for the producer session, and saying, 'Is this a sitcom?' That actually happens!"

Advice for Actors

"Study. Train constantly." Billik believes that a degree in theatre is not enough. "There are a lot of differences between what you learn in your theatre department in college and what will get you a job in Hollywood." She suggests learning audition technique, sitcom acting, the business of acting. "It would be really great if we could all be artistic, but understanding the business part of it makes the difference between working and not working."

Best Way To Get Seen by Her

An agent is the easiest way in, but Billik's office covers showcases, workshops, small theatre, large theatre, all of it.

"If you're in something—a play—or have an appearance on television, a postcard is a good idea." Billik will do general auditions for non-represented actors on occasion, "but we're a very busy office, so we tend to be more open to seeing represented actors."

Her Opinion on Alternative Submission Methods

Billik feels that electronic submission is the wave of the future, "but it's still not perfected. A lot of us are used to doing it the old-fashioned way, and so it's taking time for casting directors to get used to looking at submissions online. Maybe in about five years, we'll all be doing it." She finds immediacy to be the greatest benefit to online casting, going online almost exclusively when there is a role to fill on short notice.

Her Operating System

Working on several shows at once requires organization. "We compartmentalize. We color code. We're just very good at juggling." Billik keeps the headshots of every actor she sees, and every envelope is opened. "We don't keep all the submissions, just ones from actors we want to meet when have an appropriate part."

An Interesting Sidebar

Billik feels that all casting directors are great with faces and names. "It's the nature of the job. It's one of the weird little things. I can remember their names and faces. Everyone's. I remember everything. But, I'm also a lawyer." Yep, Billik attended law school at night while casting *Married... with Children.* "After the writer's strike in 1988, I was off work for eight months and I realized that, other than casting, I didn't really have any other marketable skills. So, I figured I'd better do something so that, if there's another writer's strike, I have something else I can do. So, I went to law school, took the bar, passed the bar, and never practiced. What ended up happening was Ellen called me and said, 'Will you come do my show?' That's why I ended up not going into law. I would've practiced, were it not for that."

Highlight of Her Week

Billik's highlight comes from outside the casting office, when she spends time with her godchildren. "They're great kids. If I have a bad day at work, I stop in on the way home before they go to bed and play with them for an hour and it puts everything in perspective."

Most Gratifying Part of Her Job

"I love that I get paid just for talking to people. I think it's a lot of fun. I find actors to be very interesting, dynamic people. I enjoy speaking with them and helping them if I can, giving them any sort of tips on how to get the job. The best part of my job, I guess, is seeing an actor who has come in and preread for me and I've given some sort of instruction to and then watching them go and nail it in a producers audition and get the gig. Very gratifying!"

EUGENE BLYTHE, CSA

Eugene Blythe was a Broadway actor prior to taking on a career in casting. "I hit New York and two weeks later, I was on Broadway," he explained. After working non-stop for two years, Blythe experienced a summer of Don't Call Us, We'll Call You. His take on that? "Well, I'm not going to do this for the rest of my life. This is silly. It doesn't mean that much to me." And that was the beginning of Blythe's long road to ABC.

First Casting Job

"I started casting in New York, actually out on Long Island, at a theatre called PAF Playhouse," Blythe recalled about his 1977 production job. "At the time, PAF was the only theatre in America that did only original plays."

Road to This Position

"Out at PAF, I was a production manager. They started welcoming my input in the casting process, so I took it over," Blythe explained. "From there, I got offers to come out here and work, and the Mark Taper [Forum] is the offer I accepted in 1980. We did a lot of really interesting stuff." Blythe went on to do short stints with Lynn Stalmaster and Universal before settling in at MTM. "I was hired to do *Newhart*, and then took on *St. Elsewhere* for six years," he said. Blythe then freelanced until Disney tapped him to be one of four executives to head their television department at Touchstone in 1990. "When they bought ABC, they combined my job tasks, until two years ago, when I was brought over to ABC to head it," Blythe concluded.

Coolest Casting Gig

While Blythe indicated that he has been "really proud" of his work at ABC, *St. Elsewhere* was his favorite project. "*St. Elsewhere* meant a lot to me. We did a lot of wonderful work and started a lot of wonderful actors. A lot of people really connected with that show," Blythe fondly recalled.

Key Things He Looks for in an Actor

Truth. "There are a million ways to say something, so I always respond to some sort of belief that that person has in his reality, even in an exaggerated reality," Blythe explained. "My instincts toward acting help me to know that truth, but I'm not sure that I was ever that good an actor to be in touch with that. I was probably destined for [casting] because of my instincts toward the process and understanding what it takes to get places, even if *I* wasn't able to get there [as an actor]," he joked.

Pet Peeves

Back when Blythe saw greater volumes of actors, his pet peeve was, "Actors who would want your opinion, your feedback, but then weren't willing to take it. I used to say, 'I have time to give feedback, but I don't have 20 minutes to defend how I feel, so if you're willing to hear what I have to say and then go away, I'll be happy to tell you what I think.' I don't have to deal with that as much in this position, so now, [a pet peeve] would be that the business sort of distances you from the art. That's not really a peeve, but it's sort of the, 'You knew it was a snake when you took it in,' kind of thing: getting the deal done, schmoozing people before you even get the actor [to] consider good material. But that's part of the landscape," Blythe conceded.

An Average Day

"We're constantly trying to get the upper hand on finding new, exciting talent—not necessarily established talent or stars, but new talent—into these projects. That involves everything from meetings, looking at tape, going to showcases, and sometimes going to theatre. I look at every picture that's sent to me. Nobody screens my mail. I look at all of it always. I may not *do* anything with it, but I look at all of it. I think postcards are the best way to put your face in front of a casting director's face with the least amount of effect on a casting director's busy schedule. A lot of times, we develop relationships with photographs, and I've met actors for the first time, thinking I have a relationship with that actor and all I've ever seen is their postcard or photograph that they've sent me over the years. I think those are much more powerful for busy people than trying to be confronted on the phone," Blythe indicated.

Advice for Actors

"I'm a person that believes that if you really want something, there's no way that it won't happen. What that means is doing everything that that responsibility entails. The only thing that you have control over, in this business, is becoming the best actor you can be. The rest of it is the lottery. I feel that, if that's what you want to do, and you don't care about the rest of it, you'll be putting yourself in the place to be ready for when opportunity actually does come. There's no reason to be in this business unless you have to. It all comes out to 50 cents an hour. If you have another choice, take it," Blythe advised.

"I think the actor's life is a very courageous life. You put yourself out in the trenches every day to be rejected. It's a very courageous way to live and it's all directed towards an art. I have a lot of respect for that. But as much as you can, be objective about your career and what you choose, what you want to be, and not just seeking the next job. A lot of actors who people respect are people who are in touch with themselves. It's a hard thing, but that's what gives you direction."

Best Way To Get Seen by Him

"That's hard. I don't see as many people as I used to. There's not enough time in the day. I'm not in the trenches. I supervise many people and I am involved in the development of projects, so I don't have time to see a lot of actors. I do a lot more generals in the off-season," Blythe insisted. "We have four casting directors here and four in New York. We have a lot of freelance casting directors that we use, a different one on every project, not to mention freelance casting directors in different cities here and in Australia, New Zealand, London."

How Much Is Going On Overseas?

"What goes on overseas is this: if we can't find people here, simultaneously, we will look at tapes from other countries to see if we can meet those goals. It's not so much that we're casting foreign projects, but that we go to every acting pool."

To that end, Blythe also participates in ABC's new Diversity Program. "We have this wonderful diversity program going on right now where the outreach is even greater. The thrust of it, right now, is toward different ethnic groups, but we hope to open the showcases up to everybody, as regularly scheduled showcases of all groups, all ages, and that's been very exciting," Blythe indicated.

His Opinion on Alternative Submission Methods

"I don't know how to deal with the computer. I send emails. I receive emails. I like my life to be simple. If I had my choice, I would just read every actor I could and be done with it. My staff uses the Internet, though. We subscribe to those [Internet casting] services and my staff is constantly doing things so that I can look at an actor online. I'd rather pull down the *Academy Players Directory* and thumb through it," he said.

Trends He Has Observed in the Casting Process

Openings for older actors. "A few years ago, I had really good friends who were older actors and I'd say, 'I've got nothing for you. It's all kids.' That's no longer true. It's really a well-rounded, diverse—and not just in ethnicity, but also in ages—pilot season. I think the family show is more *in* than it ever has been before," Blythe shared.

His Biggest Casting Challenge

"To cast writers who have written in themselves. I've been up against that a few times," Blythe joked. Then, he thoughtfully added, "It's a challenge to always keep in touch with your instincts about people, to never waiver about how you really feel about a performance. Sometimes in this business, it's easy to give in to what's commercial or the way the room is going. It's always a challenge to be true to yourself as a casting person. The only thing that drives any of us is our own instincts towards material, towards talent. That may not be good enough, but without it, you don't have anything," Blythe concluded.

What He Would Change About the Casting Process

"If I had information to impart to actors to make the casting process easier, it would be: prepare your best for an audition, go in and give it your all, ask a question if you need to at the end, and then go to the movies. Seventy percent of the reason why you're not chosen in an audition has nothing to do with what you just did in the audition. Auditions really should be seen as an opportunity to show you belong in the business, not necessarily to get the job. We're always feeding the machine. Directors and producers are always on to the next project. Have a long view toward your path, and it will help your psyche. Actors give up too soon because they don't realize how long it takes to get there and they're not willing to make the journey."

Most Gratifying Part of His Job

"The perfect fit. When it works, and I thought of it, that's the best part. That's the *only* part. The purest part, the most favorite part, is dealing with the actors. That has nothing to do with politics, nothing to do with money, it has to do with talent and instinct and people showing that they belong. That's the part I like."

KATE BRINEGAR, CSA

Kate Brinegar, former Head of Casting for Fox Family Channel is a former actor as well. I spoke briefly with Brinegar, whose credits include Men Seeking Women *and* Random Acts of Comedy, *about what it is that makes a former actor a good casting director, and what makes an actor stand out to her, from the other side of the desk.*

What Makes a Former Actor a Good Casting Director?

"We speak the language. We know we come from the same places. We speak Actor Speak. We ask the right questions," Brinegar said.

What Made You Want To Get into Casting?

"I was doing a national commercial as an actor in Chicago. I was fascinated with the behind-the-camera process," she explained. "I was at Northwestern University for Theatre and Speech. One month later, I was given the opportunity to do PA work for a commercial production company. I then became an AD, then a producer, and over a five year period in Chicago, eventually became a combination casting director-producer-sales rep. I just knew the job really fulfilled me."

Key Things She Looks for in an Actor

Professionalism. "I want you to show up, be on time, be prepared, deliver no excuses, and ask any questions you have before your reading," Brinegar listed.

Pet Peeves

Brinegar does not want to hear an actor explain that she just got the material. "Also, have your headshot and resumé ready for me when you arrive."

Most Gratifying Part of Her Job

"I am very grateful to be in the group of casting directors who are former actors. I'm very proud of that. Actors are very courageous, very wonderful, sensitive people for whom I have such respect. I am grateful to have that respect for people I get to work with—and hire—every day."

JACKIE BRISKEY, CSA

NBC's Passions *is one of the hottest, hippest soaps on daytime television. Just over three years old, its influence on other soap operas is evident, from storylines to multicultural casting. Thank Jackie Briskey for a job well done. Then take a look at her resumé. You'll see a path that may not indicate she'd end up in daytime, but certainly one filled with talent and a sense of humor.*

First Casting Job

MTM's *WKRP in Cincinnati.* "I was Meryl O'Loughlin's assistant prior to that. I had been in management/PR with the Smother's Brothers and Kenny Rogers. I worked on the Pat Paulson for President campaign in 1968," Briskey began. "It was purely by accident that I ended up at MTM and I was there in a development situation. Eventually, Arthur Price talked to Meryl and I made the step back to casting assistant with the understanding that, as soon as I learned the process, I would have the opportunity to cast."

Road to This Position

After seven years on staff with MTM, Briskey did the *Newhart* pilot then headed to Embassy to do *Gloria* with Sally Struthers. Briskey then moved on to FOX as an independent casting director, where she cast *Trauma Center*. After that, Briskey worked at Lorimar for seven years where she did *Valerie/The Hogan Family*, *Perfect Strangers*, *Our House*, and *Midnight Caller*.

"*Midnight Caller* was a favorite of mine," Briskey admitted. After Lorimar, she worked with Doug Kramer casting several Danielle Steel MOWs for NBC, as well as casting three or four projects for Aaron Spelling, including the last seven episodes of *Pacific Palisades*. It was Lori Openden (then at NBC) who suggested that Briskey do *Passions*. "I'd never thought about daytime," she admitted. "I made them very aware that I had no daytime experience and didn't know a lot of soap stars. They assured me that they knew the soap actors and I just needed to have an eye for casting. It's worked out very nicely."

"I *think* I've been able to give them what they want," she said. "Jim Reilly, creator and head writer, has a sense of humor and a sense of family. This show is unique, tongue-in-cheek, campy, and popular within the industry. It's fun for me to fill in between the beautiful people with these wonderful characters." Along with associate Don Phillip Smith, who handles Under 5s and background players, that's just what Briskey does. "That creates the look of the show."

Key Things She Looks for in an Actor

"Do they listen? The most important thing about acting is what's going on in your eyes. Are you listening and reacting or just doing your lines? I know the difference," Briskey said.

Pet Peeves

Briskey simply stated, "I detest when the picture does not look like the person. Because I bring in so many people I've never laid eyes on before, when I don't recognize you in person from your picture I am not happy."

Briskey continued, "agents will send in photos for contract players that don't match the breakdown and will say, 'Oh, but that's a terrible picture.' And I say, 'Then your actor needs new pictures!' There's a reason for the breakdown to be so specific. Actors need to police their agents a little. If you see you're wrong for a part your agent has sent you in for, you need to have a conversation with your agent about that. It leaves a bad taste in the casting director's mouth to see you on a role you have no chance for."

Advice for Actors

"Don't feel, in a cold read situation, that complete wardrobe is necessary," Briskey began. "It's a cold reading. We don't need sets, wardrobe, or props. Props are a real distraction and they show your lack of experience."

Briskey advised that actors ask questions. "Ask whatever questions you have *before* reading," she continued. "Don't kick yourself after reading by wondering what the answers would've been if you had asked the questions."

Do your homework. "Even if you're not the actor who gets the job, I will thank you for doing your homework," she said.

Briskey explained, "actors need to realize they didn't get the part sometimes because of hair color. Understand how petty it can be. Remember to do the best you can and move on. Know in your heart that you did the best that you can. That's really all you can do. Everybody in the room is rooting for you. It makes my job easier if everyone is excellent."

Her Opinion on Alternative Submission Methods

"I'm sure it's useful for some casting directors, but online casting is not useful to me," Briskey revealed. "I've been doing this for over 25 years now. I'm set in my ways." Briskey explained that she uses the Internet to look up cast lists and credits, but her source for contract roles and long-term recurring characters is Breakdown Services. "I keep files and files and files," she said, "and daily casting is too fast for Breakdowns, but for contract players, that's the way."

Best Way To Get Seen by Her

Sending your photo and resumé is good. Postcards are better. "Pique my interest in you. Tell me you're doing a play or that you're on a TV show. I take the cards home and put them in chronological order and try to catch your show," Briskey said. "Then if I'm interested in seeing more, I'll request your picture and resumé." When will Briskey *not* watch you on TV? "If you're doing something opposite *The West Wing*, no way. If you're on *The West Wing*, however, I will see you—guaranteed," she concluded with a laugh.

Briskey conceded that she attends theatre less than she used to, "but as much as I can. Twice this week, one time next week. But you can't see every show in town."

When you send Briskey your headshot and resumé, be sure to note your age range, your height, and especially if anything has changed (such as hair color or length) since the photo was taken. "It's a whole look, so I need to know before I bring you in how you'll match up. I must know your height because I know who you're playing opposite."

What She Would Change About the Casting Process

Briskey's change would be to the prime time casting process for series regulars. "It's almost barbaric, what they put actors through," she said. "It's a small room with a lot of network executives seated, seemingly daring the actor to be good. I prefer what they do in daytime, where the actors read for the producers and then they choose who they feel should be put on tape and they give them wardrobe and makeup and have them do a five minute scene with one of our actors. It's not as nerve-wracking as the same process at network. The other thing that should change is, two minutes before [the actors] walk into the room or onto the set, they're signing contracts. An actor should not have to be concerned with signing contracts before doing that final test. They're in a whirlwind," she concluded.

Highlight of Her Week

Spending time with her two-year-old grandson. "I love actors," she said. "I love my grandson more."

Most Gratifying Part of Her Job

"I like actors. I can't do what they do. I like being entertained. They entertain me and I really respect what actors are capable of doing. That's it."

MARY V. BUCK, CSA

When I spoke with Mary V. Buck, she was still partner to Susan Edelman in Buck Edelman Casting. Their Artios award-winning partnership of 20 years ended when Buck was offered the position formerly held by Barbara Miller at Warner Bros.: Senior VP of Talent and Casting. "I am a blessed human being," Buck said. "Susan is not only incredibly talented but one of the funniest people you will ever want to know. She made going to work every day a delight."

Buck, whose casting track record includes Life with Judy Garland: Me and My Shadows, Malcolm in the Middle, *and* The Wonder Years, *brings 22 years of casting experience to that position, in which she supervises casting for shows such as* Friends, ER, *and* The West Wing.

Coolest Casting Gig

Buck couldn't name just one. "*Malcolm in the Middle* was a delight. And *Me and My Shadows*, based on Lorna Luft's book about her mother, Judy Garland, was an amazing experience." Both of these gigs earned Buck an Artios award.

Key Things She Looks for in an Actor

Fun. Of course, Buck looks for professionalism, but it's a sense of fun that puts an actor over the top, for her. "I look for laughter. The actor should have done her homework, have made a choice, and should deliver that audition and then be on her way," she said.

Advice for Actors

"I'm pretty simple about how I think actors should function. To me, the only thing the actor can control is his or her performance. My recommendation is to just prepare. Study, prepare. If you're called in on an audition, get the material ahead of time. Make the choice as to what the character should be. Don't come to the audition and worry about who's in the waiting room or overhear an audition and go, 'Oh, my God, they made that choice, why didn't I?' Be prepared and trust yourself. It's too complex a process and you can't control any of it."

Best Way To Get Seen by Her

Although Buck will happily see non-union and non-represented actors, she admits that there is one way that is better than others. "The best way, honestly, is through an agent. If you don't have an agent, you can certainly submit a picture and resumé. We don't do a lot of general interviews because we don't think they really show anything."

Buck does enjoy attending theatre, when her schedule permits. "If you're performing, you can notify us. Send us a postcard and we'll try and go. I don't go to as much theatre as I used to, but I do go."

Her Take on the Artios Awards

"It's a very exciting night. It's the one night of the year that we really acknowledge ourselves." Buck indicated that she prefers the Artios environment to the stress of the Emmys. "Susan and I were nominated for an Emmy. I'll tell you, I didn't breathe for three days before the awards because it is such an honor and it is such a scary thing. My feeling at the end of it all, when we didn't win, was that it was fine it was over because I could breathe again and enjoy the evening," she laughed.

"Though the Television Academy has acknowledged our undeniably important contribution to the success of television productions with awards in three categories, the Academy of Motion Picture Arts and Sciences has chosen to ignore our contribution. It is one of our goals to continue to lobby the Academy for Oscar recognition. In the meantime, we will continue to honor our own."

Buck continued, "I want to remind each of my peers who and what we really are. We are diplomats, we are counselors, we are negotiators, we are teachers, we are artists, we are visionaries. We are a key element in the creation and success of every theatre, film, and television project ever made."

ALICE CASSIDY, CSA

I met Alice Cassidy briefly before the 2000 Artios Awards ceremony put on each year by the Casting Society of America. A longtime CSA member with many TV and MOW credits on her resumé (including The Jeff Foxworthy Show, Doogie Howser, M.D., Full House, *and* Eek the Cat*), Cassidy takes her job seriously, and thinks an actor should do the same.*

Coolest Casting Gig

"*I Know My First Name Is Steven* was my favorite project," Cassidy said, simply. As Artios presenter Tim Curry entered the press reception room, she added, "I did Tim Curry's pilot. I got star-struck when I first saw him."

Best Way To Get Seen by Her

"If you're doing a show and you get the word out, a lot of [casting directors] will come. I went to six shows in three weeks while I was casting a pilot," she recalled.

Trends She Has Observed in the Casting Process

"Trends change with the flavor of the month but I think there's been more consciousness or paying attention to the training people have and the theatre background they have," she said. "There's an awareness now that's incorporated into their thinking, to be aware of training."

Her Take on the Artios Awards

"I think the awards have raised the consciousness of the contribution that we, as casting directors, make to the creative process. I've found a difference since I started [organizing the awards] in my own relationships. People are more open, more receptive. And it helps us to know each other better, casting directors," Cassidy explained. This led us to the whole point of Artios, in Cassidy's view. "The original idea was for us to be there for each other."

FERN CHAMPION & MARK PALADINI, CSA

You'll soon understand why folks called former partners Mark Paladini and Fern Champion "The Regis and Kathie Lee of Casting." These two are a fascinating blend of New York Sass and Northern California Cool. To impress upon you their chemistry, I've stepped aside, letting their back-and-forth conversation steer itself through a few of the Casting Qs.

Their unlikely partnership began in 1989 with the miniseries War and Remembrance *and features such as* Cheech and Chong's Nice Dreams, Pet Sematary, Naked Gun, *and the* Police Academy *series. The pair joined Spelling Television in 1996 to cast* Beverly Hills, 90210. *At the time of this interview, they were anxiously awaiting the premiere of* Titans, *Spelling's short-lived drama for NBC. The partnership was dissolved in late 2001, but both remain active in casting.*

Road to This Position

Champion—Many years ago, we did a film called *Troop Beverly Hills*, and that was Tori Spelling's first movie, so Mr. Spelling was thanking us, by bringing us on with *Beverly Hills, 90210*.

Paladini—We get to do a lot of different types of projects because we moved from science fiction...

Champion—*Babylon 5*.

Paladini—...to half-hour television to gritty independents to a martial arts special effects extravaganza to a comic book movie.

Champion—We've been very fortunate to be so eclectic. I think the nature of the casting director's job keeps you from being bored. You're entertained every day. You don't have to have a nine to five grown up job. It's make-believe.

On Their 12-Year Partnership

Champion—I think we are so opposite. Mark was brought up very strict, Catholic, Italian, and I was the loose Jewess in New York. I was introduced to everybody by first names and he was introduced with last names. I will never get a last name right, but I can go, "Bonnie..." and he'll go, "Gillespie" and together, we get it right.

Paladini—I lean on her for certain things. You have different things in your life that are stressed as the way you see things, and I need her point of view on things.

Champion—Or he'll say, "You can't yell at that person," and I get back on the phone and don't yell. Or I say to Mark, "Push harder, push. Sell it."

Paladini—When we were doing *The Mask*, reading the Cameron Diaz role, we brought in everyone who could've possibly been the right one for this role, even the one who got us a good table at a restaurant. Well, the women really liked Fern, so I leaned on her to give me the female point of view. Fern liked Cameron the second she met her.

Champion—She's a broad. She's very confident. We watched her go so far. Mark, I have to say it. I keep saying I'm not going to say it, but it's such a great story.

Paladini—Go ahead.

Champion—She was my son's date to his bar mitzvah.

Paladini—So giving!

Champion—I don't know that $14 million a movie versus being my son's date is payback, but I think it makes us just about even. She stayed the whole night and she danced only with him. And she had a ball. I promised Mark not to tell the story again, but I had to. That's a real broad!

Paladini—That's okay. It's a good story!

Coolest Casting Gig

Champion—We're excited about every show we do, every film. I became a hero in my house, doing *Mortal Kombat*. We've had a good time on just about everything we've done.

Paladini—That's what's so exciting about it.

Champion—With *Babylon 5*, I had no idea what I was doing. I didn't know from science fiction.

Paladini—I loved it, just because we had to find a lot of classically trained actors, just to handle the language that Joe Straczynski was putting into it. If you had *Troilus and Cressida* on your resumé, you were seen.

Champion—That was a learning experience for us. It pushed us into theatre. And that meant we brought in quite a few people to Spelling that weren't getting seen before.

Key Things They Look for in an Actor

Champion—Talent.

Paladini—They gotta bring the material to life. Actors always ask, "What do you look for in a role?" And our response is always, "You show it to me." We don't know what we're looking for until you show it to us. The way you bring it to life is going to be different than the way another actor brings it to life. Some actors are so worried about fitting into what we're looking for when what we're looking for is diversity. If we brought in five people who did the exact same thing, if I were a producer, I'd fire us. We want to see actors bring new things to the table, then the director gets to see it, the producer gets to see it.

Champion—We're encouraged by the company to bring in various ethnicities in positive roles. Mr. Spelling would prefer to use diverse ethnicities in positive as opposed to negative roles...

Paladini—...because it was done for so long within the industry, with stereotypes. We're lucky because we came from that, with *Babylon 5* because Joe Straczynski's vision of the future was that a general could be any color, any gender. Because we came from that, and, not knowing, walking into this building, what we were going to be walking into, it became very clear that our style of casting was not only appreciated, but encouraged...

Champion—...rewarded, with show after show. That's great! And casting directors should be enthusiastic about their job every day. If they're bored with it, it's time to quit. If they're tired of doing it, move on.

Paladini—That's why we recommend term limits!

Champion—That's the way it should be. It should be up for CSA vote. "No, you're not allowed to come back. You don't love your job." Many of us don't deserve to be playing anymore. And it's a pleasure to play.

Pet Peeves

Champion—To all my SAG members out there, I would definitely move to have a reader in the room as opposed to the casting director. I should sit, as a princess, with Mark as a prince, and we should watch your scene. Between reading, and not being very good readers, and looking at your resumé, and watching your performance, it's too much. Just let me be the audience.

Paladini—The union should organize something so that actors do it, they provide readers for themselves so that we can just look at the performance.

Champion—There should be a hotline of readers. The SAG members have not made it an issue.

Paladini—They'd rather complain that casting directors can't read than actually do something about it.

Champion—It's a tough process. It's in the actor's best interest to have a reader in the room. Of course, you have to prescreen the reader so that the reader doesn't outshine the actor, but I do believe it is something that would help an actor, enormously. I've been on this soapbox for years.

Paladini—Every class we teach, we mention it. The reason it even became an issue was because we hear, "Oh, you're such good readers!" And they tell us how awful everyone else is.

Advice for Actors

Champion—It's hard. It's something requires stamina. You have to learn to reject rejection. When people tell you not to take it personally, where else do you take it? You say, "They're talking about *me*. They said no to *me*. How do I not take *me* personally?"

Paladini—There are so many reasons why people don't get the part. Actors have to understand that it's not a negation of their talent just because they don't get the part, or just because they don't get the callback. Honestly, we call back an actor because it's going to show them off the best. We won't call back an actor if we know that they're talented but this role doesn't show them off the best. We don't want to burn them with our producers. If they see someone in a role that's not the best for them, producers will make the judgment that they're not good...

Champion—...rather than not right for this role. Also, it's your audition. I've got the job, Mark's got the job. When you walk in the office, you control it. Tell me if you prefer not to talk and just want to do the read.

Paladini—I always say, if you ask a question before your read, be ready to incorporate the answer into your work.

Champion—If you start off on the wrong foot, stop right away. You know when you start off wrong. Stop yourself. It's your audition. That's what it's all about. Also, if you're going to sit and wait for your agent to do it, get a day job. To be a self-sufficient actor in this town is the ticket. Between sending postcards, trying to find the breakdowns out yourself, going to classes, doing these wonderful workshops, doing these terrific showcases, reading *Back Stage West*, and going after every God damn audition, learn your craft.

Paladini—When you're just beginning and you don't have an agent, and a manager is excited about you and wants to build your career from the very beginning, that's good.

Champion—But do your homework on that manager.

Paladini—Research them.

Champion—Young talent must be old-brained. Don't be taken in by the beauty of it all. It's hard. Life is hard.

Paladini—With pilot season, limit how many auditions you attend in a day. Preparation for an audition is so important, because things can move very quickly. A preread in the morning can lead to a producer's session, a studio session, and a network session within 24 hours. I don't agree with the mindset that you can *wing it* for the preread and if you get a callback, [then] you'll start preparing. If you connect with the material and confirm your audition, you should show your commitment from the very beginning of the process by preparing for the audition. So many times I've heard actors say, "I didn't read the script because I had four other auditions today." That's like going on a first date and saying, "I would've showered but I had a couple of dates earlier."

Best Way To Get Seen by Them

Champion—We appreciate classes and getting involved in workshops and showcases on our lunch hour. We like going to the Improv and the Comedy Store. I like the Groundlings.

Paladini—We have friends that do a lot of theatre. So, we end up seeing a lot of theatre just because our friends are asking us to go to it. When you teach as much as we do, and see our friends' theatre projects, the stray invitation we'll attend is rare.

Champion—Go to workshops. We appreciate postcards.

Paladini—Postcards!

Champion—We strongly, strongly, strongly recommend postcards. Instead of wasting money on envelopes and headshots and resumés and postage, send me a postcard. Tell us what you're doing lately. Tell us what you've just done. Tell us what agent you're with now. Tell us to watch you on a certain thing. The postage is less, and your face is right in front of us. Let your agent send your 8x10. You send a postcard.

Their Opinion on Alternative Submission Methods

Paladini—Online submissions are the future, unfortunately, we're not yet advanced enough with our computers to fully handle it.

Champion—Our assistants have that set up, but I don't know that we have the luxury to do the computer casting. I think I'm just an old fashioned kinda gal. I like what I like.

Their Operating System

Champion—We have our own books for people we've seen on every project. We try to keep very solid notes. Although, when it's late in the day, and you go back months later to review some of your notes, you really start to laugh. The notes get a little more absurd or bizarre, as the day goes on.

Paladini—And whenever we have a new assistant, I have to go, "No! No! Don't read my notes to them! You read them, then interpret my notes and give them feedback."

Champion—We have little choice numbers or checks because actors are the most brilliant upside-down readers.

Fern Champion & Mark Paladini, CSA–107

Paladini—We create code.

What They Would Change About the Casting Process

Champion—I would change the whole casting process. I hate it. When I see actors sitting in a room, staring at each other, with sweaty palms and parched mouths, they walk in here like they're just off a desert. I tell them, "Please carry water." They're parched! I hate that it never changes, that you always have to audition. Being in the same room with your competition, I think, is the toughest thing. I don't know any other way, because they would've done it already. I think it would've been accomplished.

Most Gratifying Part of Their Job

Champion—When you put together a terrific ensemble. When you've found someone that everybody's just, "Whoa! Wow! Incredible," that just rejuvenates you into being a child again. It's like getting an A on a test and being rewarded.

Paladini—There are a lot of okay actors out there who will shine in one role. It's our goal on every project on every episode to find the role that makes you shine, not just the role that makes you okay, not the role that shows you being competent, but the role that makes you shine.

Champion—You have to remain challenged in this business. So, along with stamina, it's patience. Everything comes around. I love what I do.

Paladini—I love what I do too.

Champion—Sometimes it's not a blast, and that's when you sign your own report card. Other times, it's up on the fridge.

LORI COBE-ROSS

If Lori Cobe-Ross weren't a casting director, she'd be a teacher. She conducts a weekly on-camera technique class, in addition to frequenting cold reading workshops and loves the opportunity to interact in an instructional way. Her casting credits include everything from 1989's version of Divorce Court *to the erotic thriller* Animal Behavior, *from the pilot* The Everyday Adventures of Hannah Handleman *to PBS's* On Common Ground.

With early aspirations for being an agent, Cobe-Ross attended law school rather than going the usual mail room route, worked as an agent for a short while, then moved into casting. By 1994, she was casting 20 features a year in the erotica genre. She now casts everything, including musical theatre, and says, "every day is different," which is an aspect of the job that she truly loves.

First Casting Job

Open House in 1987. It was a slasher film starring Adrienne Barbeau. "My dad was producing and I asked if I could cast it."

Road to This Position

"Jag Mundhra, the director of *Open House*, kept me very busy after that," she said. The most popular film she did with Mundhra was the direct-to-video favorite *Night Eyes* starring Tanya Roberts. Cobe-Ross was making such a good living doing erotic thrillers that she didn't want to give it up, but eventually, she felt the proverbial envelope was being pushed in the realm of simulated sex. "I had to use the same people over and over again, because they were the ones willing to take their clothes off for scale." Even though she was doing other projects as well, eventually, Cobe-Ross shifted to doing mainstream films. She cast her last erotic thriller, *Shades of Gray*, in 1997.

Coolest Casting Gig

"*Divorce Court* was fun. It was the last season they did in Los Angeles of that run before moving to Florida. We did 110 episodes in ten weeks. It was great fun, actually. We got to Taft-Hartley people. I got to cast everyone I'd ever seen who I liked, which is hard to do when there's a feature, especially independent features, with like 20 roles or something," Cobe-Ross related.

Key Things She Looks for in an Actor

Be prepared. Make a choice. "You can tell who's winging it," she said. "Get the sides as soon as you can, and really make a choice, even if it's wrong. Just let me see that you've made a choice. We can always redirect you," she said. "There's too much competition for you to do your best performance in the car. I respect actors who ask questions before they read. You need to have all the information available in order to do your best performance."

Pet Peeves

Props and pantomime. Cobe-Ross noted that she feels embarrassed for the actors that feel they need props. "Also, don't use your finger as a gun. You have the sides with you in one hand and this fake gun in the other, then you have to turn the page, so you lose the gun," she explained. "You don't have to act as though you're eating if the scene takes place in a restaurant. I know you can eat. Just do the scene."

Advice for Actors

Cobe-Ross acknowledges that this business is an intimidating one. "This is the only job where they're rejecting *you*," she said. "But you chose the job."

"I recommend that you work in a busy casting office and see just how many envelopes are not opened. Then, you'll know for sure if it's the business for you." Most importantly, Cobe-Ross noted, "You have to really want to do it. If you kind of want to do it, that's not enough."

Now, specific advice on doing erotic thrillers: "Do *one*," she said. Cobe-Ross acknowledges that the allure is strong, since the money is so good. "But it's hard to break out of that. And they try to make it comfortable for you, but the fact is that you're naked with a stranger pushing the fake sex. You don't want to get pigeonholed."

She works hard to make sure that actors who read with her are very relaxed. Cobe-Ross occasionally employs a reader, but generally reads with the actors. "It's in my best interest to get the best performance out of you. So, I want you comfortable."

Regarding pilot season, Cobe-Ross had this advice: "In casting a pilot, we are looking for someone that an audience will care about every week. Make your character special, someone we will want to care about and therefore want to see week after week."

Best Way To Get Seen by Her

Agent and manager submissions, of course, and cold reading workshops. "Make sure you have to audition to get in [the workshop] so that you'll be paired up well. Make sure that the casting directors that go there actually work. We don't need to go there for the money, because it's not a lot of money. We go there because we truly want to see talent. I can see 20 to 25 good actors at once," Cobe-Ross explained. "I book dayplayers myself, so if I know the actor is right, from the workshop, then I can just hire them."

Do unsolicited submissions work? "They don't get opened a lot of the time," she said. "Postcards are good if you know what I'm casting and you know you're right for something and they are much less expensive to send than a headshot, but if you're telling me to watch you on *Days of Our Lives*, I'm not going to. But, actors feel that it's good to be proactive," Cobe-Ross continued. "But, my husband said to me, 'If I knew that your job was this trash-intensive, I don't know if I'd have married you,'" she laughed, indicating one of the pitfalls of casting projects from her home office. "Even for low-budget films, I get tons of submissions."

Her Opinion on Alternative Submission Methods

"I use those [online services], but I like holding up the two headshots and deciding on them that way," Cobe-Ross said. "I have no fear of the technological casting methods, and I think it's especially good for commercials or things you have to get done quickly, and great for getting sides to the actors, but I like holding those headshots."

Her Operating System

"I keep binders and binders of the people I've seen and think that I can use. I go through them when I start a project," she said, "as well as going through my notes on the computer, notes I've put on their resumés when I've seen them."

What She Would Change About the Casting Process

"Well, what's to change?" Cobe-Ross acknowledged that there are elements that are uncomfortable for the actor, but that the process has been working so far. "Producers and directors need to hire the casting director that they feel comfortable talking to 25 times a day, and at midnight most times," she said. Strength in that relationship makes the best environment for casting to take place.

Highlight of Her Week

Getting to call an agent to tell them their client has gotten the job. "I just love that. That's the fun. We have to say no a lot more than we get to say yes."

Most Gratifying Part of Her Job

"Seeing the finished project and feeling that it really worked. When you go with your gut, you're usually right. That's cool."

MARKI COSTELLO

Marki Costello has a way of putting people at ease. She is genetically funny [granddaughter of Lou Costello], sparklingly charming, and intensely honest.

From the office that is her management company, casting company, and nerve center for her hosting seminars, Costello juggles casting some of the hottest reality projects on TV (such as The Bachelor, Meet My Folks, *and* Temptation Island II*).*
"I do a pupu platter of stuff. I used to hush-hush the fact that I did reality, but now I'm laughing all the way to the bank. For whatever reason, we're dying to see real people on television."

Turns out, those people who populate reality shows don't just wander onto the set. Nation-wide searches are conducted, and Costello is the casting (yes, casting) director who handles them. Call it talent-coordinating, call it reality programming, call it casting. The key to filling a reality show with people viewers love to watch? Honesty.

First Casting Job

With Chuck Berris Productions. "We were the little peons of the casting world," Costello qualified, of the job in which she cast *The Dating Game, The Newlywed Game*, and *The Gong Show.* "When we'd finish a season of one, we'd move on to the next one. I was working all the time, and that's where I got my first taste of reality casting."

Road to This Position

Costello wanted a break from game shows, so she studied for two years with Joanne Barron at the D.W. Brown Studios to become an independent film director. "I was learning a language so that I could communicate with actors. What I learned was that so many people don't know how to act," she observed. "And so many others don't know how to audition."

Costello began coaching actor friends on the craft of auditioning in the mid-1990s. "I would say, 'Are you for real? You're going in without having developed that character?' I started teaching a weekly class. And then slowly, the casting started coming back. I realized, oh wow, I miss this," she said, of the epiphany that led to opening her own company.

Costello did pilot casting for *Change of Heart, Debt*, and series casting for *Perfect Match* and *I Want a Wife: Alaska*, in addition to a dozen national ad campaigns. "I'm the real girl queen. I do reality and hosting. Hosting is a form of reality, because I'm asking you to be yourself at your best," she clarified.

After working on the MOW *Saved by the Light*, Costello was bored. "It was so formulaic. All they wanted at the network is the A-List and B-List and C-List of people with TV-Q. It was such a machine. I want to be inspired. I want people to aspire to be the best *them* they can be. Why is Oprah [Winfrey] successful? Because if she's excited about a book, everyone knows about it. Same with Rosie [O'Donnell]. She was genuinely excited to meet the people she had on her show. Viewers love to relate to people. Relatability is a huge part of reality casting."

After casting the hugely successful reality show *The Bachelor*, Costello turned down casting *The Bachelor II*. "I had worked so hard for two years with no breaks. Also, I was ready for something that wasn't a known commodity," she added.

Her Thoughts on Host Casting

"Hosting is basically taking someone and saying this is the best of you. You have to connect with somebody right away. I need beauties who are smart."

As for hosting skills, Costello is of the opinion that the skills "can be 100% learned. You can learn the Teleprompter. And then, your tape, your picture—everything—has to be indicative of where you are strong. Do what you're strongest at and *then* flex the other muscles."

Costello's credits in host casting go from TBS's bumper programming such as *Dinner and a Movie* and *Movies for Guys Who Like Movies* to feature programming such as *Speed Dating* for Universal and *Big News* for Buena Vista.

Her Thoughts on Reality Casting

"Reality is a different beast," she said. "We're not looking for someone to be the best in that role. We're looking for someone who will make for an interesting dynamic. We really have to peel that onion. We're doing thorough background research on these people but we have to be able to *get* them in ten minutes or less, if they're going to be relatable on the show."

With *Temptation Island II*, Costello spent five minutes with each couple, interviewed each person alone for ten minutes, brought them back together for another five minutes, and then edited the tapes of the candidates down to 25 minutes to present to the producers. "We put people on tape without having 20 years of history with them," Costello admitted. "So, I have to ask tough questions. I tell them to cut the crap and tell me the things they *don't* think I want to hear. I want to hear the good, the bad, and the ugly."

Meet My Folks posed a different challenge. "We were casting an entire family," she exclaimed. "I needed to find—in Los Angeles—entire families willing to do this, passing background [checks], and interesting to watch, week after week."

As for the concept that being on a reality show can launch an acting career, Costello is very opinionated. "Sure. It can open doors. But it's like you're given eight-and-a-half minutes. Can you stretch it to 15? To 20? To 40? Yeah, but you have to work it. Reality will open doors, but you have to be able to walk through them with something. The test for yourself is, 'What can we relate to?' If you provide the ultimate fairy tale, we're with you all the way."

Can an Actor Do Reality TV?

Sure. According to Costello, an actor who has a full life outside of acting, and who is not earning a living as an actor, is a prime candidate for reality shows. "I want to get to know *you* as a person. I put actors on [reality shows] all the time," she said. "Just don't tell me you're an actor all the time. In reality [shows], they'll wonder if you're acting. If you really make your living by hostessing, let's talk about that. If you're not paying your bills as an actor yet, then I can talk with you about what your real life is, and that may be perfect for a reality show." The key, according to Costello, is being real and being relatable.

Pet Peeves

Flakiness. Costello has a way to combat what she calls "a huge flake factor" with regard to reality casting. "There are hoops for the actors to leap through. There is an application process that requires a certain amount of tenacity. These people are going to be checked out mentally, physically, emotionally, and have their background investigated," she explained. "But, can you imagine being the guy who's going to meet these pre-screened women [on a show like *The Bachelor*]? You can't get such assurances from a random meeting in a bar!"

One downside to the extent of background investigation: finding out your favorite candidate won't pass the test to get on the show. "It's like falling in love with someone and discovering they aren't who you thought they were. I tell my producers *not* to get attached to anyone until they pass *all* the tests."

Advice for Actors

"You have to set boundaries in this business. Stand firm. Do your best, and trust that—if the planets are aligned—your talent will be recognized." The key to having boundaries work in your favor, according to Costello? "Stick to them."

Costello loves meeting actors who are honest and responsible. These people—whether they are actors or not—make for the most interesting relationships. And if it's not a show yet, it could be soon. Costello has plans to turn the behind-the-scenes adventures of casting reality shows into a reality show of its own. Stay tuned!

Best Way To Get Seen by Her

If you are an aspiring host, send your headshot and resumé to Costello marked "Attn: Hosting Department." If your interest is in reality programming, make sure your agent is aware of that interest, because she does release breakdowns.

"It's amazing to me," Costello began. "We're bringing people in to showcase for the heads of networks and the agent doesn't want their talent involved in reality programming. Where else are you going to get in front of the heads of networks? We had a guy on tape for *Meet My Folks* and they wanted to see him for a series. His agent said no, thinking it was reality. He missed out on the opportunity to shave a few years off his climb to network. His loss," she said with a shrug.

Her Operating System

"In this business, your word is all you have. I am a woman of my word. I return all calls each day. I have zero tolerance for people who can't return calls. If you can't get back to somebody in a week, you're in the wrong business."

Her Opinion on Alternative Submission Methods

Costello maintains a database of real people—including actors. "I can email anywhere and have 10,000 submissions for my database in just a few minutes. I keep copies of everything for five years from our submissions and searches," she noted. To get into Costello's database, call her hotline and mention that you read *Casting Qs* or just watch for information online. She encourages all of her producers to have websites available for their shows, prior to production. That way, she can put the word out online and receive submissions from anywhere in the world. "I want to be online when we *start* the process," she said.

Most Gratifying Part of Her Job

"I'll fight for someone I believe in. I'll go to network and insist that someone get in for a show. I stand firm. There is no room for being wishy-washy in this business and I'll push if I believe in you. I feel good about that. I leave knowing I've done everything that I can do."

Hotline: 888.878.2634

BILLY DAMOTA, CSA

Billy DaMota began casting in 1985, after moving to Los Angeles from San Francisco. In addition to casting hundreds of films, commercials, television shows and industrials (such as If Tomorrow Comes, Night Stalker, America's Most Wanted, *and* The Last Second Chance*), DaMota is a musician [he and his band perform most Monday nights at Babe's & Ricky's Inn], a poet [*Whispering Lunacies: 100 Love Poems *is available on Amazon.com], and an actors' advocate. His crusade to end the system of "paid auditions" in the current workshop culture doesn't just seem personal. It is personal.*

Road to This Position

DaMota's first casting jobs included assisting on studio films such as *Commando, Predator, Project X, The Running Man*, and *Three Amigos*. "I was thrown right into the mix, right away," he said. His first solo casting gig was for the feature *Miracle Mile* starring Anthony Edwards and Mare Winningham. "After that," DaMota continued, "I worked on *Colors* and *Above the Law* and then did dozens of independent films. In studios, I felt like they were more concerned with marketability than with talent. That's not to say that you don't have to be concerned with marketing, of course," DaMota conceded. It was in the early 1990s that DaMota began doing commercial casting. "Feature directors will do commercials between doing their movies and I was asked by Alex Proyas—for whom I'd done some additional casting on *The Crow*—to do a commercial," DaMota revealed. "I've now done 50 with him."

Coolest Casting Gig

According to DaMota, *Colors* was an amazing experience. "It wasn't just a creative venture, but a cultural adventure, an opportunity to see another side of the world. We cast actual gang members," DaMota commented. He fondly recalls working with Robert Duvall, Sean Penn, and Dennis Hopper. DaMota's favorite connection from the film? "The discovery of Don Cheadle."

Key Things He Looks for in an Actor

DaMota speaks of an actor's toolkit and acknowledges that there are only three things it *must* include.

"(1) Training—and not one-day workshops or weekend intensives; (2) A Great Headshot—it's your calling card, so it should be great, and you should use more than one, if you're going for character and comedy roles, but always have one excellent dramatic close-up headshot, without your hand in it, without some weird angle where I see your feet—and I don't know what this thing is with actors not wearing shoes in their headshots—just give me a good headshot; and (3) An Accurate Resumé—put what you have done it, even if it's just small theatre, student films, industrials, and your training. Do not make up credits—and it happens all the time. There's not a lot of things you need, just a few tools, but they should be good, strong ones—the best you can afford," according to DaMota.

Advice for Actors

DaMota believes that most actors suffer from the fear of taking chances. "My advice to you: break the rules!" This does not mean pulling stunts or losing all common sense for the sake of being wacky. "I'm talking about the interpretation of a role," DaMota continued. "Somebody that puts a little bit of a different spin on it, or does something different, they're the ones who book the jobs."

Why are actors afraid to take risks? DaMota believes actors become overwhelmed by the numbers. "You think there are 100,000 actors you're competing against, but really, you're competing against complacent people who are waiting for the phone to ring, who have no initiative for their career. I'd say five percent of the actors who read for me are actually prepared," DaMota said. *Five percent?* "Yes," DaMota insisted. "And *prepared* means they've looked at the script and have made character choices. Sink your teeth into the role. Don't ask for the sides five minutes before the callback. I do a lot of independent films with first-time directors and I don't want to expose them to actors who aren't sharp and ready to work," DaMota explained.

He stressed the point that actors narrow the field for themselves by being prepared, by doing homework prior to their auditions. "Actors need to know how different casting directors think," DaMota advised.

Pet Peeves

"One of my pet peeves is with casting directors who don't take a chance on unknown talent. It's intrinsically a part of their job, and to see them not do it, that bothers me," DaMota explained. Not only does DaMota feel that discovering talent is part of his job, it is the part that fulfills him. "When I bring someone new and fresh and special to the attention of the director and the producer, I come off looking like a hero," he said.

Why aren't more casting directors eager to make these discoveries? "There's a certain amount of laziness," DaMota explained. "It's easy to just depend on your agent relationships [to guide you to the talent]."

And what about Billy's *big* pet peeve—casting directors who get money for seeing actors at workshops? According to DaMota's research, "many times, it's an assistant you're meeting with, anyway—and I see that as the guy on the ground with the little orange cones, who directs in the fighter pilot in for a landing," he said. "If I want to learn to fly an F-18, I don't want to study with the guy on the ground who's doing the waving in," DaMota concluded.

According to DaMota, "actors should never pay for a meeting, a reading, or an audition. As long as there's a profit motive in selling these meetings, showcase workshops will continue. They are against SAG Rule 11, State Labor Code 450B, and were once against CSA bylaws. There's no curriculum, there's no lesson plan. How can they call these *classes*? It's so egregious. I am so vocal about my disgust over these workshops because until there is a revolt by actors, they will continue to happen." DaMota's advice? "Be proactive to get as much information to as many actors as you can. These workshops are illegal, unethical, and ineffective. Workshops are not a tool, they're a paid audition, they're a lottery. When actors stop paying, casting directors will stop charging." To that end, DaMota has developed www.DoNotPay.org.

Little Known Fact

"I've written a few movies that have been produced, such as *Energy: The Movie*, which I wrote with Timothy Leary in Italy," he revealed. "Good luck finding it, though. It's a wacky sci-fi thing."

His Opinion on Alternative Submission Methods

In his opinion, there must be enormous central databases, before more casting directors will use online technology. "Not enough casting directors or agents are using [the technology] yet. It's like email was ten years ago. Within the next couple of years, it will become part of the protocol.

It's not that far off," he predicted. Once online services offer streaming video, high quality digital video, and a powerful database, use will increase, according to DaMota. "Old Hollywood casting directors and agents may never care to log on, so it won't be universal, but in a couple of years, it'll be everywhere," he summarized.

Best Way To Get Seen by Him

Send in that headshot! "Right now, send me a headshot and resumé, with *Casting Qs* written on the outside of the envelope. I'll know you've read this piece, that you know a little bit about me and the way I work, and I'll take a look at you," DaMota offered.

Most Gratifying Part of His Job

Finding passion. "Like with any business, be at the top of your game. No matter how successful you get, you should continue to study. Take chances and be passionate! Have passion for what you do or make space in this town for those who do."

SHAWN DAWSON, CSA

Shawn Dawson is one of the two Dawsons at Ulrich Dawson Kritzer Casting, one of the busiest offices in Los Angeles. The other is Eric. Robert Ulrich and Carol Kritzer round out the partnership. A pro at casting series such as Odyssey 5, The Dead Zone, Dark Angel, *and* The Chris Isaak Show, *Dawson asks one big favor of the actors who self-submit: put the title of the show on the submission envelope. You couldn't imagine how much this helps, in such a busy office.*

Key Things He Looks for in an Actor

Preparedness. "Often, scripts are available in our office but nobody picks them up. Do your homework before meeting the producers. The stupidest thing actors can do is ask questions of the producers," Dawson explained, noting that, by the time an actor is at the producer session level, all questions should have been asked.

An important element to preparedness, according to Dawson, is being specific. "Make a choice," he said, simply.

While Dawson respects the craft of the actor, it is not something he has aspired to try. "I've never had the desire to be an actor. I couldn't do it. You're putting yourself out there and being rejected. It's like a bad dating scene. But everyone in our company is married to an actor. We empathize. We know what you go through. There's a misconception that casting directors don't like actors. It's just not true," he explained.

Advice for Actors

Training is important, according to Dawson, but it's not everything. "This girl tested for a series regular role and she was new to the business," he began. "She was one of three girls we discussed hiring. She'd trained here and here and here. The director wanted to know why she wasn't any better. Training is great, but too much of the same training can hurt you. Just because your resumé is great doesn't make you a better actor."

For Dawson, training isn't just scene study and on-camera technique. "Training includes knowing what's going on in the business. Don't come in and say, 'I don't really watch TV.' You have to know styles, tones, and what's on right now. Look up the director and the casting director on IMDB before you come in. Know what we've done," he advised.

Pet Peeves

Going too far. "There's an acting school that tells actors to do something outrageous in order to be memorable. I can tell the actors from that school. I've had my hair played with. I've been kissed," Dawson recalled. Does he remember these actors? "We remember these people... as freaks," he joked.

Best Way To Get Seen by Him

Submissions. "We open everything. I love postcards. If I like your look, I'll tell you to bring me a headshot and resumé," he said, of receiving a photo postcard first. However, make sure your approach is a personal one. "A postcard with a label and no handwritten note, just a printed invitation to your theatre performance, is so random. We like it personal. This town is about relationships," Dawson summarized.

To that end, Dawson attends casting director workshops. "I'll spend the first hour of a workshop telling our office's likes and dislikes, recommending what to do when you come in for the producer," he explained, noting that the rest of the time is used to see an actor's work.

His Opinion on Alternative Submission Methods

"I've tried [Internet casting services], but until we know that 95% of all agencies are online, it's twice the work. We do online and paper submissions because we don't want to miss anything," he said.

And, speaking of missing something, what role does diversity play in casting? According to Dawson, when an agent calls to ask whether someone of another ethnicity can be submitted on a role, he finds that refreshing. He does, however, discourage against-type submissions without a call first.

What He Would Change About the Casting Process

The rushed timing of it all. "A series is cast weekly. We'll get the script on day one and have producer sessions on day four. That's two days to preread 800 to 900 actors for one line. We'll then bring six people in for producers." Exhausting or not, Dawson's job is one that keeps him very gratified, and very busy.

PAM DIXON

Pam Dixon works alone. She has never had a partner in casting and truly loves the title of "independent" casting director. Her film credits include the Robert Altman films Dr. T & the Women *and* Cookie's Fortune, *many Alan Rudolph features, the action flicks* Vertical Limit *and* Striking Distance, *and cult classic* The Craft.

Those who employ her services as casting director trust Dixon's instincts, knowing she'll deliver the actor who is best for the role—and one whose name we'll all know, once the film opens.

First Casting Job

As a trainee for CBS Television in 1982. "We were casting the two-hour movies of the week."

Road to This Position

Head of Talent and Senior VP of Casting at ABC, then Production VP at Paramount Pictures. Next up, Production VP at Lorimar. "I started my own casting company in 1989," Dixon recalled. "I'd gone away from casting and into development, had two children and knew I couldn't do development with two kids." Dixon joked, "Since I wasn't handy and couldn't sew, I thought, 'This might be a good idea.' I was having lunch with

Brandon Tartikoff who was thinking of bringing me to NBC and he said, 'You were always good in casting. You should start your own company.' He really did influence me," she remembered.

Coolest Casting Gig

"*Zorro* is definitely one of them," Dixon said. "That was due mainly to the search for the girl; having seen over 3000 women, and really looking at the whole world, not just going along with the stereotypical confines of the role as written," Dixon recalled.

Also on her coolest list, the Alan Rudolph film, *Investigating Sex*, starring Nick Nolte, Neve Campbell, Alan Cummings, Jeremy Davies, Julie Delpy, and Robin Tunney. "I had a great time. I had to cast the fourth lead from London so I had John Light call the director in Brazil and speak to him in an American accent," Dixon explained. "The director took him sight unseen, based on the phone call and my recommendation, and now he's been signed by CAA, and he's starring in a film."

Key Things She Looks for in an Actor

"A sense of confidence, honesty, and a sense of humor about life."

Her Favorite Audition Tale

Colin Farrell auditioned for the lead in *American Outlaws*, the role of Jesse James. "I brought him in to meet with the president of Morgan Creek, Jim Robinson. Mr. Robinson hired him for the role based on one meeting, having never seen him do anything. He was just very real," she said.

A major highlight for Dixon was reading in the trades that Colin Farrell got $2.5 million to star with Bruce Willis in *Heart's War*. "I think that's great," Dixon said with a smile. [Note: Farrell was reported to earn $8 million for *S.W.A.T.* in

2002.] "The same thing happened with Matthew McConnaghey. He did *Angels in the Outfield* for scale plus ten and three months later was making three million," Dixon recalled.

Pet Peeves

Unpreparedness. "Not that one has to memorize the scene, but an actor has to take the time to decide on choices before coming in," Dixon explained. "An audition is not an attempt. You need to make a choice and go with that choice, right or wrong."

Advice for Actors

"I'm still a believer that training is important; whatever training that is right for you," Dixon said. "I think casting is about more than a look and that really good actors will succeed."

"Don't get discouraged," Dixon continued. "Anything you really want is hard to get." Being prepared and doing your best keeps you from getting discouraged. "You just may not fit that part. Step back from it. Try again. So much of it is timing."

Best Way To Get Seen by Her

"Have a really good picture," Dixon said. And what's that? "A picture that looks like you." Dixon doesn't worry too much about what's on your resumé because, "I don't know how true a resumé is. But if a picture intrigues me, I'll bring you in. I go through every piece of mail personally. If you send me something, I will see it, that I guarantee. Whether or not I'll call you, I won't guarantee," she joked.

"Using different paper is nice. It attracts my attention when the presentation is neat and looks as if it took some effort, or the letter says something interesting." So, is a cover letter really that important? "If you send a picture with no cover letter, it's just like every other picture that comes across my desk," Dixon shared.

One major point Dixon made: "I do not attend [pay-to-play] showcases in any way. Never have. Never will. I do go to theatre, but I won't do anything where actors have to pay to be in something. I have strong feelings about that."

Her Opinion on Alternative Submission Methods

"I think [Internet services] are basically a waste of time. A good 8x10, with a nice cover letter will do much better with me," Dixon shared. She does use The Link, since agents submit using it. But, again, Dixon stresses that she will use "no online casting that costs the actor money."

Her Operating System

Pretty unique. "There are maybe ten casting directors like me. I do everything myself. You read with me. I have no associates. My assistant does not preread. The organization is in my head."

An encouraging note from Dixon: "I hold generals two times each week. Half of the actors I see come in from agents, the other half from unsolicited submissions."

Trends She Has Observed in the Casting Process

"I'm not crazy about the trend where you're good looking and there's not a lot of attention paid to how good an actor you are," Dixon complained. Farrell, Dixon's find for *American Outlaws* had strong theatre and training credits from Europe. "He may have been unknown to the world, but he's not unknown in terms of craft," Dixon explained. "I'd like to think we're now reviving the trend of good acting coming first."

What She Would Change About the Casting Process

The committee aspect of it. I'm on my own and have worked for seven years as a consultant [to Morgan Creek]. That I love! In a studio, everything is on committee," Dixon said. "Try to get ten executives sitting in a room together to agree on [lunch], let alone the same actor!"

Most Gratifying Part of Her Job

"Fighting for what I believe is right. Taking a chance on new people and having them do a great job to prove me right. That's the fun of casting, when your instincts are confirmed."

MICHAEL DONOVAN, CSA, CCDA

Michael Donovan knows the "every day is different" routine of an actor's life. This actor-turned-casting director continues to work as a director, teacher, board member for West Coast Ensemble, and liaison between the Casting Society of America and the Commercial Casting Director Association. His credits include Falling in Love, Super Adventure Team, *ads for McDonald's and Mercedes Benz, and the feature film* Fudge.

With over ten years as a commercial acting teacher under his belt, Donovan also offers ongoing private coaching, kids' classes, and occasionally conducts theatrical acting classes. With all the charisma of a performer, in the new offices of Michael Donovan Casting, Donovan admitted to having further plans as a Hollywood Hyphenate. "I'm gonna write the book at some point because I have so much to say."

First Casting Job

Over 11 years ago with Beth Holmes, who was casting a spot for Payless Shoes. "I was directing a play at West Coast Ensemble and Beth came back stage and asked me to direct some casting sessions. I was an actor and someone was offering me money so I said yes," Donovan recalled. "I ended up totally winging it. The first session was totally hellacious where we had a full family group to look at every five minutes," he said.

Road to This Position

A few months later, in the same busy office, Megan Foley brought him on as an assistant. With Foley, he went through the ranks from assistant to associate to partner and was with her until 1997, when he partnered up with Jeff Hardwick, who was an agent at the time. "November 2001 marked the end of Donovan Hardwick Casting in an amicable split," said Donovan. "It was time to part ways."

In addition to casting and teaching, on some indie films, Donovan has moved into producing. "Often when casting directors come on board, there is no money and no cast. Our work is what gets the film financed. I want producer credits. It's a natural progression, especially with independent films."

On Being a Former Actor

"I understand. I'll be your best friend, and I'll be your worst enemy, because I *know*. When you're unprepared, I'm thinking of the stack of photos over there of people we didn't bring in."

Donovan continued working as an actor until 1995. "[Casting] was my survival job for the first five years I was doing it. I was doing tons of freelance work but when I partnered with Megan, I dropped the acting. I found myself thinking about what was on my desk while I'd taken off at lunch for an audition," he explained.

"As an actor, I'd gotten to the point where I decided that every penny I earned was going to come from this industry. That meant, come hell or high water, I was earning money from the industry; taking PA jobs, whatever. You have to decide to do that, or else you'll just become really good at being a waiter and you'll really care about it. And that's fine, if that's what you want to do."

"So, really, I stumbled into casting," he summarized. "Years ago, if you'd told me this is what I'd be doing every day, I would've said, 'No way!'"

Key Things He Looks for in an Actor

"In an audition, be prepared. Make specific choices. Specific choices though are not enough," Donovan clarified. "You must commit to those choices. And I'm not talking about being outrageous."

"When actors are nervous, they tend to 'bland it out.' That's when you'll hear the casting director say, 'That was fine.' That's an awful word; *fine*. If you've come to Los Angeles as an actor, you are expected, at the very bottom of the talent pool, to be good. That's not enough."

Donovan also looks for, you guessed it, professionalism. "Treat it like a business. Actors forget that they're running a small business, really. Treat your audition like a job interview."

Commercial Casting Vocabulary—Avail

"If you are put on avail for a job, check that shoot date for conflicts. Only commit if you are, in fact, available. In this office, if I put you on avail, it's serious. Other casting directors may put everyone on avail. I know those casting directors will be pissed that I'm saying that, but it's just ludicrous. The most I'll do is three [actors]. We put out avails because things happen to make an actor unavailable between the time you leave my office and the time the commercial shoots."

Commercial Casting Vocabulary—Conflicts

"If your agent inadvertently submitted you, with a McDonald's spot, on a Wendy's campaign, it is *your* job to remind the agent that this would be a conflict. May everybody get to the point where they can't remember how many conflicts they have running! Until then, you should know and make sure your representative knows before you even go in. If you don't check to be sure it's a conflict and then book the job, you are the one breaking a contract; not your agent." Some companies, such as those in the telecommunications industry, have created a major grey area, according to Donovan. "If you have Nextel cell phones and are offered AT&T cable, you'd better check to see if that's a conflict."

Acting in Commercials vs. Theatrical Performances

"Acting is acting. Good acting is good acting. The application is different, based on whether you're doing theatre, commercials, episodics, sitcoms, films. Good acting is good acting, period. And I have no problem crossing someone over from one to the other. If you're a good actor, I'll remember you."

"Just remember, with commercials, you must be trained and ready to go with strong choices—but not outrageous choices."

His Opinion on Casting Director Workshops

"The debate over workshops is outrageous. If you don't want to go, don't go. I recently hired a series regular from a workshop. It's a great opportunity. The general is a waste of time. I'd much rather see you audition for me, and not for a specific role as much as for the future. What does a mass mailing cost? $300? That's ten workshops. I would think you'd be better off getting your work in front of people instead of an ice cold envelope that may or may not get opened."

Advice for Actors

"Study, study, study, study, study. You're not going to respond to every teacher," Donovan acknowledged. "When it gets a little tougher, hang in there," he advised. "Maybe that's when you're about to have a breakthrough or make a really wonderful discovery. When you're studying, sift through what works and what doesn't work for you. Everybody will have some sort of gem to share with you, some will have many."

Donovan's advice on the business end of acting included accurate record-keeping. "Know who is in the casting office. I still get mail for people who haven't been here in years. Get the most recent guides from Samuel French. I personally think Samuel French is like a toy store for actors. Spend time there! The more information you have, the better. Read everything you can."

According to Donovan, if acting is your life's ambition, you must be dedicated to it. "I had a student in class who, with six auditions, we determined, spent 18 minutes acting that week. That's unacceptable. Six auditions is a lot, but that's still only 18 minutes spent on what you say is your passion. If you're working on acting every day, doing even small theatre, you alleviate the pressure that goes with having only one audition a week. You must understand that most of what you do, as an actor, *is* process. Once you understand that, you become a better actor."

"Check in with where you are. You're not always going to use the same bag of tricks. The bag you used as the hot babe at 25 is just not attractive at 40."

"If you change representation, update us. We're often like detectives trying to find you. Make sure we, the buyers, can get to you, the product. Call SAG's Actor Location line at 323.549.6737 and see if you can find yourself. If you can't find you, neither can we."

"Remember you are one of the few people in the world lucky enough to do what she wants to do. An audition is a chance to do your thing. We love what you do. We love watching you do what you love doing. If you're jaded and bitter, we smell that when you walk in the room."

"Walking in with one picture is crazy. Have a stack with you at all times. But don't make me choose between two different styles of headshots."

Pet Peeves

"Being late. I am very understanding if you've had your representative call to let me know you're running late. But if you're 20 minutes late and it's the last session of the day, or you had the last appointment of your category, there's a problem. There's no excuse to not have a cell phone any more. Get the basic cell phone and only use it when you're stuck on the 405 and on the way to an audition. This is a 24/7/365 job, so you must be reachable. I have booked people on New Year's Eve, on Thanksgiving Day, you name it. My first acting job in Los Angeles was one for which I was called at midnight to be on set at 6am. They couldn't reach their first choice. I was glad to be second choice—and reachable—because it meant that I got the job."

Another pet peeve for Donovan is hearing, "I haven't had a chance to look at this," from the actor entering the session. "Material is available way ahead of the audition. I put the script in the lobby, I put the sides up on the fax services. There's no excuse. We know how many people want this job, so it's awful when someone who has booked an audition isn't prepared for the opportunity."

"Get all the sides for all the characters. If you're up for a lead role, you can bet you'll learn about your character from reading all the sides."

"Don't ask what we want you to do. We want to see what you do with the material. Show me why you're the one for the role."

Further pet peeves include responsibility. "Actors say they don't watch commercials. Then how do you know what a mom in a commercial wears? Well, it's a blue chambray and khakis. You need to know what the trends are. It's a business. Treat it as such."

"If you have no interest in taking the role, please don't come in for the audition. Regarding nudity, be honest with yourself. Remember you're not naked for five minutes, but for days."

Best Way To Get Seen by Him

"Postcards are great," Donovan said, adding that theatre invitations are always encouraged. "I see a ton of theatre; a minimum of three shows a month," he continued. Donovan is the resident casting director for the International City Theatre in Long Beach, for which he casts five shows per year. "Theatre is by far still the best [acting] teacher. It is so valuable," he said.

As for mailing unsolicited headshots and resumés to Donovan, "I can tell when it's a mass mailing. We open every envelope, and I only *don't* respond to the ones with no notes. Handwritten is fine and it should be short, but there should always be some kind of note that personalizes this experience."

"A submission needs a letter inside it. Postcards are great, but if they're not sent for a particular reason, it bothers me. Invite me to something. I see tons of theatre. There are 1200 productions in town a year, so you should be doing something."

Donovan *will* look at your demo reel. "The reel should be no longer than five minutes and not include work where you were an extra."

Non-union actors are welcome to submit to Donovan. "It's no problem, but don't lie about your union status. We can Taft-Hartley you by your skills, so don't lie on your resumé's special skills section. List your skill level for what you do."

"If you have no credits, you must at least be trained. There's certain training I respect more than others. Audit classes, ask friends which coaches are respected."

An Average Day

There is no such thing, but Donovan starts his day as most casting directors do: with Breakdowns. "Breakdowns are useful for me. I'll sort the photos into yes, no, and maybe piles. I'll hear agent and manager pitches, set up audition times, and start seeing people."

"For commercials, we'll see 75 to 100 people a day and 20% will get callbacks. It all depends on the budget and how many days we have to cast."

His Opinion on Alternative Submission Methods

"I was a beta tester for an online service. It seemed to make sense ecologically and economically, but it's not going that way. There's something cool about holding headshots and resumés. But, if it's $60 a year to get in an online service, it's worth it; especially the *Academy Players Directory* online. Grab every possible opportunity to be seen."

His Biggest Casting Challenge

"Casting *Fudge*. We saw 2,400 kids."
Beyond that is the challenge of working in casting "We're one step above actors in the food chain. Trying to find the next gig is sometimes the greatest challenge," Donovan remarked.

Trends He Has Observed in the Casting Process

"We're more and more open for all ethnicities in Breakdowns. Most of my breakdowns now go out with 'all ethnicities,' especially commercials. We're looking for all kinds of mixes, depending on the market and the product."
One caveat: "I love when an agent calls and asks if I'll consider [going another way] but I don't want them to just dump it in the submission."

What He Would Change About the Casting Process

Lack of autonomy. "We'll need an actress to say one word and the producers will want to see eight people. It's frustrating. I want to say [to the producers], 'Why? You trust me. Why can't I just bring in someone for those tiny roles based on what I know the actors can do?'"

Most Gratifying Part of His Job

"Finding an actor I believe in, and having the producer go, 'Yeah!' I honestly get just as excited as back when I would book a job myself. It's incredibly exciting."

DONNA EKHOLDT, CSA

Donna Ekholdt is a former actor with a great deal of advice for those pursuing the craft. Her enthusiastically-presented ideas could fill a book—and they will—as she's currently putting one together. "In the academic world, we train actors to work, but not to gain work," she said, adding that she aims to fix that, by sharing what she teaches in a printed form.

As VP of Talent Development and Casting for Big Ticket Television, Ekholdt—whose credits include Guys Like Us, The Parkers, *and* Wolf Lake—*shops for actors in an attempt to assemble a delicious recipe, discovering new ingredients as she goes.*

First Casting Job

Intern. Ekholdt started out with Meg Liberman and Marc Hirschfeld in 1988. "I had an inkling that casting might be interesting to me. I was an actor at the time, though," she said.

However, Ekholdt *still* considers herself an actor, really. "If the aliens come and abduct me and torture me and scream, 'What are you?!?' I'll answer, 'I'm an actor!' In my soul, my thinking is that of an actor. I am very process-oriented. I love the breaking down of the scene, the trying to make that electricity occur between two people. That's my best access to what works in casting," she revealed.

Road to This Position

"I went from intern to assistant at Liberman Hirschfeld. I also worked as an assistant to Tammara Billik. I worked with Gary Zuckerbrod and then did features with Karen Rea for over two years. While I was with Karen, I was just starting to do some casting on my own, doing independent films, small films, *tiny* films," Ekholdt continued.

"I got an opportunity to work with Susan Bluestein. I was so taken with her love of actors. She has spectacularly fabulous taste. I knew, with her, I'd get to do amazing projects." With Bluestein, Ekholdt cast *The Oldest Living Confederate Widow*, *Children of the Dust*, the Menendez brothers' miniseries *A Killing in Beverly Hills*, and *NYPD Blue*, for which they received an Emmy.

"I got an offer to be Manager of Casting for NBC. I was there for about a year. Then I went on to become Director of Casting at 20th Century Fox. At that point, they began a huge investment in writers. Randy Stone and I oversaw casting on 48 pilots and five presentations in three years, in addition to the on-air programming," Ekholdt recalled.

"In 1999, as I was wrapping up a year and a half of independent casting, I was asked if I might be interested in a job at Big Ticket. It was clear that this company was about to make a little change in its focus, and I wanted to be on board for that."

As VP of Talent Development and Casting, Ekholdt oversees all development and series for Big Ticket Television. "I'm fortunate enough to be in a position where I am often involved from the pitch," she said.

Key Things She Looks for in an Actor

"Training, training, training, training, training. If you're not getting better, you're getting worse. There's no holding any ground. You're like an athlete or a dancer and you must work it every day. You're either moving forward or slipping backward at all times," Ekholdt explained.

Ekholdt also looks for marketing savvy. "Be educated enough to know—or resourceful enough to find out—what you're selling. After all, in what other business can someone who is brand new make $700 on their first day of work?"

Also on Ekholdt's list is a sense of humor. "I like to call it charm, but that's really a sense of humor about yourself or a sense of irony within the role."

When Ekholdt meets actors, she's shopping. "[Casting directors] are gourmet shoppers. The chef hasn't written the recipe yet and we're out searching for ingredients. I need all A-quality ingredients. I can bring five options to the producer and director (who we'll call the chefs)," Ekholdt clarified.

"If the script calls for cinnamon and brown sugar, I'll bring three flat-out cinnamons, one weird-ass exotic cinnamon (just off what the script calls for), and maybe one nutmeg. Now, if the chef goes with nutmeg instead of cinnamon, I need honey instead of brown sugar. Brown sugar is no longer part of that recipe." An actor must realize, according to Ekholdt, "Sometimes you didn't get the callback even though you were A-quality brown sugar because I need honey now. It's a totally impersonal choice. It's not a personal issue when you don't get cast. It's not a statement of the quality of your work. A specific combination of ingredients is required to balance the recipe."

Ekholdt continued, "Some ingredients, I have to keep in my kitchen at all times. Some, I have to go out and search for. I have a diverse spice rack, but I don't keep cumin on hand. It's good to know where I can get it, though," she laughed.

Pet Peeves

Unprepared actors. "They disrespect the profession by not keeping their tools sharp. That means they also disrespect me," she explained.

Advice for Actors

Keep a daily journal cataloging the time you spend on acting. "This includes time spent on mailings, working on monologues, scene work. When you look at that, you'll be surprised how little time you're actually investing in what you're calling your dream," Ekholdt revealed.

Ekholdt explained the financial element of an actor's life in terms of total opportunity cost. "If you're spending a lot of money on clothing, other than maybe one outfit for auditions, if you're spending a lot of money on a car or on your apartment or on anything other than your craft, it removes your ability to spend time improving your craft. You don't have time to work out with other actors, or take a class, if you're working all the time to pay for your car," she summarized.

"The single biggest weakness in actors, I think, is that they're so won over by the look of money. The truth of the matter is, every time you spend money in one place, you can translate that into the number of hours spent away from your craft."

Her Opinion on Alternative Submission Methods

Ekholdt acknowledges that an Internet casting database is around the corner. "There's limited accessibility right now, but it's growing daily. For now, actors should spend their money on class. Make sure you can audit a class before dumping all of that money on the table. Spend your money getting very good pictures," she added.

Best Way To Get Seen by Her

"I actually do read my own mail. Every Saturday morning, I go through the stack of mail I've taken home. So, if you're inviting me to see a show on a Thursday night, you'd better get that invitation to me in time for my Saturday stack the week before," Ekholdt advised. "I do see theatre. Between

Meredith Layne [Manager of Casting] and myself, we do get out there a great bit. It's great to let us know when you're doing theatre."

Do not send an unsolicited demo reel to Ekholdt. "It's like crashing an audition. It's an unscheduled appointment with me. Send your headshot and resumé with a request to send me tape. If I'm interested, I'll ask to see it," she said.

Most Gratifying Part of Her Job

"I happen to be a casting director who relishes the business of the business. I take pride in being a creative whose left brain works very well. I am very good at finances, and I take great pride in my abilities as an executive. It has actually surprised the right brain side of me!" Ekholdt laughed. "I love the fact that there are time limits in television casting. We have to get a lot done in a short amount of time. I like the challenges and I relish the process."

Ekholdt summarized, "I like what I do. I'm smart enough to have other options. So many people, especially actors, forget to enjoy the journey from A to Z. I say take the time to enjoy those middle 24 letters."

MIKE FENTON, CSA & ALLISON COWITT, CSA

As with most partnerships, the one enjoyed by Mike Fenton and Allison Cowitt includes completing one another's sentences and supporting their decisions. This was my first partner interview in which the pair spoke in unison several times. I suppose spending sixteen years together (casting such projects as Excess Baggage, Dante's Peak, *and* Arabian Nights*) will have that result. Luckily, neither half of this partnership seems to mind the collaborative input.*

How the Partnership Began

"She made the mistake of interning for us," Fenton began musing about Cowitt. Cowitt quickly clarified, "I was interning while I was in college. The week before I graduated, they offered me a job. I think they were just desperate at that point," Cowitt joked. "They needed me to replace a girl who was leaving right away. I asked if I could have a week off after graduation." "We said, 'No!'" Fenton interjected. "I started the day after I graduated," Cowitt concluded. "In sixteen years she's had one day off," Fenton insisted. He continued, explaining that then-pregnant Cowitt would work from home after giving birth. "She's taking everything with her, including the fax machine." "I'm not taking the fax machine!" Cowitt assured.

Coolest Casting Gig

Hallmark miniseries *Dinatopia*. What made that fun to cast? "The dinosaurs," Fenton said, quite simply. "They really let us cast actors," Cowitt clarified, "we didn't have to use names, which was really great" "That took about two years to make," Fenton noted, regarding the special effects for that project.

Key Things They Look for in an Actor

Professionalism. "It's really important when they come in that actors be prepared. This doesn't mean memorizing every single word on the page. They get too worried about the material that way," Cowitt explained. "Learning the material and becoming comfortable with the material is far more important than memorizing. That way you can change when asked to make an adjustment," Fenton commented. "Adjustments are so important. Be ready to make a change or an adjustment. If you've memorized the script, direction for a change can throw you," Cowitt related.

Pet Peeves

When asked what sort of things actors do to shoot themselves in the foot, Cowitt quickly commented, "Bringing a gun with you to an audition." Fenton agreed that props are out of place at an audition. Another big pet peeve for the pair? "Chewing gum," Cowitt said. "I really hate that," Fenton chimed in. "It's too casual."

"Actors can sublimate their nervous energy if they remember that we don't bite. Maybe some casting directors do, but we don't," Fenton insisted. "Some do," Cowitt exclaimed. "Speaking for us, we want the actor to succeed. We don't invite an actor in hoping he'll fail. We want the actor to score. The sooner we find an actor who scores, the better for us. Professional casting directors prefer quality to quantity," according to Fenton.

"The actor needs to be patient. Decisions aren't necessarily made on that same day you audition. Know that it takes eight or nine months to cast a project sometimes," Cowitt concluded.

Advice for Actors

"Always be early," Fenton commented about auditioning for his office. "At the very least, be on time," he said. "Prepare for traffic. It's better to be early. If people are early, we'll take them in the order they show up. We'll adjust to them," Cowitt noted. "It does get a little hectic during pilot season when actors are seeing four other casting directors that day," Fenton added. "But we can be flexible," Cowitt explained.

"Study," the pair said in unison. "Do student films to get the film experience. Student films these days are being directed by people who will be directing features a year later," Cowitt clarified.

"Do theatre," Fenton added.

"Get a demo reel together, but don't go to a corner production house and have a demo tape made. You're just throwing money away," Fenton insisted. "If you do a stage play, it's okay to videotape it for your own use, but don't send it to us. Use it to critique your own work," he concluded. "If you have to include a commercial on your demo reel, that's better than nothing. Documentaries are fine. Industrials are okay. We need to see you on film. Your reel should be no longer than five minutes," Cowitt insisted.

"Do soap operas. Soaps are great training grounds. That is truly an arena in which you learn, not memorize. It's great training. You can learn professionalism on those sets," Fenton commented. "Any on-camera experience is better than none," Cowitt summarized.

"Rather than sitting around waiting for the phone to ring, use the time. Use Final Draft, or any of those writing programs, and write. It will guide you through the process. Writing opens you up to how the system works," Fenton advised. "More and more actors are doing more than acting," Cowitt observed. "Actors like working with actors because they understand. So go ahead and do more than acting. Write. Direct. Produce."

Best Way To Get Seen by Them

"Only through your agent," Fenton stressed. "Don't fall in on a casting director without an appointment. Don't just drop in." "Can I see him? Can I see her?" Cowitt spoke, as if she were an actor stopping by. "I see him sitting there!" "It's a real no-no," Fenton concluded. "A producer, a manager, these folks can get you an appointment.

We do look at headshots and resumés, postcards," he continued. "Tell us to watch you on a show. Tell us when it's airing. I don't attend theatre as much as I'd like to, because I'm reading scripts," Cowitt explained. "We have CSA meetings, union meetings, screenings, and casting sessions into the night, so we really don't attend theatre. I'm on the foreign film committee at the Academy of Motion Picture Arts and Sciences so that takes Wednesdays and Saturdays and sometimes Friday nights. There's always something. But we do try," Fenton added.

Their Opinion on Alternative Submission Methods

"We're not really using a system yet. I think, when there's *one*, it's going to be great. But when there's three..." Cowitt began. "And not all actors are on each one..." Fenton interjected. "We can't really use them," Cowitt summarized.

"Get into the *Academy Players Directory*. We use the book. Our assistant uses The Link," Cowitt revealed. "AMPAS got smart and is only publishing twice a year," Fenton commented.

Cowitt concluded, "As for the Internet, for expediency, it's great. But the Internet isn't going to take over my habit of sitting on the floor and making piles of headshots. That's how I go through everything."

"Now, as for technology, it'd be great if we could stream our video tests to Shanghai instead of waiting four days for the tapes to get to Shanghai. It's coming. It's imminent. But we haven't seen it happen just yet," Fenton said.

Trends They Have Observed in the Casting Process

"Obviously, younger," Cowitt said. "Always younger," Fenton echoed. "The unfortunate thing is that there's a lack of work for the secondary older character right now. It's dried up. There's a gap. They can't even make a living anymore until they're playing grandparents," Fenton added.

"Budgets killed the mid-range actor. The main actor gets $20 million and everyone else gets scale plus ten," Fenton revealed. "So everyone else works for scale or they don't work," Cowitt lamented. "If the main actor would take $17 million and allow us to spread that $3 million out to those other actors, we could really do something. But no one wants to go back to that," Fenton commented. "It's just wrong." "There's no going back," Cowitt added.

"If the studios and important producers would get together and set a limit, which of course they can't do, then we'd have something. This could save the business. Films are either made for $3-4 or $100 million. There's no in-between," Fenton insisted. "But that's not always true," Cowitt interjected. "Independent films have name casts now. Look at *The Royal Tenenbaums*. Used to be, films like that wouldn't have had those names. It would've had actors that you were introduced to in that film, not actors who were already movie stars." Fenton clarified, "Well they need those established actors in order to get distribution." Cowitt exclaimed, "Which is ridiculous!

What's the point of Sundance now? It used to be..." "Introducing directors and actors," Fenton said. "It's not what independent films started out to be," Cowitt recalled with a sigh.

What They Would Change About the Casting Process

"It's nothing that we can change, but I'd like to see producers allow the casting director to create the budget for the project and determine which roles get which amount. We used to do it that way," Fenton recalled. "They would give us X amount of money and we could pitch to the actors," Cowitt added. "That way, we could provide the director with the best actors, and the money be damned! It would be much better for the projects," Fenton proposed.

Most Gratifying Part of Their Job

"Having done this for as long as we've been doing it, it's fun," Fenton said. "I agree," Cowitt added. "Seeing our names on screen with something that works is nice," Fenton said with a laugh. "But being involved with films that survive is *really* nice." "It's also nice to know that you have the right actors playing these parts," Cowitt said.

Do you ever really know? "Yes." Cowitt said, in unison with Fenton, who said, "No. Not really." Both laughed as Cowitt added, "Sometimes, you know."

JULIA FLORES

No one needs to explain the value of theatrical credits to Julia Flores. Though she has worked in film and television, her main job is casting national tour and Broadway productions for McCoy Rigby Entertainment, including Tony and Emmy-award nominated Peter Pan.

Casting for over a dozen theatre companies from TheatreWorks in Palo Alto to the Globe Theatre in San Diego, and from Milwaukee Rep to the Arizona Theatre Company, Flores strives to keep her actors as well-informed as possible. "I want actors to know everything that I know about the role," she said, after a morning of Los Angeles-based sessions. The travel involved is part of Flores' commitment to doing her best work, noting that, "When you hire Flores Casting, you get Julia Flores. I'm just that committed to my clients."

First Casting Job

Crime Story, 1987. "I was an intern at a casting office and we were working on the Vegas-based show. We were video taping everyone in town and shipping the tapes out," Flores recalled. "I had no idea what [casting] was. I was going to USC and my counselor said I would never graduate on time without doing an internship. So, I interned for Richard Pagano and Sharon Bialy. They offered me a job when I graduated and I worked there for three and a half years." After taking a little time off, Flores worked with several other casting directors, including Barbara Claman and Judith Weiner. "I really missed doing theatre, though. San Jose Rep and Berkeley Rep were very supportive and kept coming to me to get me to cast things, so I decided to do theatre exclusively." That was in 1995. Flores got her BA in Theatre, but "casting turned out to be everything I wanted: stability with creativity, structure but with each show being different. It's exciting but it's also stable, and I can use my business head and my artistic eye. There are long hours, but it's exciting. I love my job, but it *is* work," she said.

Coolest Casting Gig

"Each one of them is so special. I would have to say, the Jimmy Buffett musical, *Don't Stop the Carnival*, based on the Herman Wouk book [was coolest]. We did that show in 2001 at the Atlantis Resort in the Bahamas. This was five or six trips down to the Bahamas to do the casting with Jimmy, who makes everything fun. Luis Perez, the choreographer, and Michael Rupert, the director, did phenomenal work with the Bahamians we cast. It's Bahamian law that you have to cast 75% Bahamians [for shows playing there]. It was not easy, but it was just so much fun. So, as far as the cool factor goes, that was just cool."

Before moving on to the next Q, Flores interjected, "Either that or the national production of *Peter Pan* for the McCoy Rigby family. They're amazing people to work with. To have a show on Broadway was one thing, but to have it with them, that was a gift. Also, I have so many kids in my life—to be the lady who *knows* Peter Pan—that was great. It'll always hold a very special place in my heart."

Key Things She Looks for in an Actor

"Commitment, commitment, commitment." How does she know commitment when she sees it? "It just screams out at you. I know almost from the minute I meet an actor for the first time, whether they take responsibility for their career, whether they are doing the work in order to get the results they want. There are some actors who want the result without doing the work. I have no patience for that," Flores insisted.

A Typical Audition

"We very rarely have the actors improvise. My clients know I don't like surprises and I don't want actors to be surprised. So, as long as the actors are forewarned about something, I'm okay with that. I'll notice that a director is tossing an additional scene into auditions and I'll go down and prepare the waiting actors for that. I try to give actors as much time to prepare as possible. I want actors to know everything that I know about the role, where we'll be reading in the script, rehearsal and performance dates, money, contract, who will be in the audition, all of that. Agents always would ask the same thing, so I finally put it all in an info sheet and started saying, 'Let me just fax it to you.' I'd like it if the agents would then fax that to their clients. I don't know why they don't do that," Flores admitted.

"I love my actors," Flores continued. "I have utmost respect for my agents because I know how little money they're making on this and how dedicated they need to be to their actors to allow them to go off and do theatre for a certain amount of time."

Pet Peeves

"Laziness. Lack of commitment, lack of responsibility, lack of respect," Flores listed. At the time of our interview, Flores was holding last-minute auditions to replace the lead actor who had been cast two months earlier, but dropped out to take a smaller role in a bigger project. "I will never bring him in again. He made a commitment; he signed the contract. I cannot hire him again. It's about a work ethic," Flores summarized.

"I have fought for some of my clients to start coming to Los Angeles as opposed to Chicago or New York, but Los Angeles has such a bad reputation of actors who won't come into an audition because they want to stay available for TV and film. Or who will come into an audition and then turn it down because they want to stay available for TV and film. Or who will come into an audition, book the role, and then back out because of TV or film. My job is more challenging during pilot season than any other time because of the way actors are tuned toward staying available for TV," Flores admitted, noting that, had the interview taken place outside of pilot season, her pet peeve would simply be: laziness.

Advice for Actors

"Training." What does Flores consider the best form of training? Theatre! "Even for TV and film actors, theatre is where you learn *everything*. It's where you learn to be a better actor and a better human being, really. You can always tell a theatre actor," Flores explained. "Wonderful film actors are committed to going back to theatre. Again, it's about a commitment to grow and challenge yourself. Actors should be seeing theatre, doing theatre, reading plays. I find that actors will limit themselves by not experiencing theatre.

Krista Jackson is an actress I auditioned and used in chorus all the time. About a year-and-a-half ago, she told me she wanted to do more than chorus roles. I told her that as long as she could back that up with the work, I would support that position. She was my Evita last year and was really incredible. She made the commitment to see the decision through. She didn't just talk about it. She did a lot of really hard work. That's what I respect most in actors: hard work. The actors I hire work hard," she concluded, proudly.

Flores continued listing her advice for actors by saying, "Actors need to know we're on their side. I can't speak for all casting directors, but I go out of my way to make it easier on the actor. Acting can be so isolating. Actors need to remember that there are so many people who are on their side. The hierarchy makes it so that actors have no control and no say. Part of the reason I do theatre is because *actors* do theatre because they want to, not for the money or the prestige. Those are people I like to know."

Self-evaluation is important to Flores. "If actors don't get a job, they need to examine why. I have such respect for actors who call to get feedback, or have their agents call for feedback. Every audition is a growing experience, an opportunity to learn about yourself. If you don't get the job, it's not always about us, it's not always about them—and I hate to even put it in 'us' and 'them' terms. Learn from it. It's, again, about the commitment," she concluded.

One last piece of advice regarding auditions: "I wish actors would utilize the LORT/EPA auditions. Don't call me because you want me to see you. Pay attention to when the call is and show up for it! I'll sit here all day during a LORT audition, and just a handful of actors will show up. If you want the job, you should take advantage of that," Flores insisted.

Best Way To Get Seen by Her

No need for an agent, as far as Flores is concerned. "I am incredibly actor-friendly. Any actor who knows me knows that. I am only as good as the actors I know and the actors I love. Some of these actors I've known for the 15 years I've been casting. We've grown up together! They call me directly. I can have this open-door policy because actors call me, but they don't badger me. They're smart about it. They're human about it. Actors treat me with respect. I'll call actors directly if they're not with an agent, or I'll call them with notes after an audition," Flores included, in her description of her open relationship with actors.

Her Biggest Casting Challenge

"Finding people who are committed enough and skilled enough for the roles that I need. It's a happy challenge."

What She Would Change About the Casting Process

"I've pretty much changed everything I didn't like about casting sessions. I always hated that actors are the low man on the totem pole. In giving them more information, I'm trying to give them more control. I put a lot of thought into hiring a reader. I greet all of my actors personally and walk them into the sessions. I always say, 'It's great to have you here.' I know what it takes. Actors give up a lot to do theatre. I have no delusion over what it takes to do it. I wish there were a way I could help make actors more prepared, but I do everything I can. I try that with the info sheet and making the whole script available, giving the actors as much time as possible. I usually start making appointments at least two weeks ahead of time," Flores explained.

Most Gratifying Part of Her Job

"It's the magic. I am so incredibly blessed to have this job. I'm getting to see it all happen. I'm there from the very beginning. I miss all of the rehearsals, which is sad, but to see it all work out from the director's first phone calls with me to putting people in roles to seeing it all click in performances, it really is magic."

LAURA GLEASON, CSA

Laura Gleason is a former actor originally from the San Francisco bay area. In her pursuit of acting, Gleason attended Northwestern University, then left early to begin acting at the Neighborhood Playhouse in New York. Gleason finished her degree in theatre arts at UCLA. While in Los Angeles, she met her husband, actor James Gleason. "We lived here, both working actors, for five years and then went to New York, where we lived for 12 or 13 years. That's where I started casting."

In New York, Gleason worked as the original casting director for the soap opera Loving, *and cast a few Broadway shows and independent films. "When I moved to Los Angeles, I worked with David Cohen, who was a casting director at the time. We worked together on the pilot for* Key West *and have since done a film together." Gleason, who is a charter member of the Casting Society of America in New York, briefly moved into producing after casting the 1999 feature,* Crosswalk. *She is now hoping to head back into fulltime casting with theatre as the first stop on that road.*

First Casting Job

Associate casting director at the Public Theatre. "I was a professional actress for ten years and then decided I wanted to make a switch. This job opened up at the Public Theatre, for the New York Shakespeare Festival, and I really learned casting under Rosemary Tischler. I worked with Stanley Soble and Ellen Novack and that's how I got my start. There was no better place to learn. I got to know all of the agents in New York. Because I'd been an actress, I'd seen things from one side. Seeing it from the other side, I knew I'd found my niche," Gleason recalled.

Coolest Casting Gig

"It's hard [to select one]," Gleason insisted. "I love each one that I do! I love the theatre," she said, noting that she has cast theatre projects in Los Angeles as well as New York. "The theatre is my favorite to cast for, but of course, that's not where the money is. Still, I think my ultimate perfect job would be to be regularly employed casting theatre," Gleason concluded.

Her Favorite Casting Tale

"I almost lost a job, early on in my career, working on a Broadway show. Chazz Palminteri had created the role and then the show moved to Broadway. The show had gotten raves in its nine months off-Broadway, but the producer did not want to use Chazz in the Broadway run. I fought for months. Every time I talked to the producer I said, 'You're not letting him play the part and we've found nobody better. You've got to at least give him a shot as understudy.' Chazz was working as a bouncer to pay the rent at the time and I just knew he deserved to continue in this role. We were close to the final decisions and I was in a meeting with the producer when I brought him up again. The producer said to me, 'If you mention his name one more time to me, I will fire you!' I said, 'Okay.' Of course, the next day, I brought his name up again," Gleason relayed. "He ended up with the part, as an understudy. I still wonder, to this day, what this producer thinks of Chazz's career now," she said.

Key Things She Looks for in an Actor

Talent. "It's so subjective," she qualified. "I was really highly trained as an actress and I really have an understanding of the acting process. I totally *get* what it's about. I think, when an actor comes in who just has a freedom with their creativity, you can see it. When an actor has done their homework, they come in, they understand the role, they're not afraid to ask a question, that adds to whatever talent is there," Gleason continued. "As an actor, you need to make that audition time *your* time. It's your time. I don't care if 100 actors are waiting. Make the space your space. I'm very open to that. The only qualifier is, make sure, if you're going to do anything physical with the reader—which is usually me—that you check that it's okay ahead of time. I like to read with actors. I feel that I can tell whether they're giving anything. But I don't like being thrown around."

Pet Peeves

The wrong kind of training. "Actors take these classes where they're reading a page from a current TV show script. If you're spending that money for a class, you should spend it on a good *acting* class, in which you'll learn how to do good theatre pieces. Learning how to do theatre pieces is good because those pieces have substance. Cold reading workshops are a waste of time. Now, to be frank, I've done them, but I feel that I am qualified to teach. In New York, I taught an on-camera soap opera class. I think everyone should become comfortable with the camera, but I also think you need to have a solid theatre class. Workshops gave me a good chance to see actors, but an *acting* class should be something of substance for the actor."

A major pet peeve for Gleason is runaway production. "And it's not just [to] Canada. It's [to] Australia, England, Ireland, and even the eastern European countries. I understand why it happens but no one is doing anything about it. The only way that the problem of runaway production will be solved is by giving the same tax breaks for filming at home," Gleason explained.

Advice for Actors

"I always think of this scene from *The Days and Nights of Molly Dodd*. A wannabe actor is working as an elevator operator and asks a producer what advice he would give him. The response is, 'Keep at it.' That's really all there is to it," Gleason clarified. "Keep yourself busy acting as much as you can wherever you can. Work begets work. Classes will keep you stimulated, keep you up on your game, and help you network with fellow actors and directors. Don't let people dissuade you. If you feel a passion and you're doing this because you're passionate about it, you mustn't be dissuaded. Everybody will tell you how hard it is, but that's the name of the game. It's debilitating enough and you have to find every way you can to keep your spirits up."

"I feel very strongly that, for any actor that comes in, I want them to be wonderful. I want them to be the person that I can bring to the producers. I want it to work for them. I really feel that most casting directors feel that way. I love actors. I know how difficult the process is. I respect actors and really enjoy them as people and I want them to do so well. The thing that actors have to understand is that there are so many elements that go into casting—beyond their talents—that restrict the casting director in the decision. So often, the producer and the director have given the casting director guidelines that just don't fit with that particular actor at that particular time. I think that every actor has to go in and do the very best they can. I will always remember them. It may be three shows later, but I will remember and bring them back in," Gleason insisted.

Further advice from Gleason included knowing the importance of always working on something. "I can't stress enough how actors just have to work. Whether that means a student film, or a small play somewhere, you just don't know where an opportunity will present itself. Also, actors should be encouraged to take improv comedy classes. Not because the actor is funny but because improv really teaches you how to think on your feet. It gives you a looseness when you audition so that when the director gives you a change, you can go with the moment."

Best Way To Get Seen by Her

"Get in a good play," she advised. "When looking at a resumé, my eye goes to theatre credits, where the play was done, and who directed it. When an actor comes in the room, even for a television audition, it is obvious to me whether they were trained in theatre. It's a *good* obvious," Gleason qualified. "Also, I open all headshots and resumés that come in. I look at videos but the actor must send a self-addressed, stamped envelope so that I may send the tape back."

Her Opinion on Alternate Submission Methods

"You're talking to a computer illiterate person," Gleason joked. "I'm learning to like my computer, but there's something tactile about that headshot and resumé. That's how I learned to do it, with stacks, and I like to go back to my stacks. I would rather go to the book and look through the book, than look someone up on the computer," Gleason explained.

The book she refers to is the *Academy Players Directory*. "I cannot tell actors how important it is to list themselves in the *Academy Players Directory*. I've had a producer take the directory home, flip through it, and flag the actors he wanted me to bring in for him. It's such an important tool for the casting director. It's like your dictionary, if you're a writer. I cannot stress enough how important that is to be in the directory and keep [the listing] up-to-date."

What She Would Change About the Casting Process

"I wish that we had more time. Casting is a very fast process. I just wish there were time to see a few more people, to explore a little more. It seems to me that the casting director is the last one hired, and I would like to come in earlier in the pre-production process. The lack of time makes it hard to engage in what is really an artistic process."

Her Biggest Casting Challenge

Casting the soap *Loving*. "I did it all and I had no assistant and no secretary. They wouldn't spring for it. I did everything but cast extras and I had to beg them to buy me an answering machine! But I did it," Gleason explained. "You rise to it. It was my first television experience and I needed the job, so I did what I had to do."

Most Gratifying Part of Her Job

"It goes right back to actors," she said. "It's seeing the right actor in the right role and knowing you've succeeded. When the role goes to someone I've fought for because I know they're right, that is a wonderful feeling."

PETER GOLDEN, CSA

Peter Golden always knew he wanted to work in television. "I didn't know there was a job in casting. I was just in awe of actors and acting. My interest was behind the camera, behind the scenes. I was fascinated by people's abilities to turn themselves into people they weren't. I was somewhat star-struck,"
he explained.

From shooting 8mm film with friends in junior high to working as a PA at PBS's WNET while at Colby College, Golden worked with actors. In his current position as Senior Vice President of Talent and Casting for CBS, he works with many actors, but one former-actor in particular: Les Moonves. "Les has a keen instinct for casting," Golden said. As he shared information from his over 20 years in network casting, I learned that Golden's instincts are dead-on too.

First Casting Job

"I never thought about casting as casting," Golden began. "I knew I wanted to work in television. I watched a lot of television and I always assumed that Don Adams was Maxwell Smart and Barbara Eden was Jeannie and Elizabeth Montgomery was Samantha Stevens and Sally Field was the Flying Nun. I never thought about *how* that happened. It just was. I just saw shows and thought that was the actor that was right for that part." Through a friend of a friend, Golden became an assistant for Julie Hughes and Barry Moss in New York. "We were an across-the-board shop, doing Broadway, Off-Broadway, features, and, at the time, covering New York for ABC and later NBC. I worked up to associate and later began covering shows on my own," he recalled. Hughes Moss Casting was assembling the cast for *Endless Love* when Golden joined the staff. "They needed help for their open calls, for which they were legendary, after having found Rick Schroeder for *The Champ* that way."

Road to This Position

In 1986, Golden moved to Los Angeles, where he worked in the television casting department at Universal. He was later hired by Joel Thurm as head of casting at NBC, then by Grant Tinker to head casting at GTG. Golden later went to work as head of casting for Stephen Cannell and eventually moved into development. "Working with [Cannell] was like graduate school for writers," he recalled. Eventually, John Landis and Leslie Belsberg at St. Clair Productions hired him as vice president of development, and shortly after Les Moonves came to CBS, Golden did too.

Key Things He Looks for in an Actor

Listening. "If I'm reading with an actor and I pause, mid-line, and an actor jumps in, thinking it's his cue, I know he isn't listening," Golden said. Listening extends to the sounds indicated in the script, even when not provided in the casting session. "If the phone rings, you should pick it up after you've 'heard' the phone ring or looked to it as if the ring drew your attention there. Those details are important to the reality you should create for us," he summarized.

Pet Peeves

"Trying to figure out what I'm looking for, rather than just coming in saying, 'Here I am. This is me. This is who I am, what I look like, what I sound like, how old I am, and how I interpret this character. If that is what you are looking for, then I am that,'" Golden explained. He acknowledged, "It's a lot more complicated than just that and it's not a fair town," but in this town, according to Golden, one way to level the playing field is to know who you are and just be that, rather than trying to crawl into his mind.

Golden mentioned an agent-level pet peeve: "Agents who keep actors from auditioning. They are trying to protect the actor, and I appreciate that, but in doing so—in forcing us to make an offer before the actor even reads for us—they keep the actor from learning about the character and they keep us from learning about the actor," he said.

Advice for Actors

Golden explained that the only person who should be an actor is one who cannot *not* be one. "Remember that the real meat of the work you do is *getting* the role."

"Act at every opportunity. Go do tiny theatre out in the Valley where no one may ever come out to see you. Do student films that no one will ever see. Do the state fair. Don't do these things because they pay the rent, but to creatively satisfy yourself," Golden advised. "An actor should always, always be acting somewhere."

To that end, Golden recommended class. "Always be in class, working on your craft. Whether you're earning $20 million or you can't make the rent, you should always be working on acting," he said. "And be a good observer of people. Borrow from what you observe. It's the little things—like what an actor friend of mine said she observed strangers do on a subway—that could add to a character exactly what it needs."

Best Way To Get Seen by Him

Agents. "Agents are my saviors. They call me when they get excited about someone, and I'll see [an actor] based on that," he said. Golden also relies on his "amazing, incredible staff" of Lucy Cavallo (dramatic programming), Fern Orenstein (TV movies), and Karen Church (comedies), as well as other casting directors, to notify him of excellent work.

The Senior Vice President of Casting prereads actors on occasion, but primarily oversees the casting of all prime-time dramas and comedies, daytime programming, MOWs, miniseries, reality shows, and pilots. In assembling his staff of casting directors, Golden ideally looks for someone with whom he's worked in the past. Always, he seeks to employ casting directors with good credits, strong recommendations, and "a wide vocabulary of the acting pool," he said.

While the staff meets regularly as a group, Golden speaks with each casting director at least five times a day. He was quick to add that the "departmental secret weapon" for casting at CBS is his senior assistant, Marilyn Fischer. "She knows everything," he added.

"You never know what will happen. If you send me your headshot and resumé and it gets to me on the right day, that could be your way in," Golden explained. "However, make sure it's a realistic picture," he insisted. "It doesn't serve your purpose to send a somewhat misleading picture to me."

Put together a demo reel of your work. "I don't judge an actor on just their experience in the room [during a casting session]. That's such an uncomfortable setting for so many actors. That's why you must have tape. If you don't audition well, your most valuable tool becomes one great scene, even from a student film."

Trends He Has Observed in the Casting Process

Moving too fast. "There was a time when we would build shows around performers who had really worked, who had material, who had defined their voice. Now, the climate is so competitive, that we all take a shot on any stand-up with a good set and wait to see if it works," Golden lamented. "Performers need the experience behind them so that something happens beyond the actor delivering the words."

That being said, CBS is a good place to be, right now. "This is a very different CBS than the CBS I joined in 1995" Golden said. As he gestured toward the wall where each network's fall schedule is posted, he beamed with pride. His favorite? "I love them all," he shared. I'm very excited about *The Amazing Race*, and of course, *Everybody Loves Raymond* is the best half-hour comedy on television. *Judging Amy* is a traditional CBS situation with a hip, edgier take, and *CSI* is not how you traditionally thought of CBS four or five years ago. It's a great time, here."

His Take on Reality Television

"I see Reality Television as just another element of the divisions that already exist: News Magazine, Half-Hour Comedy, Single Camera Half-Hour Comedy, Drama, and so on. We are fortunate enough to have, as Les says, the Rolls Royce of Reality Television with *Survivor*, but I don't think it really affects the casting process for the other types of shows," Golden explained.

He expressed that, once your motivation in being on any show, reality-based or not, is fame, you, as an actor, are working toward the wrong goal. "Unless you really want to be challenged, there is no reason to be on a reality program. While it could be a step toward meeting a casting director, if you've been on a reality show, it really is apples and oranges to compare the two."

What He Would Change About the Casting Process

"Television casting is so quick. We have to deliver sometimes as many as 22 episodes very quickly. I wish we had more time to cast. It'd be more comfortable for both the actors and the casting directors. Of course, if there were unlimited time, producers and directors might never make final decisions, so the limit can be a plus," Golden laughed.

What is the timeline? "Within four to six weeks of getting the script, we're shooting the pilot, so sometimes our casting directors hold auditions with just an outline and one scene," Golden relayed. "The actor will go from reading for the associate to the casting director to the producer, do a callback, maybe read for the director, get to the studio level, and then final choices go to the network, all in just a few weeks."

Highlight of His Week

"Reading a terrific script, identifying an actor who is perfect for the role, and having that actor turn out to be available, interested, and affordable," Golden said. "And that happens more times than you'd think. It's great."

Most Gratifying Part of His Job

"I love television. I love watching the promos for the coming season and thinking that I had some small part in that. Marrying the right actor to the right role—there's something about that moment where something happens beyond the actor and the words. It's magic."

DANNY GOLDMAN, CCDA

Danny Goldman is a character actor. He has appeared in front of the camera on such shows as CHiPs, Happy Days, Soap, The Golden Girls, *and* Sabrina, The Teenage Witch. *He was the voice of Brainy Smurf and on top of all this, he has been a very busy commercial and voiceover casting director for over 20 years (clients include Toyota and McDonald's). He still directs theatre and occasionally acts to this day. He knows exactly how to put an actor at ease, as long as you can stand to hear it exactly like it is.*

What Makes a Former Actor a Good Casting Director?

"I won't keep people waiting. People keep actors waiting forever and I don't believe you get a good audition when people are pissed off for having waited an hour. You're already schlepping out all over town and spending the day in the car. Actors are treated badly, and I know that, so I want to make sure they have someone on their side, here," Goldman said.

Pet Peeves

Overdoing it. "Actors asking questions for the sake of asking questions, not to get answers. They work the room when it's a taped audition. That schmoozing doesn't translate and it makes the actor look unprofessional."

Best Way To Get Seen by Him

Come by. "I have a drop-off box in the lobby, so actors can come in and drop off a new headshot, an updated resumé, whatever. I go to showcases or the theatre about once a week. I know now what every New York casting director already knows and that's, 'You have to go out at night.' I like showcases and I like to attend comedy and sketch shows. It's a bad idea, though, to over hype a bad show. Make sure it's a show you want me to see before you invite me to it," he requested.

His Opinion on Alternative Submission Methods

"I'm old-fashioned, I don't care for it. I tried [using an online casting service]. It's a lot of work. I just don't want to sit in front of a computer all day. I know people who like it, but I'm just too fidgety! I'd rather go out into the lobby and ask if anybody knows anyone like what I'm looking for," Goldman said, gesturing toward a lobby buzzing with activity.

Trends He Has Observed in the Casting Process

"Improv, improv, improv! If you can't do improv in an audition, you're screwed. That idiot union says not to do improv in an audition, that we have to use sides. Forget it! Improv is the way we see what you can really do," Goldman explained, noting that producers are looking for improv now more than ever.

Most Gratifying Part of His Job

"We want to book someone we believe in, someone we enjoy. We'll keep bringing them in until the producers see what we see. Have passion for acting. There's lots of disappointment, lots of rejection in acting. Do it for the joy of it and not for what you hope to gain. If you're not passionate about it, don't do it."

MICHAEL GREER, CSA

For Michael Greer, casting is a family business. Her daughter, Kim Hodgert, a motion picture talent agent at CAA, led Greer into the industry. "I'm in the business because of her," Greer said, indicating that Hodgert's childhood aspirations opened Greer to the world that would become her career. With independent and studio feature credits such as Attraction, Face Value, *and* Power Play, *Greer has happily flourished.*

First Casting Job

Greer started out at Paramount Studios, working on *Webster* and *Brothers* as an associate under Vicki Rosenberg. "That's when they had a staff, but they stopped having a staff about five months later," Greer said with a laugh.

Road to This Position

"That's a long road!" she continued. Greer left Paramount along with Rosenberg and continued working with her for a few years. "Then I worked with Nan Dutton for a couple of years. Since then, I've transitioned from working in partnerships on various projects to working on my own," Greer concluded.

Coolest Casting Gig

Feature film *Attraction* was Greer's most recent favorite project. She cast this movie, starring Samantha Mathis and Tom Everett Scott, in 2000. "It was written and directed by someone I think is very talented, Russell DeGrazier. He also wrote the movie *Sunset Strip* starring Jared Leto," Greer explained. "He's very talented and he's wonderful with actors." Greer cited his respect for actors as a key factor in her enjoyment of the project. "He'd have them read the scene and then would just talk with them about their own lives. Then he'd have them do the scene again, with those thoughts in mind." Greer said she got to see actors do something even they didn't realize they could do, based on the subtle suggestions DeGrazier made in the casting sessions. "He had an ability to get actors to give their best. Invariably, when the actors left, I'd get a call a half-hour later from the agents saying, 'He really, really wants to do this,'" Greer recalled.

Key Things She Looks for in an Actor

"That's tough," Greer admitted. She indicated that there is nothing very specific that she looks for. "I like [an actor] to take it seriously and be prepared, but there are so many things actors bring with them when they read for a role that sometimes make you see the role in ways that you hadn't imagined," Greer explained. "Sometimes it may be interesting but not really work for the project. Other times, it brings dimension that suddenly makes the role come to life and often is not even what the writer imagined, making it a more interesting role. That's the exciting thing about actors; they bring something of themselves that changes how you see a role," Greer concluded.

Pet Peeves

Actors who are not prepared. According to Greer, there is no excuse for not being prepared. "Sides are available online or by fax. When I first started, [actors] had to come pick them up, and they would drive across town to do so. These days, they can get them anywhere," Greer insisted. "To come in, especially for a producer session, and not be prepared? It's inexcusable. You wouldn't do that in any other profession. You wouldn't do that with a board meeting. This is the career you've chosen. Take it seriously. It's called show *business*," Greer emphasized.

Advice for Actors

"I'm usually very truthful about how difficult this business is," Greer explained. She expressed that success is not *necessarily* based on talent. "There's so much luck involved. There are so many factors that go into why someone gets a role."

Greer's advice to the person who has chosen to work in an environment with so much risk? "Unless eating, breathing, and acting is what you have to do to live, you should do something else." Greer added, "If what I tell you discourages you, you really need to get another profession. The people who succeed are the ones who are determined to do so. They look at it as a career, they work at it, they study, they're in plays and doing anything they can to put themselves in front of an audience. They may not become big stars, but they'll work in this business and they'll have a career, because they're determined to. If you are determined to succeed at *anything*, you will," Greer concluded.

Her Opinion on Alternative Submission Methods

Greer certainly sees Internet submissions and online casting resources as the future, and one that's not too far off, either. "It isn't used as much at the moment because many casting directors aren't computer literate. That will change," she said. Once casting directors realize the power of holding a casting session in another state over the Internet, according to Greer, that change will come quickly. "It's a more efficient way to submit actors, but casting directors themselves need to look at it. That's the holdup at this moment. There's a snowball effect with technology. In a very brief time, we've come to rely on fax machines, answering machines, and cellular phones," Greer explained.

In addition to the lag in adopting new casting methods, Greer detailed a very practical reason that casting directors do not utilize the tools already in place. "Most of us are independent. We change offices. Not every casting director is provided with computer access in each production office." Is Greer cyber-savvy? "I'm becoming a techie! I don't understand how it works, but I understand what it can do. I want everything that is out there. I'm lusting over the new Mac laptop."

Best Way To Get Seen by Her

"It's hard to say," she began. "If you're with an agent who I know really well and who has taste I respect, if they recommend you strongly, I very definitely will see you. Otherwise it's getting yourself in front of audiences as much as possible; doing workshops, doing plays. If you're with some obscure agent, I may not see you [through that agent's submission]. I love theatre, and I attend theatre as often as I can," Greer revealed.

What She Would Change About the Casting Process

"I don't think I would change anything. I've often said it's a strange process, but it's the only way that we can do it. I sometimes think to myself, after a casting session, if people believed that this is what I do for a living, that people walk in and I say hello to them and then they might lie on the floor and writhe in pain, for example, and then they get up and say thank you and leave, you'd think that's a very odd thing for me to do for a living. But it's the only way we have to judge, really," Greer said, shrugging.

Highlight of Her Week

Casting sessions. "I do enjoy reading with actors."

Most Gratifying Part of Her Job

Assembling a cast of actors whose personalities create a relationship of its own. "You don't always have the resources to get the actors you want, with money and scheduling, but it's wonderful when you have something in mind and it comes together and it works really well."

IRIS GROSSMAN

Iris Grossman's first job as a casting director is her most recent one: Senior Vice President of Talent and Casting for Turner Network Television, where she oversaw casting of all TNT original films and specials. She joined up with TNT in 1993 and worked in a supervisory capacity on projects such as Gettysburg *and* Frankenstein. *She casts by instinct, and is rewarded by doing so.*

Road to This Position

Grossman was an agent at ICM for over 12 years. "The opportunity arose and I decided to make a career change—which wasn't that much of a career change," she explained. "Instead of selling a small client list, I now have a very large client list. Now it's every actor in the city." The major difference between her job at ICM and the one at TNT is what Grossman qualifies as a "fun" difference. "Instead of telling actors they didn't get the job, I get to tell actors they *did* get the job."

Coolest Casting Gig

Grossman refers to her many projects as her children, insisting, "All my children are my favorites." Grossman was nominated for an Emmy in casting *George Wallace* and she won the CSA Artios Award for miniseries casting in 1998. "That was a real turning point in my career," she said. "I realized that I could do it. The acknowledgment and the validation of working on that project was incredible."

In addition to the professional acknowledgment, Grossman holds a special place in her heart for her work with *Nuremberg*. She explained, "the whole concept of the Nuremberg Trials and the Holocaust and the justice that was performed on a humanitarian level was really quite moving for me."

Grossman continued, "but there's not any of my kids that I don't love in their own way. They each were special. Even the ones where I may feel I made a mistake, when I thought I was casting it right but didn't—when I went with a certain name instead of going with the actor who may have been perfect—[the project] is still one of my kids and I love them all."

That statement caused me to ask about the importance of instinct in the job of casting director. Grossman's response was simple, "The job is 85% instinct and 15% luck."

Key Things She Looks for in an Actor

"I love working with smart actors. I love working with actors who love to act," she said. "I had the pleasure last year of working on *The Mists of Avalon* with Joan Allen, Anjelica Huston, Samantha Mathis, Julianna Margulies, Caroline Goodall—extraordinary actresses—and to get to cast a piece for actresses and to hire that many women for such great roles, that was wonderful."

Pet Peeves

Grossman mentioned the same thing that is on the pet peeve list of every casting director, "People who aren't prepared, who didn't do their homework." Additionally, Grossman wants you to treat the audition process with respect, meaning that you dress for your audition. "I see so much inappropriate dressing; like they're going to the beach. Dress like a professional. I'm not saying you have to wear a suit and tie, but be clean."

Advice for Actors

At a recent seminar, Grossman commented that the biggest piece of advice is to be prepared and professional. She elaborated, "Know what you're doing, make a choice, come prepared, study your craft, and if you're coming in to read for a nurse, you don't have to wear a nurse's uniform. We have an imagination too."

Doris Roberts, who also spoke at that seminar, gave the "most incredible advice," according to Grossman. "She said you have to go in with a positive attitude. A negative attitude—they smell it coming through the door. Take the chip off your shoulder, take the negativity and leave it outside, go in, do your best," Grossman recalled. "In casting, we want you to be the one who's going to get the part because then the job is done. I want you to come in and get it."

Continuing her explanation of the damage actors' negativity can do, Grossman revealed, "When I was an agent, it was my fault that the casting director appeared the enemy to the actor," and she speculated that this is still the case. "Depending on the level of the actor's experience, the casting director will never ask a huge star or someone with an extraordinary amount of credits to come read for them just because it's an ego trip. If a casting director asks them in, it's to read *with* them, not *for* them." Grossman explained, "I've been in enough readings where I'm going to help you with your reading. You have to give the casting director some benefit of the doubt that we're there to help the actors," she said. Further clarifying the role of the casting director, Grossman asserted, "we're not just people who make lists and check off names. If it weren't for certain casting directors—and a lot of actors acknowledge it—they wouldn't have had career chances."

So, what can agents do to soothe the perception that the casting director is not on the actor's side? "Agents have to be a little less protective of their clients and a little more trusting of the casting director," she replied. Quickly, Grossman added, "of course, there's always going to have been one bad experience that makes someone think that all of them are bad experiences. I heard the stories as an agent about the casting director who conducted an audition never looking up, eating lunch, talking on the phone. That's inexcusable. That's not somebody who should ever get another job. They have to have respect for the actor and the actor has to have respect for the casting director and the process," she concluded.

Her Opinion on Alternative Submission Methods

Grossman described online services as "interesting, but I don't think we're all really savvy on it yet. Do I look at the [*Academy*] *Players Guide* online? Yes, but it's faster to look it up in the book. There are certain websites that are sophisticated, or I'll go to SAG online to check who someone is with, but as far as those companies that want to come in and make me buy their equipment in order to give me the service that [the actors] have to pay for, I'm not going to do that." Is electronic casting the wave of the future? According to Grossman, "it's coming, but not yet."

Best Way To Get Seen by Her

"I go through agents, I go through managers. I open their submissions." What about the non-represented actor? "I attend theatre, so you may drop me a note if you're doing a show. I do have a staff and they'll go see a great play, as will I. We're limited, in that we can't see every showcase, but we'll hear about it if it's a good show and we'll see it," she affirmed.

What She Would Change About the Casting Process

Grossman quoted the all-time favorite casting director statement from Barbara Miller, "Everyone has two jobs. Their job and casting," and followed that with a laugh and the comment, "it's the truest thing!" Grossman said she would change the level of input from non-casting directors. "I would change the fact that people who do not know what an actor's ability is make a decision on them. When actors are pigeon-holed based on something they [were] in, but I've seen them do remarkable theatre work and I know what's *in there*, it's frustrating." She continued, "We want the whole business to trust that we know what we're doing, in casting."

I asked about Grossman's opinion of the lack of awards for casting, and the potential for change. "It won't take away anyone else's glory to give an award to the casting director or to even thank them for the ensemble that they've assembled," she said. "[Those who do get the awards] can't do it alone. And there are directors that use the same casting director time and time again—they wouldn't think of doing a film without that person at their side. So, there is some reward for it, but no awards," she summarized.

Highlight of Her Week

Grossman quickly laughed, "Friday! That's the highlight of my week. Look at me, going for the joke!"

Most Gratifying Part of Her Job

"Seeing an actor come in and nail it. Seeing the actor light up a room and get the job and change their life. Or seeing someone who's been doing it a long time find a new shade or new level or reinvent themselves. Those discoveries are the rewards."

KIMBERLY R. HARDIN

According to Kimberly R. Hardin, an actor's job is to bring herself to the material. "An actor can only do his take on it," she said. "One of the most important things about being a casting director is having an understanding of your director so that you know what he's looking for and you can communicate that to the talent. That way, the actor can take those notes and make the material come alive."

With credits ranging from CB4 *and* Baby Boy *to* The Fast and the Furious 2 *and* Biker Boyz, *Hardin has helped thousands of actors through the process of bringing out their best take on the material. The one thing she requires actors bring to the session: Passion. "It's key on so many levels. I really enjoy meeting people who have passion and integrity for the work. When you have passion, it's not about how you look or about being a star."*

In that requirement, Hardin asks no more of actors than she brings to the session herself. Her passion for the craft of casting is evident.

First Casting Job

I'm Gonna Git U Sucka, as assistant to Robi Reed-Humes and Jaki Brown Karman.

Road to This Position

"I fell into casting. I originally thought that I wanted to be a production manager. That's what I had been involved in in my college days," she began. Hardin attended Pasadena City College and Cal State Los Angeles. "I had been involved in theatre in high school and at both colleges. A producer put a bug in my ear about casting and that's how I learned there was even a job called casting."

"I worked as an assistant to Jaki on a couple of films and also worked on [HBO series] *Dream On*. Then I worked with Gail Levin when she was partners with Lauren Lloyd at Paramount. I worked with them as an associate on *To Sleep with Anger*, *The Hot Spot*, and *Switch*," Hardin recalled. "I came back around to work with Jaki again as an associate and we did the Jackson Five miniseries [*The Jacksons: An American Dream*] and *Jason's Lyric*, to name a couple."

"Everybody works differently," she said. "Working with so many different people helped me tremendously. Not only did I learn different actors, I learned a work ethic with each casting director. I learned how to get that tough skin and find out whether I could hang or couldn't hang in this industry. I was fortunate enough to work with really good people. I try to carry that over with my people too."

Coolest Casting Gig

Friday. "I literally came from casting a film in Florida to being thrown into the situation where I had to cast *Friday* in three weeks. I had already cast Chris Tucker in the film I did in Florida. He was supposed to do one scene with Eddie Griffin. He had like two lines. He came in and auditioned for *Friday* and he just wasn't getting it. I gave him some notes and told him to work on it, put his own spin on it. He came back in and blew us all away. I brought him in to Ice Cube and F. Gary Gray. Then I had to go through trying to pull him from the other movie. That other producer was George Jackson, and, after a lot of work, I was able to get him out of that one scene so that he could be the lead in *Friday*. Look at how that turned out!"

Unable to name only one gig as her coolest, Hardin added, "I also had a lot of fun with a search that Fox hired myself and Jaki and Leah [Daniels-Butler] to do for *In Living Color* right before they were going off the air. We did six cities in six weeks. We had an open call in each city and saw thousands of people in Atlanta, Chicago, Houston, New York, Los Angeles, and Detroit. I had an associate who did nothing but prep for the open call we would be having in the next city before we left the one we were in," Hardin recalled fondly. "It was so much fun. We saw so many interesting people. They ended up not picking up the show that season, but Fox did pick up an option for the guy we found—Chris Kattan—through an open call. The next year, I put him on the pilot for *Def Comedy Jam Prime Time* with Cedric the Entertainer. A few months later, Chris got *Saturday Night Live*. That was great to see," she admitted.

Pet Peeves

"Actors who aren't prepared. Actors who don't take the time to prepare for the meeting and who do not take the craft seriously. Especially out here in California, they feel if they're half-way good looking they should be successful because of that," Hardin complained.

Another peeve, that ever-popular *not-you* headshot. "Please make sure your headshot is how you're looking these days! It's a huge disappointment when you come in and don't look like that photo. Speaking of coming in, don't be chatty and try to shake my hand. I know you're trying to be nice, but I see 100 of you. I'm trying to get a job done. So, if I don't shake your hand, it's not personal," Hardin remarked.

As for your read, Hardin is fine with you needing to start over. "If you need to make a restart, *one* is fine. Three to four times is not going to fly. I'm here to help you do the best job you can and a false start is understandable."

Advice for Actors

"I tell every actor to spend six months to a year in New York doing theatre. If you don't want to do theatre, then what are you doing [acting]? That's the core of acting. You get your immediate response right there. You have immediate feedback, you get such direction in rehearsal, that's where you get it all," she insisted, adding, "Los Angeles is not strong when it comes to theatre. It's sad, but true. New York is a great training ground for theatre. There's really great culture there."

Further advice from Hardin included training. "Actors shouldn't be afraid to have coaching. Some people think they get past the need to train. The oldest actors, even, should always think of themselves as a work in progress," she explained. In Hardin's opinion, training is a cure for several traps of the industry. "Training keeps you humble and takes away the ego. Ego is so unnecessary. Life's too short. I will only bring someone to the director if they have the talent and skills. An untrained actor with ego will not go beyond the first session," she added.

Best Way To Get Seen by Her

"Submit your headshot. I literally go through every picture. I go through everything that comes in. I make the time to do it. Ask any of my crewmembers. But don't send a submission unless I'm currently working on a project. Otherwise, I have nowhere to keep your submission," Hardin explained.

Her Favorite Casting Tale

Putting Halle Berry in 1991's *Strictly Business*. "I was associate [casting director] on that one. From sessions, we had it down to three people: Holly Robinson, A.J. Johnson, and Halle Berry. The director asked me, 'Who's your pick?' Halle was always my pick. They hired A.J. Johnson for her dance skills. For whatever reason, they fired the director and hired Kevin Hooks to take over a week before shooting began. He went back and looked at the finalists and selected Halle. Although she had done a small role as a crack addict in one of Spike Lee's films, this was her first lead. She skyrocketed from there," Hardin recalled proudly.

Her Operating System

"I'm lost without her," Hardin said of her associate, Leah Daniels-Butler. "And Billy [Murphy, their assistant] is a godsend."

"It's a creative process. There's a lot going on at one time. I work best like that. I'll be good with ideas for every role, but keeping up with the technicalities of who is with what agent and how to get in touch with everyone, that is my crew's job. I limit the amount of time that I'm on the phone, because I'll agree to see everyone. I want to cover all of my bases. I'll check out theatre, schools, I'll put Post-It Notes in magazines and my crew will find these people for me."

Her Opinion on Alternative Submission Methods

"We'd use [Internet casting] if we had a solid office space. But we're gypsies. Have box will travel! We move with each project. I like that element, but it makes technology difficult."

Hardin did take a break from her nomadic tendencies for about six months as Director of Talent Development Programs and Casting for ABC. Hardin left that position in March 2002. "I'm very proud of what I've done in helping them get the diversity project going, but it felt different being in the same office every day in that corporate situation. I like the constant change and the travel."

Most Gratifying Part of Her Job

"Being involved in movies is almost like people's dreams coming true. I really like being a part of that. I like to pop 'em. That's the fulfillment I get. When actors come back to me after having made it and say, 'Thanks for giving me my start,' that really touches me. When it all comes together, we have an extremely happy director and an actor who went through a gazillion auditions and finally got it and I sit there at the theatre with a real audience and see the enjoyment; that's really cool."

CATHY HENDERSON, CSA

Cathy Henderson's name is often mentioned by other casting directors as someone who was a mentor to them on their path to casting. Henderson, along with partner Dori Zuckerman, has been nominated for multiple Casting Society of America Artios Awards (including two in 2001 for Comedy Central's That's My Bush! *and Sundance hit* What's Cooking*).*

As one of CSA's first members, Henderson has seen the business of casting weather many transitions and trends. She rides each wave with the ease of the skilled surfer she is: with grace and strength.

First Casting Job

Nearly 30 years ago, Henderson was employed as casting secretary to Linda Otto at Spelling-Goldberg Productions, working on *Charlie's Angels*. "Both of my parents were in show business, so it was second nature to me." Henderson's mother, Dorothy Dells, was an actress for 30 years. Father, Jack Voglin, worked in production on *Gunsmoke*, *Bonanza*, *Have Gun Will Travel*, and *Rawhide*. "I felt comfortable in that environment and I was a young mother in need of a job. I fell into this and it was perfect for me," she recalled.

"I love talent of all sorts," Henderson revealed. "I am in awe of people with talent. It excites me just to be around talented people, so it seemed natural for me to be the liaison between the talent and the producers and directors."

Her Take on the Craft of Casting

"Casting directors work every hour we're up and even sometimes in our sleep. This field has such rewards, but the hours are rough. Between seeing plays, attending showcases and workshops, screening films, and reading scripts, I barely have time to surf with my husband [Sandy Martin]," Henderson shared with a laugh.

"I feel so grateful to be in a career I love so much. My only disappointment after 28 years of casting is our lack of a union. We are execs," Henderson insisted. "We have a lot to do with putting deals together. And with no union, we have no pension, no medical, no scale. My hope for younger casting directors is that CSA will get a union together to enable [casting directors] to get the same kind of benefits that other people in the industry have."

"We can't possibly get hired again unless the actors who come in do a good job. Our job is to find talented people, give them the information that we have, and make them feel comfortable so that they will do their very best performance. [Casting directors] have to audition for work too."

"It's a joy to work with folks who understand and respect the casting process," Henderson confided. "Just like acting, casting is at its best when you are appreciated."

Road to This Position

Henderson and Zuckerman have worked together for eight years. "We hooked up when we were both looking for new partners. We told one anther what films we were working on and discovered that we were individually hired to do the same film," she laughed. "So, we decided to have a meeting to figure out what exactly was going on. Turns out—and it happens a lot in independent films—the guy was 'hiring' casting directors all over the place and basically taking their lists and not hiring anyone!"

"We have different opinions about things," Henderson remarked. "That's what makes our partnership so strong. We work well together as a team. We'll have debates on which actor is best for a role and we'll have to 'agent' each actor on our list to one another. It makes our list really diverse. We really cover all the bases."

Coolest Casting Gig

"My first project was a favorite. *Rock Follies*. It was an English show about a girl rock-n-roll group back stage. I had worked with the Rolling Stones and Led Zeppelin, and lived in England for seven years. Martin Stargar knew I loved music, and he hired me to do the show. It's where I met one of my best friends, Ellen Green (who played Audrey in *Little Shop of Horrors*) as well as John Shae. After that experience, and working on *Grease* with Joel Thurm, I knew casting was for me."

Most recently, 2001 Sundance favorite and Artios Award nominee *What's Cooking* was a favorite for Henderson, mainly because it came to her with no names attached. "I have to give credit to [agent] Steve Doranville for helping get Mercedes Ruehl, Kyra Sedgwick, Julianna Margulies, and Alfre Woodard," Henderson recalled. "In independent films, we really count on agents to help us put unfunded projects together. We all have to really believe in our projects," she said.

Advice for Actors

"Be diligent. Be professional at all times. Get a good day job, maybe live with a group of people in order to shave costs. Meet in groups and network. Work at acting with such a passion that nothing gets in your way. Have camaraderie. Share information. Be positive," Henderson advised. "Casting directors don't want to help people who don't help themselves."

"A good picture is your first priority," Henderson recommended. "Good pictures are extraordinarily important. And don't let your lover or your mother pick the one they want on the mantle. Your headshot should say, 'I'm a very good actor,' to me, when I look at your eyes. Let us figure out what to do with your hair. Just look like you can act."

"Take acting classes and do lots of theatre. Participate in theatre, not for who will see you there, but as a way to hone your craft. Casting directors check to see who you've studied with and look at your theatre credits. This tells us how hard you're working to be a competitive working actor. We need to see who you're currently studying with. We don't care that you're in the business because you were the class clown and someone told you you were cute," she concluded.

Her Opinion on Alternative Submission Methods

"Dori and I have used Internet services for last-minute casting needs," Henderson revealed. "It's difficult to cast just by a picture," she said. "But I'll use the Internet to find ethnic actors, actors with accents, older actors, or very young actors. If you're a run-of-the-mill, good actor in a standard age range, I'm not going to look for you online."

Pet Peeves

"When you're in the audition, please don't act unprofessional. Be prepared to take an adjustment during your read. Be on time. Have your material ready. Ask questions of your agent or come early to our office. Don't ask your questions about the part in front of the producer and director," she advised. "They will want to see *your* take on the material."

"Props are distracting and annoying. Forget about props," Henderson directed. "Don't wardrobe yourself specifically unless you are asked to [dress for the part]. Leave your stethoscope at home! Just be comfortable and give the feeling of the role by your dress. Always be pleasant and make [the audition] about the work," she concluded.

Best Way To Get Seen by Her

"Have a good agent whose opinion we respect," Henderson asserted.

Other than that, an actor can send postcards. "Postcards are much better than 8x10s. They hang around longer because of their size. If you send a [demo] tape, please call a week later and pick it up," Henderson requested.

Another good avenue: workshops. "Both Dori and I [attend] as many workshops as we can after a full day's work," Henderson said. "I've seen some terrific actors in well-run, well-organized workshops. I'll bring them into the office based on the workshop experience. Dori and I have cast anywhere from 15 to 65% of non-star roles from workshops. Actors need to be ready before they do workshops for casting directors. It has a lot to do with the effort the actor puts into it," she qualified.

"Casting directors who don't work at studios or networks need a way to do general interviews more efficiently. From that, we already know what the actor is about, more than we would from a picture and resumé in a mailing. That's what the workshop is, for us. It's an amazingly wonderful way for actors to see casting directors who are working in an environment where phones aren't ringing off the hook."

Regarding the controversy of workshops as paid auditions: "I always thought workshops were a good idea. Nobody twists the actor's arm to do it," she summarized. "It's my job to do talent scouting. Workshops are just one of the ways I do that."

Her Biggest Casting Challenge

"We're big on changing the ethnicity, the gender, the age of a character, so that the project will look real," Henderson explained. "That's why independent films are so much fun. Often the writer is also the director, and we can break down the concept of ethnicity as we're casting the project. It's about the best actor for the part, so we'll break that down from the beginning so that the director will watch the read, rather than looking for the person that fits the physical description they're so attached to."

Most Gratifying Part of Her Job

"Discovering new talent and watching their successes. Billy Bob Thornton called me and said, 'I stayed in town because you always brought me in, even when I wasn't right.' Hearing that," she said, "is gratifying."

MARC HIRSCHFELD, CSA

Marc Hirschfeld, Executive Vice President of Talent and Casting for NBC Entertainment, began his casting career with Norman Lear's Embassy Television. In his partnership with Meg Liberman, he assembled ensembles for 3rd Rock from the Sun, NewsRadio, MadTV, *and* Party of Five, *as well as the Emmy award-winning miniseries* From the Earth to the Moon.

In 1999, Hirschfeld assumed his current role, in which he developed PS-NBC, an experimental performance space in New York. The geographical choice for this project has generated local controversy [see Los Angeles Times, *June 21, 2000 and July 10, 2000]. Hirschfeld generously offered his answers to the usual* Casting Qs *and set the record straight on "edgy theatre" in Los Angeles.*

First Casting Job

Hirschfeld was the casting receptionist at Norman Lear's company in 1980. Yep, he started out at the front desk! At Embassy Television, he and Robin Nassif became assistants for Eve Brandstein, then became casting directors themselves. Hirschfeld worked with Meg Liberman for 11 years before heading off to NBC.

"The first things I cast were *One Day at a Time* and *The Facts of Life*. Embassy was sort of a mom-and-pop store, so we kind of did everything. Not only did we cast the guest stars, but we cast the extras. We were de facto casting directors and then we were given the title."

Coolest Casting Gig

The original casting of *Seinfeld*. Putting together the ensemble for a "clever little show that no one believed was going to get much of a following" and then seeing that show become the "seminal sitcom of the '90s, that was enormously satisfying," according to Hirschfeld.

Key Things He Looks for in an Actor

The main things Hirschfeld looks for are strong persona, charisma, distinct choices with the character, and that intangible star quality. "I don't care if it's just one line, I want to see an air of confidence about you."

His Favorite Audition Tale

When Hirschfeld was casting *The Nanny*, a woman who read for the part of a high school gym teacher came in wearing sweats. "It's okay to indicate with clothing, but you don't want to wear scrubs coming in for a doctor audition. Also, I totally discourage the use of props in an audition. I just think it's a crutch that people use when they haven't put a lot of energy into the character." So, when the woman pulled a whistle out from a lanyard around her neck and began blowing the shrill whistle in a small room filled with people, everyone burst out in laughter. "It was ear shattering! But she felt like she got a response out of it, so she did it again and again, and every time we were like, 'No! No!' Needless to say, she did not get the part, but it was one of the funniest and most tragic auditions I have ever been witness to."

Pet Peeves

Props, clothing that distracts from the performance, not having your headshot and resumé ready. "I don't want to see the actor fumble for it for 15 minutes. Oops, wrong resumé! No. This is your job. Get it together. Be ready."

Actors who stay in the room too long also annoy Hirschfeld. "My attitude is, you go in, you do your thing, and get out gracefully and quickly so that we can start talking about you while the audition is fresh in our mind. Otherwise the audition fades."

Advice for Actors

Have passion for what you're doing. Persevere. Take your craft and the business of the craft seriously. Be responsible and prepared. Do your homework. Make strong choices. Don't second-guess yourself. "The worst thing an actor can do at the end of an audition is say, 'Boy, that sucked. Can I do that again?' I say, 'How confident is this actor in their work or their choices?' If you have a question, ask it beforehand, not after.

Best Way To Get Seen by Him

Get in a good play, showcase, stand-up club. Get a referral from an agent, manager, or another casting director. Send your demo reel. And in that tape, remember, less is more. "I want nice, tight, short pieces that show the different things you can do, not three scenes of you being a hooker or a cop or a nurse."

The Truth About "Edgy Talent" and Los Angeles Theatre

Truth is, Hirschfeld attends a lot of theatre in Los Angeles, "and not just the major theatres like the Taper and Music Center. I go to a lot of Equity Waiver theatre." That means, specifically, attending shows at the Coronet, the Tamarind, the Groundlings, ACME, California Institute of the Arts' Disney Theatre, the Hudson, Actor's Gang, Highways. "And, by the way, an inordinate amount of it is inferior. Not the majority, but more than should be, is inferior. But I haven't stopped going. I still go! I'll talk to my counterparts at ABC or CBS and they are shocked that I go to these things because a lot of it can be disappointing. But I still go religiously because you never know."

Yes, Hirschfeld feels that much of the work he sees in Los Angeles is "showcasey" and that the nature of the "See me!" presentation affects the purity of the work. Still, he's seen a lot of good theatre here. "I'm not lazy and I'm certainly not ignorant. I make an effort. More than most casting directors do out there. The bottom line is, if actors are doing work to be showcased, if their primary interest is they're doing this to get an agent to be seen—whatever—it is going to have an impact on the work. That is the bone I have to pick. It shows."

Still, if you're in something really wonderful, have no fear. Hirschfeld will hear about it. "Word spreads like wildfire. Good stuff is energizing and there's very little of it. But if there is something good going on, I will hear about it. I will be there." Hirschfeld believes that many actors put themselves in front of him before they are ready, with sub-par material, or with scene partners who do not complement them. "They're just shooting themselves in the foot. But I still go. I've found a lot of people that are good. There is positive reinforcement. Just remember, [making] no impression is better than [making] a negative one—and a negative one is longer lasting."

Why Not Start PS-NBC Here?

Since there are already so many venues for showcasing and even developing talent in Los Angeles (such as HBO Workspace), Hirschfeld targeted the "lightening rod for artists of all kind. They may not have the ability to harness what they do. We give them a venue where all they need is the creative idea and we provide the technical expertise, the space, and the audience. We don't pay these people. And we don't charge them either. All we ask is a 30-day period in which we get to negotiate a deal with them in good faith. In New York, there isn't a really big presence of talent executives and agents, so we can help develop these performers kind of under the radar. One of my beefs about Los Angeles is that if you're a stand up comedian with three good minutes of material, suddenly you have a development deal because everyone is so hungry to sign the next big thing."

His Opinion on Alternative Submission Methods

"It's gonna happen. Online [casting] is gonna happen. I personally want to be on the leading edge of technology. I'm on the wireless web. I have the PalmV with the OmniSky wireless modem. I can surf the web wireless. We're changing our department so that 50% of the things we do in this department are going to be on the web. This is the wave of the future."

Most Gratifying Part of His Job

Hirschfeld supervises casting for the entire network and develops talent for each new season, so amidst plenty of gratifying experiences, the most gratifying is going to the table read of a new series. Hirschfeld's involvement in putting together the cast rarely gives him the satisfaction of seeing the actors all in one place, doing what he's hired them to do. In addition to the table reads, he loves the discovery process that the public goes through in connecting with these actors.

"The American public discovers them and loves them, even the guest stars on *Seinfeld* like Newman and The Maestro and J. Peterman, they became icons. It's very exciting to me. I love finding actors and making them into TV stars!"

HAL HUNDLEY

Meeting Hal Hundley comes with a warning: he's a real piece of work. He'll say so himself! A former actor and former agent who has spent most of his 50 years in the business directing major theatrical productions, Hundley sees casting as a lost art. He is attempting to revive this lost art through working on low-budget SAG films using "good, solid actors."

From his history-filled Old Hollywood office, Hundley expressed his desire to direct another musical and shared his sometimes-unpopular opinions on how casting should be done. "I've been told, 'Oh, you're a bastard,' and my response is, 'You're right. I am!'"

First Casting Job

Hundley's background as a theatre director gave him much experience in casting. He had a major voice in casting each of the plays he directed (36 musicals in eight years, to be exact). *Isle of Lesbos*, which screened at the Cannes Film Festival in 1997, was the first feature film he cast. Since then, he's cast a dozen films, including *Dumped*, *Eating L.A.*, and *The Black Rose*.

Coolest Casting Gig

"I don't have a favorite project," Hundley said, noting that the coolest gig is always the one he's working on at the moment. "Then I go on to the next one."

Key Things He Looks for in an Actor

"Professionalism," Hundley summarized. "And I can't tell you how little I see it. Two-thirds of the actors in Hollywood aren't ready yet." In fact, Hundley has taught a workshop entitled "How *Not* to Piss Off the Casting Director." He distinguishes the class he teaches from cold reading workshops. "This isn't paying for an audition. This is a seminar on the biz," he explained, "and something every actor needs to learn."

An actor should always look nice and neat. "You could get an audition standing in line at the post office," he said. "I want to throw actors out when they come to an audition all grungy."

He looks for that spark, that level of energy so many casting directors describe. However, "don't give me attitude," he continued. "And don't let your agent be a pain in my ass."

Hundley continued, "I look for theatre on a resumé. If theatre's not on there, I wonder!" Also, on a resumé, you send to Hundley, be sure to get the exact name of the production right and, c'mon, do a spellcheck! "People think I'm being picky, but it's not that. It's simply attention to detail," he continued.

Pet Peeves

Photo postcards. "Don't send them. I'll throw them away," he insisted. "A picture is an 8x10 with a resumé attached. Period."

A pet peeve regarding directors: "I wish young filmmakers would keep the damn cameras still. Let the actors do the work and just keep still!" Hundley begged.

Advice for Actors

"Don't pick your own picture," he advised. "Let your agent choose it for you. If they're working, they know what they're doing."

Best Way To Get Seen by Him

Get into his file. Okay, how do you do that? "If your resumé strikes me, I'll call you in." What about inviting him to your shows? "I go to theatre, but not to showcases."

Once you're in his file cabinet, he knows what you can do and he'll call you when he knows you're right for a project he's casting. "I work so that I can pick up the phone to the actor directly, and I won't call them unless I have something for them," Hundley stated. "People may not agree with my approach, but I know what the actor can do, and I don't need to see 1000 people for one role."

His Opinion on Alternative Submission Methods

"I like to handle the picture, or go to the *Academy Players Directory*," he said. "I don't even own a computer."

His Operating System

"I do it the way I bloody well want to," he summarized with a laugh. He won't work on television shows or with major studios. "I've been my own boss too long," he concluded.

Trends He Has Observed in the Casting Process

"This will make me sound politically incorrect, but I do not believe in [the current trend of] colorblind casting," Hundley said. "There are times when ethnicity doesn't matter, but when it does, [the casting] better be done right," he explained. This is most important when casting pieces we've seen before. "I don't believe in revising the material. But, with an original film, you're creating the history of the story, so the characters can be anything."

What He Would Change About the Casting Process

"Actors are afraid. Casting directors have scared them into thinking they can't control their own destiny." When Hundley was an agent in Denver, he'd go on auditions with his actors. "We work for the actor, not the other way around."

Most Gratifying Part of His Job

"That's easy. The director saying to me, 'You were right!'"

JULIE HUTCHINSON, CSA

Julie Hutchinson, VP of Features Casting for Universal Studios (formerly 20ᵗʰ Century Fox's VP of Features Casting), is challenged by the need to consider creative and marketing elements when casting. "Casting is not magic. We are satisfying all of the creative entities involved in the project. There are a lot of people who need to be satisfied. While we are looking for talent, we are also visualizing the one-sheet for the film, knowing that profitability is a consideration. It's a balancing act between art and commerce," she explained.

Hutchinson acknowledged that there are times when commerce wins, times when art wins, and times when her team strikes a balance between the two (such as with recent projects Like Mike *and* X-Men 2*). While laughing about the absurdity of it all, she summarized, "We're basically looking for a star that nobody's heard of who has the power to bring in an audience and who will work for scale."*

First Casting Job

Hutchinson started out in New York as an associate for now-retired casting director Barbara Shapiro. "I worked with her for five years. I cut my teeth there on 57ᵗʰ St. We cast hundreds of commercials while I was there. We worked on many of [director] John Sayles' films, which was a magnificent experience for me. We cast a little bit of theatre at the Arena Stage in Washington as well. It was a spectacular experience. It enabled me to learn the business, while starting my casting career in New York. That was just extraordinary," Hutchinson described.

Hutchinson studied acting at UC Santa Cruz. "Clutching my bachelor's degree in theatre, I went to New York to be an actress," she recalled. Hutchinson met Shapiro through a friend and started working as an assistant to her right away. "It was perfect. I needed to learn more about the business and I needed a survival job. I frankly did not know what I wanted to do, except to be in New York doing something." At the time, Hutchinson had no idea that her survival job would turn into her career.

Road to This Position

Hutchinson took a break from casting. "I unsuccessfully explored journalism for a while," she joked. When she returned to Los Angeles to resume casting, she started off doing freelance casting assignments. She connected with Donna Isaacson, current Executive VP of Casting at 20th Century Fox. "We did [1991's] *Father of the Bride* together. Then I went on to work with Amanda Mackey and Cathy Sandrich on *Patriot Games*," she recalled. Hutchinson and Isaacson got together again to cast the Sean Connery and Wesley Snipes action thriller *Rising Sun* from an office on the 20th Century Fox studio lot.

"Donna and I were there, thinking, 'Wouldn't it be great if they had a casting department right here at Fox?' Little did we know at that time that a few years later, we would be there," Hutchinson said. Before the department opened up, Hutchinson was Director of Casting at CBS for three years. "I spent three to four nights a week at comedy clubs, scouting for our shows. I had a fantastic time learning about television.

It's a totally different world." Hutchinson, the VP of Features Casting, was with 20th Century Fox from 1996 to 2002.

Coolest Casting Gig

Hutchinson named her coolest gig in *recent* history: the feature *Unfaithful*. "I got the opportunity to be hands-on with that film before we put our casting directors on. I got to spend time in the room with [director] Adrian Lyne, who was fantastic to work with. We got to audition all of these young, up-and-coming and established actors for the lover role [ultimately portrayed by Olivier Martinez]. I love reading with actors, and reading with actors for that role was quite memorable," she indicated.

Key Things She Looks for in an Actor

Preparedness. "I respect an actor's need to do the emotional work required for the role, but those choices need to be all worked out before the actor comes into the room. An actor going through the emotional process in the room with us is disruptive," Hutchinson explained. "That is not to say that we don't make time for work in the audition process, but an actor needs to be as prepared as possible."

"It is a good idea for the actor *not* to be off book when he reads for us. Being off book causes the actor to be locked into the way he memorized the material. We need actors to be fluid. Actors should be as fluent with the material as possible, have their choices ready, know their objective, understand the point of view of the character, but be ready to make changes when directed to do so," she said.

Pet Peeves

"Tardiness, lack of preparedness, and attitude. We're remembering this stuff. We are paying attention to the actor as a whole. We can see if an actor is trouble. I've said to a director, 'Great performance, but life is too short [to work with this problematic actor].' You need to be somebody we want to work with, not someone who is phony or obsequious. The set is an artificial but very intimate situation. We have to figure out how you are going to get along with the whole crew," Hutchinson explained.

Advice for Actors

"Be prepared. Be on time. Check your ego and attitude at the door. Remember that we want you to be good," Hutchinson stressed.

She noted that her office is very supportive of actors. "We like actors. We want them to succeed. Our fantasy, as casting directors, is to make a major discovery and stop looking. The way actors can improve their chances for that is to do as much work in advance as they possibly can in terms of figuring out the character: read the script if it's available, make choices about the character, ask their agent to help getting information on the storyline or character breakdown," Hutchinson listed.

Hutchinson added that actors should not over-extend themselves. "Don't ask too many questions. Keep your antenna up when you're in this room. A couple of concise questions are fine, but if you have a need to really explore the material, you should call ahead of time and go over the details with your agent."

Best Way To Get Seen by Her

When Hutchinson was in New York, she attended Off-Broadway shows and actor showcases three or four nights each week. She is not as actively attending theatre in Los Angeles. "However, if you get in a good play, I will come see it. Here's my theory: if you are talented, people will notice. If you are not talented, you will go unnoticed. Ultimately, talent will rise. But, truthfully, the best way to get seen by me is through an agent we have daily contact with and we have respect for. There are a lot of talented people out there without representation who deserve to be seen, but it is more difficult. It is up to those actors to figure out how to be seen," she explained.

Hutchinson recommended that actors keep her updated with postcards and flyers for shows they are doing. Regarding unsolicited headshot and resumé submissions, she requested that actors include a professional cover letter, noting, "Since September 11th [2001], we've cut down on the amount of unsolicited mail that gets to us. We really do prefer agent submissions. You are more likely to be paid attention to if you have representation."

Her Opinion on Alternative Submission Methods

"I am sure that's the wave of the future, but it's a wave I haven't caught yet," Hutchinson mused. "We are still casting the old-fashioned way. I go to my own lists and to the [*Academy*] *Players* [*Directory*] book more than anything else. We have a pretty good handle on the talent pool, nationally. If we are looking for something very specific, or someone overseas, we will go online, but for an average casting assignment, we're not going to go online."

Hutchinson justified this by saying that, in 20 minutes, she could have agents send 20 actors over to her office, just by hitting a few buttons on her speed-dial list. The Internet does not give her that level of reliable service at this time.

Highlight of Her Week

"To find an actor for a role and close a deal. To meet somebody I know is going to be a star. My heart will race when I know something is there. My gut tells me. It's a visceral response to the Star Gene. It's impossible to define, but I do think you are born with it."

Most Gratifying Part of Her Job

"To have an actor walk in, nail the audition, and book the role. I also love to see on-screen the growth of an actor I've supported from the beginning. It validates my instinct about them."

DONNA ISAACSON, CSA

Donna Isaacson began her career in theatre as an actor. She attended the High School of the Performing Arts and NYU School of the Arts. "I was working, but I wasn't so easy to cast," she recalled.

Her no-nonsense style and eye for talent is evident in features such as Quills, A Life Less Ordinary, Broken Arrow, Dirty Rotten Scoundrels, *and ten years' worth of Joel and Ethan Coen films, including* Raising Arizona *and* Barton Fink. *As Executive Vice President of Casting at 20ᵗʰ Century Fox, Isaacson may have a supervisory role, but she's still as hands-on as she was over 20 years ago.*

First Casting Job

Isaacson reminisced, "I was typing scripts, working freelance to make money. I went out as an assistant to the writer and producer for a Broadway-bound show. Actors were fired from this show on a regular basis and I was assigned the task of organizing the replacement of these people. I realized I was pretty good at it."

What she refers to as her first *real* casting job was at the Manhattan Theatre Club, where Isaacson started in 1980.

She did freelance casting on other independent projects and then formed her own company in 1983.

Road to This Position

Isaacson began, "In 1992, I was hired by Hollywood Pictures to do a feature film. They canceled the picture while I was out here, pregnant, and I was told I had to stay in bed. I was stranded in Los Angeles!" Within a few weeks of giving birth to her daughter, Isaacson received a call from 20th Century Fox to start a casting department. "I came in to talk about it, and I never left."

Coolest Casting Gig

Isaacson wouldn't name a specific film as her coolest, with good reason. "In over 20 years of casting, I've done ten years with the Coen brothers and ten years with Phil Kaufman. I love to work for them. Those are gifts. It's the people, not the project sometimes."

Best Way To Get Seen by Her

"It changes. Timing has a lot to do with it. We're doing several pictures right now, and I oversee all of the divisions," Isaacson revealed.

Will a mailed submission get to her? Yes. "If you don't have representation, it's challenging. We get so much material. That being said, an eye-catching headshot will help. A demo reel is good. Enclose a self-addressed, stamped envelope if you want it returned. We do generals all year long. We are always available for generals unless we're swamped. Send a flyer for your show. We cover as many as we can. Between my staff and myself, we try to see everything."

According to Isaacson, theatre is a great way to get seen, to work out, to launch or restart a stalled career. "Theatre really impresses me," she said. "It's a great route you can take to really hone your craft."

Key Things She Looks for in an Actor

A sense of humor and a sense of irony. "That ability to access wit separates a lot of people from the megastars. There's a mystery: that thing you can't put your finger on," she explained.

Also important is what Isaacson identified as a work ethic, of sorts. "I'm concerned that I've seen a lot of talented people over the years self-destruct. You wish they could just keep their eye on the work," she said, noting that some incredibly talented people find it hard to accept the level of attention that is thrown at them. "Know what your body and mind is telling you. There's no logic to the industry. Just realize that and go with the flow," Isaacson advised.

What about a bad audition experience? "I never say that a person can't change. I couldn't do this job if I didn't love actors. If an actor failed, I say they failed at *that*. I will really try to give the actor another shot. I'll put you on tape if a producer or director won't see you. If I believe in you, I'll go to bat for you."

Pet Peeves

No-shows. Isaacson explained, "The agent or manager pushes and begs and gets to get an appointment for the client. Then they call back and say, 'Oh, he read the material and doesn't respond [to it].' I'd have thought, if you were campaigning for an appointment, you would've exposed your client to [the] material before pushing me to see the actor. 'No, no. I don't want to show them the material until I'm sure I can get them an appointment.' So, I'm left tap-dancing for the director when there's a hole in the schedule that could've been filled by an actor who had seen the material and had responded to it and really wanted to read for it. This is a huge pet peeve. Never no-show with a director. It's a very compromising position."

Another item on Isaacson's list of pet peeves is the ever-popular response; unprepared actors. "Directors want to see what you came up with first. If you haven't made a choice, the director doesn't know where to begin making adjustments with you to see if you can take direction," Isaacson explained.

Advice for Actors

"Be responsible. Be prepared, but don't be over-rehearsed. If you read with someone, you can't predetermine their reactions. So, be open to listening and responding. Be loose enough to adapt to what they give you rather than carving out immutable space," she advised.

Isaacson firmly believes that if you get off on the wrong foot in your audition, you should stop immediately and ask to begin again. "You'll get one restart. After that, there's no grace period. I have a lot of respect for someone who needs a restart and nails it on the next shot," she said.

Bring *one* headshot and resumé with you to the audition. "Make it one. Don't come in with a portfolio and force us to make the choice of which headshot we want to keep. Choose a headshot that is close-up and that is representative of you."

Isaacson tries to defer to the actor, in terms of where she would like to stand or which scene she would like to read first. "What I find is, they're so terrified to be wrong and to have no one to blame but themselves, that even though it's their time and their space, I'll sometimes make the choice for them because it's obvious that they're uncomfortable with choosing which scene to read first," Isaacson admitted. "It's your time. Make it work for you. Never apologize. Never qualify. Come in from a position of strength," she continued.

How is that accomplished? "Sit in the waiting room with blinders on. Don't look at your competition. There *is* no competition. Keep your eye on the work at all times. There are 90,000 things that will come in to distract you. The director might be late, the phone might ring, the camera might break, the mic may be a little too far away from you. You have no control over anything but your connection to the material," Isaacson insisted. "When I look at Kobe Bryant at the free throw line with all of those squiggly things waving at him from the stands, I think that's the level of distraction you, as an actor, must tune out."

Isaacson further advised that the actor be professional. "Know who you're reading for. Treat yourself like a business. Make notes from auditions. Use index cards. You are a business and you should create a file on everyone you meet. I do my homework on you when you come in. You should do the same thing. If you get up every morning and remind yourself that you are a business and you are not getting rejected, you're just running a business, you can get past taking the rejection personally," Isaacson explained.

Most Gratifying Part of Her Job

"To find someone new, give them an opportunity, and then see them succeed."

JANE JENKINS, CSA

Jane Jenkins and Janet Hirshenson, the partners that make up The Casting Company, began working together in 1979. Their lobby walls are decorated with posters of films they've cast, including Ransom, An American President, Apollo 13, In the Line of Fire, A Few Good Men, and Stand by Me.

Jenkins has co-chaired the Casting Society of America's annual Artios Awards for 16 years and is a major advocate for the recognition of casting directors by groups such as the television and motion picture academies. While Emmys are now presented in the casting categories of episodic, miniseries, and movie of the week, Oscars are still withheld from casting directors. This situation will be corrected, according to Jenkins, when Academy members "participate in the way casting is done in the year 2000." There is a great deal involved in this process, some of which Jenkins shared with me in our run through the Casting Qs.

First Casting Job

The film *On the Nickel.* "I cast it for $100 a week, off the books, so I could continue to collect unemployment," Jenkins said with a chuckle. This was over 20 years ago. "I became an instant casting director."

Coolest Casting Gig

"It's really hard to say," she said. "One of my favorite scripts was *The Princess Bride*. I had a great deal of fun saying those lines all day long," Jenkins continued. "I had a lot of fun doing *Parenthood*—finding all those kids." Jenkins mentioned that she and [partner Janet] Hirshenson have been "very privileged to work with some very talented people."

Key Things She Look for in an Actor

"I look for a level of confidence in your own ability," Jenkins said. Jenkins acknowledges that the auditioning process is "nervous-making" but believes that one must have a level of security that is visible. "It is the biggest part of the actor's job to come in secure, with a grasp on the part, and with the confidence to convince me he's the best one for the part," she said.

Jenkins doesn't want to see an actor needy or rushed. "Even if you just got the lines this morning, say so," Jenkins continued. "Actors tend to fling themselves into the foray without asking any reasonably intelligent questions that would color the way they would say the words." Jenkins believes this is simply a result of the actor not thinking through the final results of these choices. "If you have a question, ask your agent, ask the assistant, ask the casting director. At least ask someone," she pleaded.

"You hear a lot of actors say the same words over and over again and frequently, you begin to feel the writing isn't very good because you hear similar readings and think the material is so boring," Jenkins explained. "Then one person comes in and personalizes the words. They bring their own persona to it." Jenkins believes that a combination of intention, attitude, and purpose create the best audition. "And there's no difference if the read is for a small part or a substantial role."

Her Favorite Audition Tale

"I have vivid memories of Vincent D'Onfrio's audition for *Mystic Pizza*," Jenkins began. The sides called for the character to roll around on the floor with Lily Taylor's character in a heavy make out scene, followed by an abrupt confrontation by her father. "Most actors felt the need to grope me, grab me, or roll around on the floor by themselves," Jenkins continued. "Vincent got down on one knee and did the whole scene as if it were his close up." This tactic truly impressed Jenkins, as she shares this audition tale at her occasional seminars. "When you have one of those physically demanding, complicated scenes that is impossible to do in an office, do your close-up," she summarized.

Pet Peeves

Not being prepared. "Ron Howard says, '*getting* the job *is* the job,' and he's absolutely right," Jenkins said. "That's the work. Once you have the role, that's playtime," she elaborated. "If you do the best job you can, and for whatever reason you're not right for that part, but you've made an impression, I'll remember you for the next job," Jenkins revealed. In this sense, according to Jenkins, there is a "residual effect" to an audition.

Advice for Actors

Relax! "It's not life and death," Jenkins said. "Take a deep breath and enjoy it. Nobody forced you into this career. It's not like your family said, 'No, don't be a doctor. Be an actor!'" Jenkins mused. "Have a good time doing it."

Best Way To Get Seen by Her

Through your agent. The best agent, according to Jenkins, is tough, smart, and feisty. "Every once in a blue moon, a postcard will work," Jenkins shared. For instance, one of the actors Jenkins cast in *Backdraft* came to her attention through a photo postcard he'd sent in. "There's no place for me to put all the pictures and resumés [we receive], but postcards, I'll hang onto," she said. However, according to Jenkins, unsolicited mailings are an "expensive long shot. You're trolling like a fisherman, casting that net out as broadly as you can," she summarized.

Her Opinion on Alternative Submission Methods

"I use The Link and I love the *Academy Players Directory*," Jenkins revealed. "Internet casting is a useful thing, but until it develops further, it's not essential," she said. Jenkins suggests that the Internet submission process has to become more uniform in order to have mass appeal.

As for video submissions, Jenkins said she is eager to see broadband allowing for more online reels of good quality. "I feel responsible for all the money actors spend on tapes," she said, noting that she could never possibly watch them all. Jenkins does not want to see your unsolicited tape. "Save your money," she advised.

Her Operating System

"We put more and more actors on video during their auditions," Jenkins said. "Our directors don't have the hours to see 30 bodies, but tapes, yes." Jenkins keeps all of the headshots of those actors she's seen. "Janet and I have quite a collection of pictures from over 20 years of actors coming through," she revealed. She has kept notes on actors' resumés, on index cards, on session sheets, supplementing a "strange process of memory," Jenkins said. "Having a partner really does help!"

Trends She Has Observed in the Casting Process

Jenkins is always looking for good actors. The main trend she sees is in how business is conducted. "Now everyone can have a manager and an agent," she lamented. While a legitimate manager can "help you push things through at a certain time and is helpful early on, a manager is part of a team," according to Jenkins. "The business is overwhelming and the right agent is hard to find." Finally, Jenkins noted that the business of the business has gotten more difficult due to the fact that there are more actors but not a proportionately greater number of productions going on.

What She Would Change About the Casting Process

"I don't think there's anything to change," she said. "There's gotta be an easier, less painful way for the actor to get there, but I don't know what it is." Jenkins noted that everybody works a different way and is emotionally invested at a different level. "There's no way to make it painless," she summarized of the casting process.

Highlight of Her Week

"I love making that phone call to the agent to tell her the client has the job," Jenkins said. "I love to hear the squeals of excitement."

Most Gratifying Part of Her Job

"When you look back at the careers you gave a start to, it's nice," according to Jenkins. "But the first cast read-thru, when it's the only time they are all together and the project is still filled with promise, that's the moment I really love. It's better than the premieres!"

CATHY KALMENSON & HARVEY KALMENSON

Cathy and Harvey Kalmenson have a combined fifty years of experience in the world of voiceover. "We are totally over-qualified to do what we're doing," Mr. Kalmenson (also known as "da harv") said brashly. "You'll find I'm brutally candid."

Mrs. Kalmenson is a perky complement to her husband. Their combined skills have clearly established a well-oiled machine of a production facility. In their Burbank studio, the Kalmensons teach classes, hold auditions (over 20,000 voiceover auditions in 2001), and produce spots for clients from all over the world. They welcomed me into their studio for our interview and some observation of the Kalmenson Method: truth-casting.

First Casting Job

Kalmenson & Kalmenson first entered the market with a Miller Beer spot.

Road to This Position

The Kalmensons met while working in a Los Angeles agency in 1981. Mr. Kalmenson came from a theatre background and, as an agent, headed up the voiceover department at Abrams-Rubaloff & Associates. Mrs. Kalmenson was also on staff at Abrams-Rubaloff after having started in advertising with Leo Burnett in Chicago. She also worked with the Tischerman Agency and Special Artists Agency before moving into casting in 1990. In 1992, the two married, and one year later, launched their own company.

Coolest Casting Gig

The Budweiser frogs. "We also really enjoyed casting the Harry Potter line for Warner Bros. Consumer Products," Mrs. Kalmenson said. The partnership was named the exclusive casting and project management team for all talking products marketed in association with *Harry Potter and the Sorcerer's Stone.*

Key Things They Look for in a Voiceover Actor

"Strong acting skills and genuineness," Mrs. Kalmenson quipped. The duo mentioned the importance of an actor's comfort with herself, awareness of her personal signature, and the ability to translate her truth to commercial copy. A vocal signature is a voiceover artist's defining sound. It indicates the way in which that voice is "typed." Mr. Kalmenson added, "You'd better have a sense of humor and flexibility."

The Kalmensons stressed that actors must know what they best present, vocally, and hone that skill. "With so many choices in the voiceover talent pool, Los Angeles is a market of specialists, not generalists," Mrs. Kalmenson explained.

Pet Peeves

"Actors calling to 'check in,'" Mrs. Kalmenson mentioned. "There's no time," according to Mr. Kalmenson. The pair would prefer contact in the form of postcards, letters, and even email.

Another pet peeve at Kalmenson & Kalmenson is the lack of labeling on demo CD spines. "We need to file your CD! Make sure we know it's yours from all angles," Mrs. Kalmenson advised.

Their Operating System

I observed, firsthand, what the Kalmensons refer to as a "tight ship" in their studios during auditions for Nike and Einstein Bros. Bagels. Each voiceover actor was greeted at the door by a member of the Kalmensons' efficient staff, who checked the actor in, reviewed audition sides, and answered any questions. With almost no downtime, each actor was escorted into the booth, greeted with warm familiarity by Mr. Kalmenson (who sat on the other side of a sound-proof window, controlling the recording equipment), and provided with a custom-adjusted microphone for the audition. "We get professional sound out of every audition," Mr. Kalmenson revealed. Mrs. Kalmenson explained that, on occasion, clients like what they hear on audition session CDs so much that they simply use a selection for the ad itself. "It's great because the actor gets a call that they not only booked the job, but have already done the job, and they sign the contracts and get the check. It's great! So, we strive to get performance-level auditions here," she concluded.

Mr. Kalmenson's direction between takes was specific and well-received. Each performer made the requested adjustments and delivered another take on the audition material, while Mr. Kalmenson made notations on the log sheet. "That's the one," he indicated to me, after a particularly fine read.

"I like to talk with the actors," Mr. Kalmenson said. "Sometimes, they're so stuck on the way they've rehearsed the spot that I'll need to get them talking about their day in order to get them to try another direction. It's different for each person." Mr. Kalmenson asked one actor to deliver a line with more of a reward to it. Another was told to open up the pronunciation of a certain word. These cues were interpreted by the actors and, upon the next take, Mr. Kalmenson said, "Great. That's it. Thank you." In under three minutes, each actor had performed several takes, had a friendly exchange with Mr. Kalmenson, and left feeling encouraged by his comments.

"The actor's job is to be the most authentic person he or she can be," explained Mrs. Kalmenson. "There is no other you, so don't try to come in with a lot of, 'I can also do...' type stuff. Just do you and do it with truth."

For each job, a team captain at Kalmenson & Kalmenson's business office in Encino is assigned to get as much information as possible from the client. "We'll do a conference call to make sure we get, right from the horse's mouth, what it is that they want," Mr. Kalmenson revealed.

"Voiceover is a postproduction job," Mrs. Kalmenson explained. "Money is tight by the time the client gets to this part of the process. If the client says, 'Send the 20 best voices,' that's exactly what we want to send." Mrs. Kalmenson went on to explain the range of material sent to the client. "We do 'bracketing.' We'll send something that is dead center of what the client asked for, and then a little flavor on each side of it."

A Kalmenson & Kalmenson staffer entered the studio with a status update on an actor who was 17 minutes late and not yet in the production facility. "What's the cut-off? We've made our numbers," he reported, indicating that the 20 best voices the client had asked for had been attained. "With a late actor, we'll be on the phone with the agent," Mrs. Kalmenson said. "We can't keep bringing a late actor back."

Once the session was complete, we took a break from the ongoing interview while Mr. Kalmenson burned copies of the master CD made during the auditions. Next, the staff affixed custom labels to the CDs and packed them up in a FedEx pouch, along with a copy of the session log and the studio's recommendations, based on the auditions. Both Kalmensons signed off on the package, and Mr. Kalmenson resumed the interview by commenting on the silence. "We don't multi-task around here. When we are putting these packages together, we are not doing anything else. It's too important."

Trends They Have Observed in the Casting Process

Compassion, resiliency, and patriotism. "Actors are a part of our nation's recovery," Mrs. Kalmenson said, indicating the American flags displayed throughout their studios. "Our spirit as a nation is strengthening, and our clients want voices that speak that truth."

Clients of Kalmenson & Kalmenson request attitudes, rather than specific vocal qualities. "The attitudes include irreverence, sarcasm, honesty, invitation to indulge, playfulness, vulnerability, dry, offbeat, edgy, and genuinely spontaneous," Mrs. Kalmenson listed. "But truth is the bottom line, with any of those," Mr. Kalmenson added.

"Voiceover is an acting craft. It's less about vocal quality than people think," Mrs. Kalmenson clarified. "When I'm on the phone with a client, I hear them describe an attitude, a type, a nature, an essence."

Advice for Actors

"I try to constantly encourage actors," Mr. Kalmenson said. "The economy is down, and advertising has been the first business to fall off and it's the last business to recover. I want actors to relax and know that we still love them."

"Do not make a voiceover demo tape prematurely. Make your tape at the end of focused study, when your coach, your agent, and your heart tell you it's time," Mrs. Kalmenson advised. Mr. Kalmenson added, "A bad tape could cost you your shot at our company."

There is a difference between animation and commercial voiceover demos, according to the Kalmensons. "Unless you are an animation specialist, your tape should represent who you are by nature. We will always bring in the actors who *are,* by nature, the role we are casting, rather than the ones who can *do* the role," Mrs. Kalmenson elaborated.

Further advice from the Kalmensons included: choose an attitude, be prepared to ad-lib and improvise when asked to do so, show commitment to your work, and understand that luck and timing have a great deal to do with it. "Impose your personality on the world," Mrs. Kalmenson instructed.

Best Way To Get Seen by Them

"Showcases, demo tapes with an agent pitch, and education are the three ways we see people," Mrs. Kalmenson listed. The Kalmensons teach eight classes per week at their Burbank studios. "Our students are confident, when they come in here to audition. They're using the same professional equipment and are already comfortable in this environment."

The Kalmensons have over 16,000 voices in their voiceover database, all indexed by searchable keywords. "Because we already have access to so many great voices, we do not take meetings, interviews, or hold generals. A demo tape serves as our screening method," Mrs. Kalmenson explained. "A demo tape should be under two minutes, and should showcase an actor's strengths and defining signature," Mr. Kalmenson insisted. "Remember, we call it 'truth-casting,'" Mrs. Kalmenson stated.

Most Gratifying Part of Their Job

Mrs. Kalmenson summarized, "Seeing our training contribute to an actor's career success is really wonderful. When we hear a student on a spot, we know we've affected someone's life."

ELLIE KANNER, CSA

Casting is a collaborative process, according to Ellie Kanner. She knows that many actors feel like the casting director is their enemy, when that's really not the case at all. To her, casting is all about teamwork, and a casting director's job includes both suggesting people and guiding the decision-making process that the producers and directors experience. Kanner believes that every casting director wants the actor to get the job. Best-known for casting Friends, *Kanner has cast and directed such series as* The Division *and* The Dead Zone. *Her recent leap into directing could mean that Kanner is casting you to star in* her *next project.*

First Casting Job

Kanner started out as an agent with Irvin Arthur Associates, where she specialized in representing comedic actors. "My boss' friend was producing a play called *Marvin & Mel* in a theatre in the Midwest and asked me to cast it in 1986," Kanner said. Her next casting job, was for Roger Nygard's short, *Warped*. Kanner soon realized that she was not a salesperson. Since a sales mentality is required, in agenting, she then knew that casting was her preferred line of work.

Road to This Position

Kanner began meeting with development people who encouraged her to follow this new path. "Fern Champion and Pamela Basker were looking for an assistant," Kanner said. "I worked for them for a year, doing pilots, films, everything! I learned so much in that year." Next, Kanner was an assistant at Lorimar and was soon promoted by Barbara Miller, staying on through the transition from Lorimar to Warner Bros. TV. "I did the pilot for *Friends*, for *The Drew Carey Show*, and, with Geraldine Leder, *Lois and Clark*," Kanner shared.

Eventually, Kanner partnered up with her then-assistant, Lorna Johnson, with whom she cast features, pilots, episodic television—including *Dawson's Creek*—and then began a shift into directing. "I loved working with the actors and going to the set," Kanner recalled.

"Robby Benson mentored me," she continued. "He had me on the set as his informal assistant, when he directed episodes of *The Naked Truth* and I learned quite a lot. He encouraged me to direct something—anything, and I decided on a multi-camera, ten-minute pilot presentation which came out of a pilot my husband had written for HBO Independent Productions," Kanner continued. "I got these great actors, we shot the presentation in about two hours, and suddenly, I had a reel!" Alas, Kanner discovered that no one really cared about that reel, so she continued forward by directing a few plays at the HBO Workspace, all the while continuing casting with Johnson.

Her feature-length directorial debut, *Face to Face* was the opening night film at the Taos Talking Pictures Festival in 2001. "Lorna helped cast it," Kanner recalled. "Directing this film was the most incredible experience of my professional career. It was Scott Baio's screenplay about fathers and sons, and he wanted a director to give the female perspective."

Coolest Casting Gig

Without a doubt, Kanner was thrilled by the process of casting something she would also direct; so *Face to Face* is her favorite thus far. "I'm just so happy with how it all turned out!" she exuded. The cast she and Johnson assembled? Dean Stockwell, Joe Viterelli, Alex Rocco, Thomas Calabro, Carlo Imperato, Meat Loaf Aday, Julie Bowen, Ellen Travolta, Jonathan Banks, and—of course—Scott Baio.

Advice for Actors

Use your VCR. "Tape every show currently in production," she said. The benefit to this task is that you will be aware, when called to audition for any show—other than a pilot, of course—of the show's pacing, its style, and the type of performances expected of its actors.

Also, you might want to read her book, *Next! An Actor's Guide to Auditioning.* Kanner co-authored this book with Paul G. Bens in 1998, so she acknowledged the material may be somewhat dated. "But go to Samuel French," she advised. "They have lots of books that every actor should go and read!"

Additionally, actors need to "let it go," according to Kanner. "I know an actor who rips up his copy of the sides after each audition, as sort of a ceremony to the end of the process," she explained. "You have no control, and you must let it go. Just do your homework, connect during the audition, and then move on."

Most importantly, actors must keep in mind that every casting director is different. "We all have our own opinions and our list of pet peeves," Kanner said. "Figure out what works for you, use common sense, and do your homework."

What She Would Change About the Casting Process

If Kanner had a magic wand, she'd want to see everyone prepared, taking their job seriously, and treating each other well. "It would be a nicer process that way," she said. "I mean, it's never easy. Never, ever! No matter what, it's always difficult, but it could be *nicer.*"

Her Opinion on Alternative Submission Methods

"I'm not used to [Internet casting], but that's just me," Kanner revealed. "But you *must* have a demo reel," she insisted. However, bad tape is worse than no tape, according to Kanner. So, unless your tape is of broadcast quality, with good writing and talented actors playing with you, don't use it. "Remember that the tape could be the last thing a producer sees on you."

Best Way To Get Seen by Her

Through your agent or manager. "Showcases are good, if they're put together by a group of actors who are well-connected and renting a theatre to put something up," she said. Kanner also attends plays and one-person shows. "Go do it!" she insisted. "Who's stopping you from joining theatre companies and being in class? Learn from the people you're most impressed with and ask everybody for help. We're so afraid to do that!"

"Additionally, when watching a show that you've decided you want to be on, send a note to the casting director for that show, explaining why you think you'd be right for a role on it. It may work. There are no guarantees, but if, at that *one* time, your photo gets in front of me when I need your type, it was worth doing," Kanner said.

Most Gratifying Part of Her Job

"Working with the actors. Watching their final performance and knowing I had a part in helping them get the job."

LISA MILLER KATZ, CSA

Lisa Miller Katz feels that she has the best job on the planet. She loves casting Everybody Loves Raymond. *The people she works with are talented and enthusiastic, two words that describe Katz as well. The passion she feels toward casting is obvious, and her eagerness to do the best job possible is paying off. The entire cast of* Everybody Loves Raymond *has been rewarded with nods from Emmy. Here's to Katz—casting director for shows such as* King of Queens, Blossom, *and* The Fresh Prince of Bel-Air—*for assembling a family that is everybody's favorite!*

First Casting Job

Assistant to Peter Golden at GTG Entertainment in 1987. "We did the original *Baywatch*. It was on NBC. We did the pilot and then a year of the show," Katz recalled.

Road to This Position

Katz went with Golden to Stephen Cannell's office as his associate, then became associate to Cheryl Bayer during the casting of *A Different World, Herman's Head*, and the Pauly Shore film *Son in Law*. In 1994, Katz set out to cast the last two seasons of *The Fresh Prince of Bel Air, Space: Above and Beyond*, and *The Last Frontier*. "Then I got the pilot for

Everybody Loves Raymond and all 100-plus shows since then. I also did the pilot and the first two seasons of *The King of Queens*, plus the pilot that became *The Geena Davis Show.*

Coolest Casting Gig

"*Raymond.* This little show which was incredibly well written and so real and so identifiable has become this huge hit. It's very gratifying in that respect." Of course, there are many ingredients to a hit show. Katz explained, "In addition to the show being really fun to work on, so many people are still with it who started with the pilot. That's completely unusual. It's really a joy. It's really familial around here. It's incredibly gratifying to have the world agree with the 120 of us who work on the show," Katz said.

Key Things She Looks for in an Actor

Enthusiasm and a vibe that they're happy to be there. "I get hundreds of pictures for every role. The number of people who I can't hire is mind-boggling to me. So, when someone comes in and it feels like they don't want to be there, I think, 'You must pick another career.' Your job as an actor is to audition. And if you audition well, your reward is getting the part."

Her Favorite Audition Tale

Katz enjoys seeing a non-union actor start out in an audition with her and move forward rapidly to stardom. She said, "I love it when I turn to my producers and say, 'All right, listen, he's not SAG. We're going to have to Taft-Hartley him.' And my producers go, 'I don't care. It doesn't matter,' like this guy was so good and fun and interesting and different and new and fresh. I brought in a guy on a pilot who'd been doing tons of theatre and he's, since then, appeared in a big movie, and he works all the time now. That's incredibly gratifying!"

Katz reads with auditioning actors, even in the producer sessions, and she prides herself on giving the actor a lot to work with. "I was on a movie of the week and it was about this man who was attacking this woman and the actor had said to me, 'Do you mind if I kind of go for you a little bit?' And so, he'd forewarned me. All the execs were all around and he actually pinned me to the wall and it was scary. It was inappropriate." The audition becomes less about the performance and more about the physical contact in those situations.

Katz has seen producers virtually ignore actors because they become so concerned over what they feel is behavior that crosses the proverbial line. "A lot of people are very intense about their personal space and I think you really have to respect that. If your sense is that it might not be received okay, go with your instincts. If it's someone you've only met a couple of times, I think you have to really trust that the urge may be possibly wrong. Respect the space. Make a move toward someone, indicate, reach for their hand, but don't grab them. I've had a woman sit in my lap! I'm all for confidence, but it's quite astonishing sometimes."

Pet Peeves

"At this point, if someone hasn't seen an episode of [*Everybody Loves*] *Raymond* and they come in and say, 'I don't watch TV,' I hate that one! Like TV's beneath them! They sit in their room and read sonnets all night. But TV is what I cast!"

Katz will give you time to prepare for your reading, "because cold readings show. I can smell a cold reading in an instant, generally at the end of the actor's first or second line. I'm more than happy to give you the time to work on it," Katz said.

One more thing: "This is going to make me sound like a crazy person, but I think wearing perfume is inappropriate. That's just my pet peeve."

Advice for Actors

"If acting is what you have to do or else you feel that you will crumble off the face of the Earth, then this is totally the right town for you. You have to be prepared to do whatever it takes. I've met people who seem to mistake fame for an acting career. I think there's a difference between the two. I think some people are attracted by the pretty shiny lights and the cameras and the money and the excitement and the glamour and I think there's a difference between the person who wants to be handed all that and someone who comes here and gets in a class and becomes a member of an ongoing theatre group or takes workshops at the Groundlings or workshops to get in front of casting directors they've never met or will work three days for free on a student film just for the tape because they don't have any—that's the person who came here to be an actor. That's what you should be doing. I talked with someone a couple of months ago who was frustrated with his career and I asked him all of these questions about things he's doing. 'Well, I got these headshots.' This is not your permission slip to the acting club! It's just not! You have to do legwork. This is why you came here, right? That's what frustrates me about this. People think these are steps that can easily be bypassed."

Katz had further advice specific to the whirlwind that is pilot season. "Try to be as prepared as possible during pilot season. It is about the only time of year that a script should be readily available in the casting director's office, so there's no excuse for not having read and prepared the script as much as possible. Ask questions of your agent or of the assistant in the casting director's office. Know the tone of the show. Is it similar to something already on the air? There's no such thing as too much information. All of this will be helpful during an audition," she said.

"Many people have multiple appointments on busy days during pilot season. If you feel the need, ask for more time. Usually that will be an option. If you're an actor who seems like you don't care about giving a cold reading, you'll be quickly dismissed during pilot season; a time when reading 100 actors a day is the norm."

Best Way To Get Seen by Her

Theatre. "When the flyer comes in the mail, if I recognize one of the names, I'll pick up the phone and make a reservation. I'll even go by myself. That's my job."

Also, send your headshot and resumé to Katz. She looks at them all. "It's all very random. Sometimes I'm just looking for someone I've never seen before." Of course, comic timing is an integral part of sitcoms, so your resumé should spotlight your comedic skills.

Her Opinion on Alternative Submission Methods

"I'm very slowly acclimating to the computer age," said Katz. "I love to sit with a stack of pictures on the floor. I like the physical act of going through my old lists, stacks of pictures, books." Katz feels that it is her job as a casting director to know who's right for a part. "I don't want the computer to make that list for me," she said.

Her Operating System

Sitcoms require quick casting decisions. Katz uses Breakdown Services and opens "every submission that gets to us in time, regardless of the return address label. We go over the submissions all at once, no matter who they came from."

Highlight of Her Week

"Every element of my job is a highlight! I'm a very lucky girl. I work on really great shows and I work with great people. These are smart, funny shows and I'm incredibly proud of that."

Most Gratifying Part of Her Job

Working on a show "that I actually like to watch, even though I've read the script half a dozen times, been to each table [read], each run-thru, and the taping and still watch it on television and appreciate it for the television show that it is, apart from the fact that I work on it."

DINO LADKI

I'd been told that Dino Ladki was an "up-and-coming" casting director. To me, that term means someone who is early on in their career, who hasn't cast many big projects, and who is willing to take some risks, as their most influential casting decisions are yet to come. After meeting Ladki, I'd say he's more the "next wave" of casting director: young, intelligent, and ready to take risks by nature. I don't think his "up-and-coming" style will erode. Those qualities are the very things that give him his edge.

First Casting Job

Ladki started out as a receptionist at Lorimar Television casting in 1993. He would certainly recommend starting out at a big place to get in the door. "It's not really hard, getting a casting assistant job because they want fresh people," Ladki said. "I mean, the jobs are few and far between but you don't have to have a lot of experience."

Road to This Position

In his three years at Lorimar, he worked as casting assistant first to Mark Sachs and then to Pamela Basker. "She treated me as an associate, even though that wasn't the position. I was making my own lists. I wasn't in readings, but

I had a mental Rolodex of actors and I could make appropriate suggestions." Ladki indicated that he didn't want to skip the step of being an associate casting director. "I wanted to learn more."

He started working for John Aiello as his associate, where *Sliders* was his assignment. "It was so much fun. One week it was kings and queens, the next week it was vampires." With Karen and Mary Margiata, he worked on *Hollyweird* and *The Adventures of Rocky and Bullwinkle*. "I did the pilot for *Undressed* for MTV and was then hired for a year contract to cast six or seven pilots for MTV. Those were acting pilots, not reality television," he clarified. "After that, I did a Canadian pilot and indie film and then became an independent casting director at Carsey-Werner," Ladki explained.

Coolest Casting Gig

Locust Valley, a pilot for MTV. While it didn't get picked up, Ladki was "very fond of it, the cast, and the producer, John Feldman. He's a really smart guy who knows what he wants, understands the casting process, knows actors," he recalled. The shows *Live Through This* and *Lyricist Lounge* did get picked up, and Ladki remembered those as "fun to cast" too, as was the pilot for *Undressed*.

Key Things He Looks for in an Actor

Smarts! "It's my opinion that there are no stupid people that are brilliant actors," Ladki revealed. "I'm a big fan of 'under-the-top' acting. Subtlety is everything, even in comedy. It's knowing how to get the joke from behind and surprise people." He feels that acting is a very important, noble profession. "I'm a big fan of actors and acting. They portray what goes on in our world and in life and that's such an important thing," Ladki explained. "As much as they talk about how much shit is on television, the same basic moral stories are told over and over again. It's basic right from wrong, from children's shows to adult shows. They have these moral themes."

His Favorite Audition Tale

This one, for Ladki, is bittersweet. The lead he'd first cast for the *Locust Valley* pilot had never done anything. "I found her in a preread and she went through the whole process. I worked with her a lot," he remembered. "The day before the final audition was a Sunday and I worked with her for five hours. She got the gig. After the first table read, she got fired. They were on a tight schedule and didn't have time to give this 16-year-old girl from Colorado a week of rehearsal. She was nervous and didn't do the table read well so they fired her and I had to replace her, which I did—with someone else I liked very much—but it was hard," Ladki explained. The moral of the story? "It was important lesson for me because those five hours I worked to make it perfect for her, well, you can't do it all for the actors. If I have to do that, then maybe I shouldn't, because it's not really helping anybody."

Advice for Actors

"Persevere. Have confidence. Confidence is 90% of it," he calculated. Oh, and if you want to shake someone's hand, shake their hand. "If they don't want to, don't be offended because there's a million reasons they may not want to. Be courteous, but ass-kissing is never necessary," Ladki indicated.

He also recommended that the actor take acting seriously by studying constantly. "Be selective. Talk to a lot of people before deciding who to study with," Ladki said. "Also, work as much as you can. Constantly perfect what you do by doing plays and showcases." And lastly, Ladki suggested that the actor treat acting like a business, "in every situation except for the audition. In the audition, be the artist."

Best Way To Get Seen by Him

"I look at every postcard, but I've cast very few people that way. I haven't done a workshop in a while, but I have cast plenty of people in small roles from workshops. I look at some, but not all, unsolicited headshots and resumés. The thing about casting is, it's always, 'Hurry up and get a cast.' It's always a rush, there's never enough time. I know a lot of people say they look at every single thing. I don't believe them. It's a nice answer, but they don't," Ladki revealed. In terms of priority, he looks at submissions from the top agencies first. "If I don't see it there, I go deeper through the stacks, and sometimes that gets to the people with nothing on their resumé. If they have a good look and at least have representation, I'll see them," he explained. Bottom line: the best way to be seen is through an agency's submission.

His Opinion on Alternative Submission Methods

"I've tried to do some casting through [the Internet], but it's not comprehensive enough to really do that," Ladki said. "But for submissions, I do think the Internet is the future. In about four years, that's the way everyone will submit."

Trends He Has Observed in the Casting Process

"I think the trend is going away from 'Teen Everything,' if it hasn't already," he predicted. But, more than any trend, Ladki explained that substance is what we keep coming back to. "People get sick of the bullshit and eventually they want quality. They want the real thing." He feels that mainstream producers have taken a cue from independents and that they are putting more substance into their big-budget features. "However, I think there will always be people who will make crap to make money." Why? "Only because there's people who will pay money to see crap."

His Operating System

"I've worked on my mental Rolodex for quite sometime, watching credits on every single thing I see. I've learned to read the names in credits so I'll recognize them next time," Ladki explained. "I have a terrible memory, but I've worked on it. I remember actors' names. That's my mental thing. I make myself remember them."

Highlight of His Week

"The only part I really like about casting is being in casting sessions. I love working with actors, bringing actors along. I think I'm proficient at raising someone's performance if they need that. I think hopefully one day I'll be a good director. I've got my five-year plan. I would love to do that, eventually, and I think casting is an avenue to help me do that. It certainly provides me the opportunity to work with actors and see what I can do with them at different levels of talent."

Most Gratifying Part of His Job

"When the person that I want most gets the part and they deserve it."

RUTH LAMBERT, CSA

If Ruth Lambert, former Director of Feature Animation Casting at Disney, could describe her old job with one word, it would be "fun." Along with Mary Hidalgo, her then-partner (who now runs the department), and Matthew Beck, their associate, she has cast such features as Fantasia 2000, Toy Story 2, Lilo & Stitch, *and* Monsters, Inc.

Still busy in the casting business and serving as vice president of the Casting Society of America, Lambert remains positive and passionate about her job, matching the best actors to the coolest roles.

First Casting Job

Over 20 years ago, Lambert met Gretchen Rennell-Court in Milwaukee. Lambert was a stage manager and Rennell-Court was interviewing actors for *Winds of War.* They hit it off, and three years later, Rennell-Court, along with Bonnie Finnegan, received a promotion at Paramount Pictures. They needed an associate. Larson had moved to Springfield, Massachusetts, since their meeting, and Rennell-Court wasn't sure how to find her. Over dinner with a mutual friend, she said, "We want someone like that Ruth girl." The friend said, "Why don't you just hire her?" He got the two in touch, and a career as a casting director began. Lambert left Stage West and moved to New York. "The first thing I worked on might have been getting Michael J. Fox's new girlfriend for *Family Ties* maybe."

Coolest Casting Gig

Without a doubt, that's her former job at Disney. Larson was with Disney for seven years. But what was the coolest film she cast there? "I think *A Bug's Life* was the most fun."

Key Things She Looks for in an Actor

Training is important. Larson zeros in on voice and speech training, specifically. Training, paired with improv experience, makes for a strong audition, and a strong performance to follow. Obviously, your look, as an actor, is much farther down the list, since your character must come through you via only your voice. Larson notes that this aspect can be difficult for those actors who have long-relied on being beautiful to get a foot in the door.

Her Favorite Audition Tale

Dave Foley, who played Flick in *A Bugs Life*, was originally called in for the part of the walking stick bug. On the day of his audition, the session was running way behind. As he waited in the lobby, a celebrity came in. Larson had to go to Foley and ask him to reschedule. His response? "Oh, yeah. I just saw [that person] walk in. It's fine, Ruth." He agreed to come in on another day, but by that time, David Hyde Pierce had already won the part. Larson had to work very hard to get Foley seen for Flick, as no one had visualized him in that role. Once he came in (again) for his audition, he had the job before he left the room. "He was exactly the kind of person that they love to hang out with. Those Pixar people love to hang," Larson said. Not only was it a great audition, but everyone adored Foley, and, as Larson noted, "You don't want to work with someone that's nasty. Our process takes so long. For the actor it's two-and-a-half years, and so who wants to keep bringing someone in that you don't like?" According to Lambert, an animated feature is a much longer commitment than twelve weeks on a film set, where you can pretty much endure personality conflicts. There is no room for that on these projects.

Duration of Her Job

Larson got involved at the very beginning. Along with Hidalgo and Beck, she began the process of casting right along with the story people. Her team was constantly casting and recasting as changes were made, usually up until six to nine months before the feature is released. "I learned a long time ago that it's never finished being cast when they say so," she mused.

Pet Peeves

Of course, if every actor booked for an audition would show up prepared, Larson would be elated. Unfortunately, many actors enter their audition with excuses about not getting the material—or they don't show up at all, even after being confirmed. Larson attributed that to a feeling of embarrassment over not being prepared. But she'd rather you show up anyway. Or at least call. Her assumption, when she doesn't get a call and an actor no-shows, is that they've been in a car accident. She can't imagine that someone would just blow off an audition, disrespectful of the other actors, of her, of their agent's work in getting them the appointment. Once, an actor *was* in a car accident on his way to his audition. Larson felt awful when she found out he'd been hospitalized, since she'd assumed that's what had happened when he didn't show up. "But y'know what? I found out quicker about him than I did about the people who just didn't show up."

Advice for Actors

Larson acknowledged that acting is a very tough business to break into, and that the voiceover industry, in particular, has changed. Looking back at *Beauty and the Beast* or *The Little Mermaid* reveals very few celebrity voices. Now, famous voices are required to sell tickets. Despite that fact, there are roles for the non-celeb. "You just have to be patient. I try to get a couple of people into every movie who've earned their jobs, who've auditioned. And that's very exciting for me to be able to do that."

Best Way To Get Seen by Her

Through an agent. "I am covered at every agency."

Her Opinion on Alternative Submission Methods

Okay, so if you don't have an agent and want to go another route, know that her office does open unsolicited submissions. "Everything is opened, everything is given a listen," she said. One very important point, though, is to be sure your tape is geared away from commercial pitching. "When people call and say, 'Can I send you a tape?' I always say, 'Make it short, make it a poem or a story or something interesting.' Commercial tapes get you a commercial but it's hard for me to hear that and translate it into this."

Her Opinion on Alternative Submission Methods

There is a database of information, but Larson would rather pull out the *Academy Players Directory* or her own book of headshots and resumés. Yes, headshots! Even though she's casting voices, Larson wants to see your mug! It helps her "place you" if she's seen your work before. It rounds out the feeling your voice provides. Larson is from a live action background and is set in her ways of flipping over a headshot and resumé while listening to tapes, keeping books of pix, and referring to handwritten notes. "I know it's very old-fashioned, but I've been doing this so long, I like having paper in my hands. I like having someone's picture and resumé in my hands, I like turning it over. I love my computer and I use it all the time because they make me use it here and that's excellent. But I like having a session sheet in my hand. I pay more attention to it." When Internet submissions come in, Larson will print them out right away. "What if my computer crashes? Then I'm screwed!"

As for organizing casting sessions, there are few variations on the "typical" protocol. Breakdowns are released to agents. Then, instead of sending sides, Larson puts out sketches, synopses, and character descriptions, "because we don't have scripts. And, even if we do, we don't send them out." Once agent submissions are in, they are organized according to priority, sessions are set up, and, once they begin, they run the same as on-camera sessions. Except for one thing: no camera. "We tape people, it's just a different tape."

Highlight of Her Week

"I love auditioning actors. I love meeting actors. The highlight of my week is when we have sessions."

Most Gratifying Part of Her Job

"Oh, my God, I get to go see these movies. My name's on them. And they make loads of money. And the actors that I hire love working on them. Ninety-eight percent of the people that are in these movies love them and love working on them and love their experience on them. The best part is when I get a note from an actor thanking me for their job. The best part is how thrilled people are with the product."

CAROL LEFKO

Many times, actors think that casting directors are not on their side. "We are," insists Carol Lefko. "We want [the actor] to succeed. We have a problem and they are our solution!"

Lefko, who has cast such films as Pushing Up Daisies, Ice Cream Sundae, *and* Kleptomania, *matches problems and solutions using an Old Hollywood sensibility, understanding that talent, perseverance, professionalism, and an unwavering sense of self are the keys to staying power in this business.*

Road to This Position

Lefko started in the mailroom at CBS. "The head of casting was the only female VP at CBS at the time. I remember her entire office was blue and maroon," Lefko explained. "I was the only female working in the mail room, and I put myself in charge of everything. I was Little Miss I'll Do It around there," she recalled with a laugh. "I pushed my little mail cart around like it was very important business. I wore a dress every day—with all of these guys in jeans." Lefko soon became aware of an opening for an assistant in casting. "I went home at lunch and changed my dress so that, when I went by the VP's office to deliver her mail, I was wearing blue and maroon. I went in and told her I wanted the job. She didn't ask about my skills, she just said, 'Oh my God! You match my office! You've got the job!'"

From there, Lefko has worked in production, in casting, and as a writer (three of her sitcoms have been optioned). "I've been working a long time," she admitted. "If you can still make a living at this after doing it for any length of time, then you're okay."

Key Things She Looks for in an Actor

Preparedness. "Read the whole script if you can. At the very least, read all of the scenes your character is in. If you want the part, you should want to know the journey of that character. Reading the script means that you are ready if you are asked, in an audition, to do more. At a callback, *know* all the scenes your character is in. That doesn't mean you should memorize every word, but you should know the scenes," she explained.

Pet Peeves

Excuses. "I don't need to know why you're late, why you have no picture, why your agent didn't tell you about the sides. If you're not going to work as a grownup, then find a new job," Lefko insisted. "Take responsibility in every way. Acting is not a hobby. If your heart is not in it, you need to examine what course of action to take. If it's not at the fiber of your being, then don't do it."

Once you've determined acting is your calling? "Persevere. Don't beat yourself up. Remember that there's always the next role," Lefko assured. "Acting is a hard job. I give actors a lot of credit. You can be the best listening actor around, but if you're not given a chance to *be* a listening actor, what good does that do you?"

Back to pet peeves: "Don't show up for your audition with a gun, with a knife, on drugs," Lefko listed. "I'm serious! Be professional. Shake hands with the casting director only if she extends a hand first."

Lefko is somewhat distracted by actors who bring their children with them to an audition. "It's not that the kids are poorly behaved, it's that the parent is such a mess over it, because they couldn't get a sitter at the last minute. It removes their focus from the job they're there to do," she commented.

Advice for Actors

"Do something to help yourself in your career every day. Read a play, get the right hair color, fix something that is somehow holding you back. I'm not pro-implants, but if you want to do the kind of films that your body is not made for, go to a really good doctor. Attend screenings. Do the socializing that's so important in this profession. The more you can network, the better."

"Read out loud every day for 15 minutes. Read, enunciate, articulate, project. This is so important, even if you're not planning to be a stage actor," Lefko concluded.

Lefko also mentioned the importance of staying true to who you are. "Be smart. Regarding the auditioning process, don't get psyched out in the waiting room by another actor. Actors come in a mess after having encountered someone in the waiting room who makes them feel like less than who they are. Don't sit there letting your energy go into the chair. Stand up, move around, keep your spirits up."

"When you enter the room, find the power person in the room. It's very important. Who is the director? You may think the camera operator is no one important and it turns out, that's the director. Know who you're dealing with. Ask before you go into the room. Ask *in* the room. It's okay. And since so many directors are also writers, don't critique the script. If you do, you put yourself in a bad position, and the casting director who brought you in looks like an idiot."

Study. "It's hard to find a really decent teacher," Lefko admitted. "A lot of coaches are just out there for the cash. Go to different classes. Audit if you can. See who the actors you respect are studying with."

Know your strengths. "You need to know what you excel at. Is it comedy? Drama? Do you sing and dance? Be honest with yourself as an actor. Do you want to do community theatre? There's nothing wrong with that, but you need to know that's what you want to do. Ask yourself if you're best suited for commercials, if you have a great voice and should do voiceovers, if you should work on soaps, if sitcoms are your market, if you're best-suited for films—but you have to know who you are. A sense of self-truth is key to that. Keep a journal and reexamine yourself every few weeks if you're not doing something toward your acting career. Be honest with yourself."

"If I could boil my advice down to just three items, I'd say, when you walk into the room to audition, have a genuine smile on your face. If you're not having a good day, it'll show. So, feel good. Smile and let it show. Second, learn how to walk away from an audition and let it all go. It's the hardest thing to do. You do need to learn from it, and fix what might have been wrong for the next time, but then just let it go. Last, always be professional. Be a pro. Those items encompass everything else I could possibly say."

Best Way To Get Seen by Her

"You need representation," Lefko insisted. "Your manager or agent can submit appropriately based on the [character] breakdown."

"I do like [casting] new people," Lefko admitted. "In sitcoms, you'll see the same people over and over again. I don't like that. I love loyalty, but I don't like laziness."

Trends She Has Observed in the Casting Process

"Since I started working in this business, the agent has become more powerful than the studio. As with everything, there's a good side and a bad side to that change. I think an actor needs to take a more critical role in his career. You don't see a plumber calling his agent to see if it's okay for him to fix that toilet. As an actor, say to yourself, 'No one should make a decision on my behalf. That's too much power.' And take that 90% role you have seriously. Make sure your agent is running things past you, rather than making decisions for you."

Her Opinion on Alternative Submission Methods

Regarding Internet casting services, Lefko said, casually, "Just don't get ripped off."

"Spend your money on the best headshot that looks like you. Look around. Look at a photographer's book. Shop around like you would for any major purchase. Check your appearance in the mirror and know what will help get you a job. If you need to rectify your appearance by changing your weight in either direction, changing your hair color, getting plastic surgery, visiting a makeup consultant, getting new wardrobe—whatever—do that so that you can properly market yourself. Men should be masculine looking and women should be feminine. It's so important. And it's good to have a look that will allow you to work in period pieces. Tattoos and piercings keep you from being able to do that."

Most Gratifying Part of Her Job

"It's fun to put someone in a movie that will then propel their career."

MICHAEL LIEN, CCDA & DAN COWAN

Michael Lien has been in the casting business for over 20 years. Dan Cowan, only five. Each man came to casting by way of other entertainment industry jobs. In fact, Cowan still works occasionally as a set and technical designer for Los Angeles theatre.

Their individual offices are end-to-end in the patio area of their Beverly Blvd. location, where two dogs meander around to investigate all goings-on. Cowan leans back in his chair, eyes moving back and forth from me to the computer monitor throughout the interview, while Lien is up out of his chair more than in it, giving much of the interview from other rooms. Casting sessions take place around the corner from their business office, and assistants buzz from room to room, displaying the volume of business this commercial casting facility enjoys.

Road to This Position

Cowan was working as an AD for a children's theatre company five years ago, when he was referred to Lien. Cowan was hired as an assistant, and three or four years ago, the two began talking partnership. Lien explained, "Dan purchased a share of the company. A vested interest is really the only way a partnership can work." I asked Cowan when he was sure that casting was for him. "I'm still not sure," he said with a laugh.

Lien came into casting by way of production. "I fell into it. I was doing production work in the early and mid-'70s. I was working on a Clairol commercial and the client requested me when they couldn't find a casting director on their next project, which was for Pillsbury's Hungry Jack," Lien recalled. Why he left production? "Being a casting director involves better hours and better pay than producing, so I stuck with it."

Coolest Casting Gig

Many casting directors say that their current casting gig is the coolest. No exception here. "This current director [for a Bank of America commercial]—I love working with," Cowan said.

Key Things They Look for in an Actor

"The specifics depend on the director and the job," according to Cowan. But self-confidence is always at the top of the list. Also on that list? "A sparkle in the eyes, personality, strength."

Pet Peeves

For Lien, it's mail. "Don't make work for me by putting a headshot and resumé into an envelope, sealing it, double-sealing it, taping it shut. Send me a postcard. There's more of a chance I'll remember it," Lien said. He then sorted through a stack of postcards to show me which were too busy, which were clean, which he'd remember, and which were not worth sending. A rule of thumb, according to Lien, "I shouldn't need an Evelyn Wood Speed Reading Course in order to read every word on your postcard. Tell me when you've switched agents; thank me for a job—not an audition. That just seems like you're sucking up and says to me that you never get out on auditions."

For Cowan, pet peeves include the same old jokes and what he calls false friendliness. "Be yourself. If you're not, it shows so much in auditions. The false friendliness sticks out to directors and everybody," Cowan said.

Advice for Actors

Lien's advice? "Prepare. At the bare minimum, read the script," Lien insisted. Actors don't read the script? "Yep. You'd be shocked," Lien explained.

Lien suggests that the actor consider how far he or she has come, rather than focusing on failure. "Just to get to the audition, you've beaten out 1000 people. That was a feat! Don't be discouraged by lots of people in the waiting room. They could be there for other jobs."

And, finally, on Lien's list, "be kind to people. If you're painful in the audition, we have to assume you're going to be painful on the set. Assistants tell us who's a pain, so just be kind," he advised.

Cowan began sharing advice on keeping at it, being persistent and then stopped and said, "Scratch that. Have fun. Have fun doing it. It shows." And if the actor is not having fun? "Angry actors, don't come here."

Lien added that, when attending an audition, you'd better know if you're the last slot of the day and not be late. "By 4:30pm, we're already dubbing tapes to send to the client. You need to know that you're holding us back from getting an entire day's worth of sessions to the client, if you come in late."

Their Opinion on Alternative Submission Methods

"You don't need to go online to find anyone," Cowan summarized. "If every single actor and every single agent did it, if SAG made it a requirement, it would be worth it. The agencies with rosters online, especially modeling agencies or those that specialize in kids, those are useful."

"Dan's the techie, I'm the dinosaur. He got us networked and on all those online services," Lien revealed. Lien's specialty? "I talk to agents. I'm hands-on with all the headshots." He picked up a stack of headshots as he explained a current casting method, "We were doing an ABC Summer Campaign and it was not about the look. It was about the personality. And I *know* these people." Does he see the point to online casting? "Yes. But there's so much to be involved with. I didn't want to buy *a* computer, much less have one at every desk. Now we have an incoming and outgoing fax machine," he laughed. "Yes, I think it's an interesting tool for actors, but no one has been able to implement it properly. Actors should, however, be on *one* of them. None of them have won exclusivity in the field. No one is using them exclusively. Honestly," Lien continued, "it's almost easier to just go through the pictures. We still can't download pictures fast enough."

Until one system "wins," Lien suggests that actors get in the *Academy Players Directory.* "It's a good tool, it's highly respected, it's reliable. It's not the only source, but we go to it, in print or online, at least once a day."

Their Favorite Casting Tale

"Searches are fun," Cowan said, especially for actors with specific qualifications. For example, Cowan conducted a nationwide search for Kemper Insurance, a company that needed an actual family—three generations—all of whom could ice skate. Additionally, Cowan recently found a blind actress with a black belt in karate in Brockton, New York for that current Bank of America spot.

Best Way To Get Seen by Them

"Through agents," according to Cowan. Of course, he does open unsolicited headshots and resumés. "You never know what might be in there, so I open everything." Postcards are great in this office. "Especially if you have an interesting update and the timing is on," meaning, you could just so happen to have a postcard on his desk when Cowan is looking for your type. So, go ahead and send an update, when you have something happening, like a change in representation or a new show premiering.

Lien maintains his position on mail. "I don't want to say never send a headshot and resumé, but postcards work better for me."

Highlight of Their Week

"The busiest day is the best day. Being busy is the most fun," summarizes Cowan.

Lien's highlight? "Sessions. Pulling the sessions off is great."

AMY LIPPENS, CSA

Amy Lippens recalls working as assistant director on a school production and taking copious notes for the actors on stage. In college, Lippens studied Sociology and Women's Studies. Her interest in the intricacies of performances and human nature have blended perfectly to give her the edge in casting projects such as Meet the Deedles *and* Catch a Falling Star. *Her work as casting associate for the pilot of* My So-Called Life *kicked off her relationship with Marshall Herskovitz and Edward Zwick, who would later hire her to cast the pilot and series* Once and Again.

"I love actors. I have a sense of actors. And I believe that the person who is most right for the part will get the part. With my sociology background, I always focus on trying to reflect the real world," Lippens said, noting that diversity is on the minds of everyone in the industry. With a warm, caring personality, and the willingness to share every lesson the industry has taught her, Lippens is an expert at casting—and working with—children.

First Casting Job

Casting assistant on Alan Parker's *Come See the Paradise*. "I had been a PA on *Tin Men* in Baltimore before that. I learned so much: what the jobs were, respect for each of those roles. With *Come See the Paradise*, we were doing a major search for kids who had to age through the movie. We had to delve into Asian Boy Scout troops, looking for non-actors," Lippens recalled.

When casting young performers to play characters who will age over the course of the film, does Lippens scout a similar *look*? "More of an essence," Lippens replied. "I see a lot of people and I look for the common charm, the sense of the actor that will be playing the adult role. It takes a lot of focus to get a sense of who they are."

Road to This Position

"I studied acting as a young girl. After college, I worked in production on projects such as *Back to the Future 2* and *Tequila Sunrise*," Lippens explained. It was on these projects that Lippens was told that she would be good at casting. "I worked as a runner on a TV show and then assisted Henry Winkler on a film he directed." Mary Goldberg was Lippens' mentor. "She took me under her wing and gave me my first screen credit," Lippens said. The project was *Milk Money*, and it included a huge search for the five children in principal roles.

Coolest Casting Gig

Once and Again, the pilot. "It was an amazing experience," Lippens said. "We cast in September, so there wasn't the pressure of pilot season. So many actors were available for us to see." Out of ten series regular roles, four were children. "[Executive producers] Ed [Zwick] and Marshall [Herskovitz] really empowered the heads of departments. They were very supportive of my choices. Finding the right mix of actors for these families was a joyful experience. When the writing is so good, and you have been empowered with the trust of the series creators, you can be the best that you can be," Lippens explained. A reason the series itself was a cool gig, for Lippens, is the fact that her office was just off the set. "I loved doing set visits, to see how the actors were working.

To watch them work, to see the growth of these young people—as performers and as people—was just wonderful for me. I will always hold that experience in the threads of who I am," Lippens concluded, wistfully.

Key Things She Looks for in a Young Performer

A unique essence. "Kids are who they are. They don't bring a lot of baggage. So, I look for what that actor will be bringing to the part. Are you genuine? Are you funny? Kids will say the things that come to their heads, and that's great. I also look for a young actor who really wants to be here, who really wants to be an actor," Lippens explained. That means, to Lippens, that the young performer is not pursuing acting due to parental influence. "The actor needs to find performing fun, not stressful, not a chore."

Most importantly, according to Lippens, the young performer must have stamina. "This is someone who is going to be working *and* going to school at the same time. They must have the energy for both," Lippens insisted. "Young actors should come in, do the best they can, be polite, be professional, and then be on their way, ready to enjoy the rest of their day."

How Parents Can Contribute

"I know it's hard, but let your child make his own decisions with the material and with the roles he's up for. This process has to be about the individual who wants to be an actor. What you can do to support that is make sure your child is active, eats a well-balanced diet, is healthy. Make sure your child knows it's okay to *not* go on that audition when he's tired, has homework to do, or feels the role isn't right for him. Young performers are taking on a job, so they have to want it. They have to be able to speak up. They are the drivers of their careers," she said.

"I assign young actors the job of watching TV and writing down the roles they could play. Children who want to perform professionally need to go see movies with a different eye. Reading is very important—and I mean great literature—reading keeps the imagination from getting lost," Lippens commented.

Lippens added, "I always ask where the family is from. People forget that the parents are schlepping these kids all around town. I remind the children to go outside after the audition and thank their parents. It's a big commitment they've made. They sometimes have to relocate or separate from one another. It's important that I am informed about who the parents are before recommending the child to a producer or director. They're not just hiring a child, but a whole family."

Pet Peeves

Gifts. "I don't need a bribe to see you. I'll see you because it's my job to see as many actors as I can for every role."

Advice for Young Actors

"Live your life. Acting is *one* extra-curricular activity. First there's family, then school, and then all of the rest. One element of that 'all of the rest' part may be acting. Those priorities are very important. You need life experiences so that you can bring them to the role and expand upon them," Lippens said.

"Remember that we want you to be good. We want you to be right for the part. If you have a question, speak up. Take your time and be present in the moment. Be prepared, be professional, and remember that this is always a win-win situation. Every audition is cumulative. There's too much pressure to get the job, and that makes kids think they're performing because they have to. No. It's about being creative and having fun."

"Know that it's okay to stop for a while. There is so much that is important to a child's life that only exists through high school graduation. After that, many of the athletics, extra-curricular activities, and honors are all gone. Acting will always be there, so know that it's okay to take a break from it."

Best Way To Get Seen by Her

Lippens provided a list, in order of importance. "Through agents and managers, at showcases, by viewing films and TV shows, by attending theatre, and from producer and casting director recommendations. I am open to seeing actors through individual submissions," Lippens insisted. "Postcards, I look at. If the timing is right, I'll make a note of when to catch your show. Postcards remind me that you're still around."

Her Opinion on Alternative Submission Methods

"I use the IMDB, the [*Academy*] *Players Directory*, and all of the sides services online. Things are really just beginning with this, though. I am very open to [links to] reels sent online," Lippens said. She suggested that, for young actors, a well-done—but inexpensive—headshot is a more important tool. "Kids need new headshots at least once a year, more frequently if there is a drastic change in their looks." Lippens also recommended that young actors utilize the acting classes available in their schools and at community theatres. "Kids should be doing scenes with other kids, just like adult actors get together to workshop scenes."

Her Biggest Casting Challenge

Her first solo film, *Camp Nowhere*. "I had to cast 21 kids in seven weeks. All of them were 12 years old. Everyone is changing at that age. I couldn't use Jessica Alba in a major role, but I kept her on as one of the camp kids. Years later, just before *Dark Angel* went into production, I saw her at a party and asked if she remembered me from her childhood. She said,

'Of course! You gave me my SAG card!' That's a wonderful feeling," Lippens recalled.

Most Gratifying Part of Her Job

"To be able to give people jobs. To call an agent or manager, or sometimes even the actor directly, and say, 'You won the job. You did a wonderful reading, you embodied the role, and you are the choice.' Just knowing that they're getting to put food on the table, put money away for their future, pay for college, it's wonderful."

BEVERLY LONG, CCDA

Entering Beverly Long's casting office in Studio City is like visiting her at home. Members of her staff greet visitors warmly as they buzz around the nerve center of the office: the kitchen. Snapshots are splattered on the walls and all over the refrigerator. Abbey, the chocolate lab, sniffs her approval and then flops on the floor for a nap. According to Long, "You've gotta have a dog!"

At a moment's notice, a rush job for a hair-care product has come in. "Wow! There's a lotta hair in here," Long exclaims as she passes the waiting room, ushering me to the table where we'll have our chat. "We cast a lot of journeymen here. Lots of workaday worker bees." Translation? Real people, get in front of Beverly Long.

The office walls display thank you notes from actors who've visited this unique space. There are gifts of cookies and potpourri on the kitchen table. Long's six-week commercial workshops take place here and she theorizes that actors are somehow put at ease by the presence of the dog. I'd bet it's more than just Abbey that gives this office that family feel.

Road to This Position

First an actor, then an agent, then a casting director. Long had a recurring role on *Father Knows Best*, was a regular on *Those Whiting Girls*, and co-starred in a little film called

Rebel Without a Cause. "They cast two girls and four boys to support James Dean and Natalie Wood. I was one of the two girls: Helen," Long revealed. She and fellow actor Corey Allen [master teacher at Margie Haber Studio] were working in the play *Pick Up Girl* at the Players' Ring, where the director spied them and brought them in to audition for the film. "Five hundred kids auditioned!" Long recalled.

At the age of 17, Long originated the role of Susan in the play *Susan Slept Here.* Fast-forward ahead through a marriage, three kids, and a divorce, and Long's realization: "I have to have a *job*-job." Luckily, Long's agent asked her to be a subagent for the summer. "I figured, I may not know how to be an agent, but I'm an actor. I can *act* an agent," Long insisted. "After two years, I realized I'm too much of a gypsy to sit behind a desk that much," she explained.

Norman Greiner, a now-retired casting director that she'd met while agenting, was doing so much feature casting that he was losing commercial clients. He asked Long to step in and assist. "After a year in the role of feeble-minded assistant, I became the sole commercial casting director in that office," she joked.

Key Things She Looks for in an Actor

"A Can-Do attitude," Long explained. "There's a positiveness that I look for. If you're negative, no one wants to work with you. Honestly, no one wants to work with a depressed person, even if they're talented."

Long also looks for an understanding of the process the actor is experiencing. "They need to know what they're being sent in that room to do," she said.

Pet Peeves

"Actors who don't show up for the audition," Long asserted. "The lack of responsibility shown by actors is shocking." In fact, Long invites students in her commercial classes to sit in on auditions, so that they may see how obvious it is to identify the actors who take the process of auditioning seriously.

"So many actors are not dressed appropriately when they come to an audition," Long began. "If the breakdown calls for a woman in a bikini, show up in a body-conscious outfit. Don't make me send you home to change." Long attributes much of this carelessness to lack of communication between actor and agent.

Regarding unsolicited submissions of headshots and resumés, Long explained, "We're pretty loose around here, but if you send your headshot and resumé to me, please God, do *not* address the letter to, 'Dear Casting Director.' It looks like you did a mass mailing and you don't know who the hell I am." Long continued, "You want me to pay attention to you but you don't even know who you're writing to. It's like a form letter, and I'll put it right in the trash." So, to get past that fate, know Long's name. Know her credits. "Do a little research," she said.

Advice for Actors

"Be someone who grasps what it's all about," Long advised. "Have an idea of what you're coming in for." To that end, actors should do their homework, be prepared for anything, and be flexible enough to make changes on the fly.

"When you send me a postcard, make sure it's something personal or it's a notice that you're in a show somewhere. Again, don't do a blind mailing to just say hi. I really don't have the time," Long explained.

Another piece of advice Long offered involves gratitude. "Send flowers if you book the job!" she insisted. "Booking a national is a big deal. Thank me for it!"

Her Opinion on Alternative Submission Methods

"I don't go online, but my associates do," Long revealed. "The computer screen is a bore to me. It doesn't feel right."

Long reached for a stack of headshots and fanned through them, then said, "I need to hold your picture. Besides, organized people use the Internet. That's not me!"

Best Way To Get Seen by Her

"The best way is through your agent, but sometimes it's serendipity. It's just a fluke," Long began. "One day, I was here all alone after a long day of taping sessions for a Red Lobster ad. It was the end of the day and this guy just walked in. He came by to drop off his picture and he was the match for what I'd been looking for. He got the job!" Now, sometimes an actor can't get in the door, so Long did not, by any means, encourage the casual drop-by. "A drop-*off* of your photo, though, is okay," she clarified.

Most Gratifying Part of Her Job

"Teaching, I like," Long summarized. "The commercial workshop we do is so rewarding." After 20 years of teaching, Long finds those rewards on the small screen. Recent Super Bowl ads starred several of Long's former students. "To see these money-makers when they're just starting, that's great," she said.

"And I love the audition process. A lot of casting directors never go into the sessions. I would go mad if I didn't get to do that. I enjoy meeting and working with actors, seeing what they can do."

"A casting session is like a party. It should be festive," Long shared. "You, the actor, are my invited guest. If you throw the lawn furniture into the pool, you don't get invited back. Remember, your goal is not to see every casting director *once*, but to get invited back to these parties over and over again."

If you sense that Long loves her job, you're right. "We have a good time here. It's fun. Hey, if I didn't enjoy it, I'd get out of it."

ELLYN LONG MARSHALL & MARIA E. NELSON

Occasionally, I get the opportunity to interview a partnership: two casting directors who have worked together for years, who have a certain simpatico, and who—together— have stronger casting instincts than either would alone. The women who comprise Orpheus Group, Ellyn Long Marshall and Maria E. Nelson, are two such casting directors. Their extensive work in New York theatre has lead to what appears to be a can't-miss instinct that the pair has brought to feature film casting. If you haven't heard of Orpheus Group yet, you will. Marshall and Nelson assembled the casts for such independent hits as Girlfight *and* Real Women Have Curves.

First Casting Job

Marshall—I was a casting director before Orpheus Group was formed in 1986. I worked as a casting assistant at The New York Shakespeare theatre, doing general auditions. I was sent to Los Angeles to cast *The Pirates of Penzance* in 1979. My first casting job with Orpheus Group was at The Crossroads Theatre.

Nelson—I started casting in 1987. I was an agent prior to actually going into casting. Once Ellyn left the Public Theatre, we did not really decide that we'd go into casting until friends started calling. People were starting to ask us to cast their projects.

Marshall—We both had a wide vocabulary of talent. Theatre had been so much a part of our lives. That's why people would call us for suggestions. So, we asked ourselves, "Why not? We know everybody!"

Coolest Casting Gig

Marshall—I think it's the same for both of us. *Another Person is a Foreign Country*, a theatre piece written by Chuck Me and directed by Anne Bogart.

Nelson—This was site-specific theatre, which is a wonderful idea. They performed this show in a meatpacking plant, an old abandoned nursing home on the Upper West Side, places like that.

Marshall—The theme of the piece was all of our differences and how we're all the same. Chuck went to extremes. Our casting chore was finding a blind choir, a deaf legit actor...

Nelson—...little people...

Marshall—...a giant—we didn't quite do that. It was an amazing experience. It was not only a challenge but an enlightening experience for us both. Things we took for granted as casting directors we really learned to look at, such as how to leave phone messages for deaf actors, how to put the sides where the little people could reach them when they came into the lobby.

Nelson—That was the piece that made the media conscious of all of these people with all of these differences. The show got wonderful reviews. It was so incredible. *The* [*Village*] *Voice* called and said they wanted to meet the people that had cast that show, and that marked a real beginning for us: for the actors we cast to get such recognition.

Marshall—It really put a new spin on the casting process and made it a more meaningful process for us.

Do Casting Directors Act as Producers?

Marshall—We think as producers anyway. Even with theatre. We always I do. Casting is a part of that.

Nelson—With first-time directors, we'll take them by the hand. For example, with *Girlfight*, this project came to us two years prior to us working on it. We fell in love with the piece and committed to it. Karyn Kusama was a new writer-director and we really tried to steer it in the right direction. That required many, many meetings with Karyn. We really dissected the script. That was rewarding for us.

Marshall—As a casting director, if you're really doing what you're supposed to be doing, casting bleeds over into producing. We're all working very closely to have the same view as the writer-director. We're making sure that all of the components are right, and that goes beyond the cast.

Key Things They Look for in an Actor

Nelson—Commitment. We take for granted that the talent is there (or we *hope* it is there). We're looking for actors who are well-prepared for an audition, both with the material and emotionally. One of the most important things for us is that, when you walk into that room, you leave whatever baggage you have at the door. Leave it outside. The minute you enter that room, you have our eyes on you. Take us on a journey. Whatever you are feeling, we pick up.

Marshall—Our eyes and our minds and our hearts want you to be what we need. It's not known what is needed. You bring it in and show it to us.

Nelson—You make it happen. You give us the answers. It's very true. It's very important. Actors have a way of beating themselves up after an audition. It's very important for us to let actors know that the audition is something they should enjoy. Just come in and do the best you can do.

Marshall—There is no right and wrong. Every person in that room is a part of a whole, including the auditioning actor.

Nelson—The audition should not only be our experience but the actor's experience. They're offering us something very special. We like to work with producers, directors, and writers who make the actors feel special. The actor has to leave the room having taken something from us. Otherwise, what is it about?

Advice for Actors

Marshall—I'd like to encourage actors to perform as readers. We receive letters saying, "I'd love to work as a reader." We call those actors in. We encourage it. It's such a learning process. It also helps you as an actor by taking the pressure off the audition situation.

Nelson—The actors will say, "This has been such a rewarding experience, being a reader for you." It is very important that you go out of your way to be a reader.

Marshall—Plus, we need readers!

Best Way To Get Seen by Them

Nelson—For us, it's a constant search. Because of the amount of film that we're dealing with right now, we don't get a chance to go to as many showcases as we would like. The actors unions invite us to come in and speak to the actors. That's very important to us. We sometimes cast actors out of those situations. We absolutely open every envelope and we read every resumé and then we file it. We will sometimes find someone very interesting and call them in. Postcards are a wonderful way to keep in touch with us. We're very conscious of that. When I first started agenting the owner used to say, "What you throw away today you're going to need tomorrow." So, I keep everything.

Marshall—We seem to be getting most of our films for very young newcomers. That's another reason to open all of our mail. We find people that way. I'm looking at the industry showcases we attended to scout for Josh Masden's first film, *Maria, Full of Grace*. We went wherever there's a strong Colombian population. For this film, we dealt with the real community as well—not just the actors. We did something similar with *Real Women Have Curves*. That was cast out of Los Angeles, and we went to Mexico. Maria went to Texas. That's happening more and more.

Do You Attend Theatre To Scout Talent?

Marshall—Yes we do. We cast theatre. We love theatre. It's where we come from. Theatre is a good injection between films.

Their Opinion on Alternate Submission Methods

Marshall—I think it's very effective. It's necessary. The world is small and getting smaller. We're not quite up to Internet casting yet, but we're in the process of making that transition.

I think everybody is. It's as accessible, more so, than opening the mail.

Nelson—We did a project in London quite a few years ago. Today, Internet casting would be completely essential to that. It's a link that you cannot, at this stage, do casting without.

Their Biggest Casting Challenge

Nelson—*Real Women Have Curves*. It was a real search for us to find a young girl who was talented, but who was not in the mainstream because of the weight issue. We really had to go to the schools and colleges and programs where there were just young people who maybe, at times, didn't have a very good self-image.

Marshall—We needed a young girl who was overweight but who had enough self-confidence and talent to carry a film. Even with *Girlfight*, it was difficult to find someone age 17 who had the maturity that shows on the screen, within her eyes, right away.

Nelson—We're dealing with a visual medium, so it's hard to strike a balance. Casting *Real Women Have Curves* was very tricky and took us so long. We were very fortunate to have a lot of help. We zoomed into the different programs in the communities. Community leaders helped us a lot.

Marshall—That was true with *Maria, Full of Grace* as well.

Nelson—When I went to Texas for *Real Women Have Curves*, I called around and found someone who had a connection with a casting director in Texas who had done searches. We set everything up before I left so that I could cover a lot of ground in a very short period of time. It all came together. The Internet allowed us to link and communicate in a very short period of time. Once you get one person who is connected to the community, getting the information back to the office is the easy part.

Most Gratifying Part of Their Job

Marshall—For me, it's seeing the finished product. We hadn't seen anything at all on *Real Women Have Curves* until it screened at Sundance 2002. I just couldn't settle down for days after seeing it. I just thought it was beautiful. All of those months of biting my nails and wondering where we were going to find all of these women who form a family in that factory... I just thought it was so beautiful. That's the most gratifying part, to have an end result like that: beautifully edited. To see those actresses up there, I was in heaven.

Nelson—For me, every once in a while, I'm in an audition situation and someone walks in the door and is so brilliant, I have to pinch myself. It's heavenly when it's all there. That's when I think, "Aren't I lucky to be sitting in this room right now?" I love actors and have such respect for them. Actors do a thankless job. The world of their discovery is the most wonderful part of my job.

MELISSA MARTIN, CCDA

As an actor, there are times you sit across the desk from a casting director thinking, "You have no idea what I've gone through to get to this audition." Turns out, Melissa Martin does know. She made a career out of acting before becoming a casting director, casting ad campaigns for Coca-Cola, Visa, and Sony. She knows what it's like, she feels for you, and she also has some pretty good advice, having been on both sides of that desk.

Advice for Actors

"I have a lot of advice! Your picture is the only thing— the *only* thing—you have to buy. Make it the best it possibly can be. This is where you should spend some money," Martin explained. She added that you could spend all the money in the world on photos, but if she can't call you, it's money gone to waste. "Put your phone number all over everything. This guy brought his headshots by and dropped them in all the commercial casting director bins here [at Chelsea Studios] and everywhere else in town, and there was no contact information at all. What a waste!"

Martin recommends that you pay special attention to the detail you put in your resumé. "Get very specific with your skills. The more specific you are, the more likely you are to get in front of me. Leave off the goofy, cutesy stuff." Martin is also interested in the training section of your resumé. "I look for people who are studying, and not just staying with the same instructor for five years. It gets cultish. I want to see you working with a bunch of different people. I want to see you doing improv. It makes you quick on your feet and that really pays off. If you don't have credits, you'd better have a lot of training."

Pet Peeves

"Actors who don't look like their headshots. Men will use the same headshot for ten years and they've gone bald. Women will gain 20 or 30 pounds and not change their headshots. Eighty-five percent of the actors I see come in not looking like their headshots!" Martin continued, "You *must* do your hair and makeup the way it was done in your headshot. Clients cannot imagine what you might look like with your hair and makeup done if you show up sloppy."

Best Way To Get Seen by Her

Martin accepts unsolicited submissions from non-union and non-represented actors, but she admits she can't possibly keep every headshot she receives. The best way in? "Have your agent submit you to me. There is a difference between the smaller agency and the larger one, where commercials are concerned. The smaller the agency, the later we get the submissions, sometimes even after the job is done. You have a better chance of getting in front of me when you're with an agency that uses a messenger service and gets your headshots to me right away. If you're with a smaller agency, you'd better be helping them with your marketing."

How does an actor go about that? "I'm a proactive person from my acting days. It's a numbers game. Make the rounds. Go to Westside Casting, go to Chelsea, go to all of the commercial casting facilities where more than a handful of casting directors work. Do not walk in the door and say hi.

Just drop your stuff off and go! Do this once a week," Martin advised.

Her Opinion on Alternative Submission Methods

"Online submissions are the future. It's a good resource. I'll go look for something in The Link, but I do not look at emailed submissions. Still, I do think online databases are coming around," Martin explained.

"Oh, and I don't have time for postcards, so save your money. I know some casting directors respond to them, but I do not. If you've only got so much money, spend it on your pictures, full-sized."

Trends She Has Observed in the Casting Process

Diversity. "If you're in an ethnic minority, your time is now. You'd better be ready. You'd better be properly trained and ready for the opportunity that's here *now*. You may not be used to getting out frequently, but every breakdown is saying 'submit all ethnicities' and you'd better be ready to go! We're ready to hire you. Be ready."

Most Gratifying Part of Her Job

"I love the people. I love to help people make a lot of money. I don't let anybody screw anybody, since I come from acting. I will negotiate a deal and try and get as much money as possible for my actors. To reward someone—someone who wants nothing more than to act—with that big job, that's amazing. So much of it is timing and technical work and I'll ask actors to take an extra beat somewhere or something. It's all about getting people work, so if they just need their performance tweaked, I'm going to make a suggestion because I want to see them get the job."

ANNIE MCCARTHY, CSA

When I glanced at Annie McCarthy's IMDB.com entry, I prepared myself to meet a casting director of Old Hollywood. With over 50 credits (from mainstream films such as Can't Hardly Wait, Spy Kids, Cruel Intentions, Three Kings, Scary Movie, Training Day, *and* Scooby-Doo *to Sundance darlings* The Slaughter Rule, Pumpkin, *and* Requiem for a Dream*), McCarthy, on paper, has been around a long time. When we met, however, I was genuinely surprised.*

McCarthy, who couldn't possibly be 30 yet, popped into the room with her hair piled on top of her head and curled her flip flop-clad feet up into her lap, trying to get comfortable for an experience she rarely endures: an interview. When I took a longer look at her list of credits, I realized that all of her IMDB-listed work had taken place over the course of four years. At that moment I thought, "I just may be sitting across from a member of the next generation of casting director." You be the judge.

First Casting Job

Intern for Mali Finn. "It was a happy accident, actually. I didn't have aspirations to be in the business. I'd just been going to school and didn't even know there *was* a business, really. A friend who is an actor knew the head of casting at HBO. We all went out to dinner after a taping one night and I was like, 'What's casting?'" McCarthy joked. "She told me all about it and said she knew someone who needed an intern and I said, 'No thank you.' But a couple of weeks later, I didn't have a job and I was bored, so I interviewed with Mali's associate, Emily Schweber and then worked there for a year. While we were doing the search for the little girl for *A Time to Kill*, I moved up to assistant," McCarthy recalled.

Road to This Position

After casting *A Time to Kill*, Finn took a break, leaving McCarthy open to work for Ronnie Yeskel and Mary Vernieu, who were partners in 1994. McCarthy then partnered up with Vernieu and Felicia Fasano for a few years prior to heading out on her own in 2002.

Director Jim Stern hired her to cast *It's the Rage*, which earned McCarthy her first producing credit. "A lot of what we [as casting directors] do is producing anyway, especially when you're working with new, independent filmmakers who may not know the business as well. You really do teach them as much as you can and you do actually earn those producer credits. So, it's nice to *get* them."

Coolest Casting Gig

Requiem for a Dream. "That was really challenging," McCarthy said. "But, even though it was challenging, I thought it was the coolest. Darren [Aronofsky] was really creative and amazing. It was really educational, from that point of view. We worked on it for a year. Darren took his time. It was challenging because Darren was very particular about what he wanted," she recalled. McCarthy qualified this as her pick for "coolest gig" by saying, "I understood when I watched the movie, much more than while we were casting it, the reason he was so particular during the casting process."

What Casting Indie Films Is Like

"It's great, seeing new, up-and-coming filmmakers come through the process. They need [casting directors] to give more. Casting is harder because we don't always know where the money is coming from, but it is so wonderful to put together an ensemble cast for these projects. The process, with indie films, is more collaborative and really rewarding. There's something about getting to help a first-time director see his vision come to life and knowing you're a key element to that. There is no better feeling than that," McCarthy revealed. "Also, to cast an actor—an unknown—and then to participate in that actor's happiness is really awesome. There is nothing more rewarding in my job than those *two* elements."

Key Things She Looks for in an Actor

"Definitely, the details of what I look for are role-specific, but generally, I'm looking for good energy, being open to trying all different things, not being scared of anything," McCarthy listed. "Even if you think you're not right for it, go for it," she advised. "I find that just being natural and being true to yourself is important. Being nervous makes it tough, but I like the whole 'picturing everyone in their underwear' technique for that," McCarthy hesitated, "except for me!" she insisted.

"We're all people. Don't be scared of failing. You can't be *on* 24/7. Everyone's going to have a bad day and a bad audition every now and then, so just come in and be yourself," she continued. "I know actors who say they only feel as good as their last audition. That means, to me, you should always give your best, so that you feel your best all the time."

Pet Peeves

Props. "It usually takes away from what you're doing. They're distracting to me and to the actor," McCarthy said.

"The actors don't even realize that *they* are being distracted by the props they've brought in, but they put their energy into that *thing* instead of into their performance," McCarthy explained. "Sometimes it works, if it's natural, but most of the time it doesn't, so just don't do it. Pantomime instead."

Another peeve, "Don't throw me around," McCarthy commented. "I don't remember the movie, but there was one scene that required the actor to hit someone with a newspaper. It may be no big deal to you, but by the end of the day, I've been hit with a newspaper 40 times," McCarthy clarified. "And after seven or eight years, you've been hit by a newspaper forever," she joked. "Don't do it."

Advice for Actors

"Be yourself. Be real. Don't sit in the waiting room and get intimidated, thinking, 'I don't look like that,' 'I don't have that shirt on,' 'I didn't think to wear those glasses,' about every other actor in the room. Just don't look around. Everyone's got their own thing. Whatever you're doing differently is what makes you special. Don't be intimidated by anyone else around you. They're all doing the same thing you're doing and probably looking at you and going, 'I don't look like that.'"

Best Way To Get Seen by Her

Submissions. "I'm open to seeing pretty much anyone who is right for whatever I am working on, even if they're not represented," McCarthy said. As for postcards, McCarthy is not a huge fan. "I prefer headshots and resumés. There's more information there." McCarthy does attend theatre to scout for new talent. "I go as much as I can, or I get someone in the office to go. The hours that we keep are so crazy sometimes, but we do try to see as much as we can." McCarthy also relies on the *Academy Players Directory* as a resource for finding actors.

Her Opinion on Alternative Submission Methods

"We've started to use [Internet casting services]," McCarthy revealed. "Environmentally, it's very cool," she said. "More importantly, it saves people a lot of money on messenger services, postage, printing. Headshots are expensive. We can get the headshot online and print it out, if we need it. We'll let you know if you should bring one in, but I'm always online, so it's fine to get it that way, for me. I just feel horrible for the environment with all of the tapes and headshots we waste in this business," McCarthy commented. "When I release Breakdowns for a role, submit your headshot because the director wants a hard copy. They like that physical picture in their hands. But if I'm doing generals, I can get everything I need online," she insisted.

Trends She Has Observed in the Casting Process

This trend could be indicative of McCarthy's involvement with more mainstream projects, after having worked on so many groundbreaking indie films, but her experiences have led to less freedom. "It's frustrating that I don't have the freedom to cast a great actor when an actor who means money will be attached is also up for the role. I wish we could give more unknown actors more opportunities. If I really believe in an unknown actor I've seen, I'll work with them and give them hints, pointers, tips, whatever it takes," McCarthy insisted. "When you believe in someone, it's just what you do."

Most Gratifying Part of Her Job

"Giving actors their shot. Giving that opportunity to an unknown actor, having that moment. Usually, I have to call the agent, but then the actor will call me and say, 'Oh my God!' There is nothing better than that phone call. It's really awesome."

ROBERT MCGEE, CSA

Robert McGee and I spoke briefly at the 2000 Artios award ceremony held by the Casting Society of America. Later that night, he would win the award for casting Sofia Coppola's The Virgin Suicides *with Linda Phillips-Palo. McGee has cast* Growing Up Brady *and* The Audrey Hepburn Story, *to name just two. Our conversation was a quick one, but his responses were indicative of his passion for casting and for seeing actors work.*

First Casting Job

"I started as an intern, working for free, on and off for a year. That's how casting begins, really," McGee summarized.

Coolest Casting Gig

"There will always be a special place in my heart for *Billy's Hollywood Screen Kiss* [1999's Artios winner] because it was my first movie on my own. It was exciting to see that go on the ride that it did, with Sundance and everything," he said, of the fiercely popular independent film.

McGee was also very complimentary of director Sofia Coppola, with whom he worked on *The Virgin Suicides*. "She was terrific. She had wonderful ideas. She adapted a beautiful screenplay and was open to all of our ideas."

Key Things He Looks for in an Actor

Simply put, McGee said, "I look for actors who feel completely comfortable being themselves and who are able to bring their own qualities to the reading."

Advice for Actors

"Study. It's so important to study with good teachers. It's the most important thing you can do."

Best Way To Get Seen by Him

McGee recommends submissions. "We open all our mail. We go to submissions on every project."

His Opinion on Alternative Submission Methods

"I think it's definitely something that will take a while for people to get used to, but [the Internet] will definitely be the future method of casting."

BOB MORONES, CSA

Bob Morones is a storyteller. After 30 years in casting, he has quite a few stories to share. He cast the award-winning feature Platoon, *but has most recently received accolades for his work on the cable television series* Resurrection Blvd.

With intense attention to detail, Morones follows the work of actors he plans to hire. His level of investment in discovering the history of an actor's work pays off time and again, as he uses his knowledge of an actor's range to cast him in a non-traditional role. This risk advances the actor's career, confirms Morones' instincts, and provides quality entertainment for everyone.

First Casting Job

Night Gallery in 1973. Morones assisted Ralph Winters—who was head of TV casting at Universal Studios at the time—after graduating from UCLA's film school. "They were hiring student workers and I went over there. I'd been in the service and had let my hair grow long. I had this big beard. I looked like Fidel Castro," Morones laughed. "I never thought I'd get called back. What was going to be a summer job turned into five-and-a-half years with Universal TV."

Road to This Position

After doing series work and MOW casting, Morones was ready to do some feature casting. "I hung my shingle at a space in the Melrose Theatre and became an independent casting director," Morones said. "It was hard to get into feature casting from television, although I was well trained at Universal, because all I had was television. But little by little, I did get opportunities and I did end up returning and casting three features back at the studio."

Coolest Casting Gig

Oliver Stone's *Salvador*. "We met in 1981 when I was casting *Scarface* and he called me later in Texas—where I was working on a project—and asked me back for *Salvador*. It was a low-budget, cinéma vérité feature that he had planned to cast with non-professionals," he said. "I stretched my neck out and said, 'Hey, Oliver, I've got a novel idea. Let's use real actors!' We started casting, the budget got a little healthier, and he made me associate producer. I put James Woods in as the love interest and cast Jim Belushi in his first meaty role," Morones continued. "James Woods was nominated for an Oscar and he really deserved it. After the success of *Platoon*, *Salvador* was re-released. It had been shelved until after *Platoon* had its success."

Key Things He Looks for in an Actor

Depends on the project, the genre, the types of actors he's auditioning. "I do a lot of tracking," Morones explained. "I see three to seven movies a week. If I see an actor I like, I track them, I track their career." Morones feels this research is an essential part of his job as a casting director.

Morones has certain opinions on the "look" of a star. "I come from Old Hollywood, so I believe that a leading man should look like a leading man, walk like a leading man, talk like a leading man. A handsome rascal," described Morones. "And a character [actor] should have that swagger, that different way of going."

Most of all, Morones expects commitment. "I want to see an actor committed to developing a character that is different from the last character he or she played. When you start seeing a body of work with range to it, you know you've got someone who can do the work."

His Favorite Casting Tale

"I sent a script directly to an actor because his agent had passed," Morones began. "The actor loved the role but would need to lose 50 pounds to be right for the role. The agent called me, 'You schmuck, you went around us, we told you he wasn't available, but now he wants to do this, so what are the terms?' The actor began working with a trainer in Belize one month before we started shooting, lost 60 pounds, and played the love interest in *Beyond Desire*." The actor? William Forsythe.

Pet Peeves

"I only have one pet peeve and that's unprepared actors. Actors who come in and say they just got the material, they're not prepared, they're just going to do it on a whim, they're not ready," Morones listed. "It's like showing up for a major league ball game and just striking out. It's so obvious! The attitude, the body language, it all shows whether you're ready."

Morones recalled a time when actors were running from studio to studio, picking up sides, so they could be prepared as far in advance of an audition as possible. "Now, there's no excuse. Now, when there's Breakdowns and ShowFax and Sides Express and fax machines and email and all these ways to get the sides quickly, there's this laziness where actors are still not making the effort to get the material," Morones said. "You put all that money into your career, training, pictures, and then wing it in the audition? That's not wise. I want to see you invested in your career. I want a performance, I don't want to see you doing a cold read. Some wonderful actors cannot cold read," Morones insisted.

Advice for Actors

"You hear about the actors who come into it half-assed and make it from some chance meeting, being at the right place at the right time," he said, "but that's random. Put the odds in your favor by training." Scene study work, according to Morones, is not enough. "Get improvisational training, study the classics, study music and movement. If you're looking at acting as a career because it gives you a line that's good in social intercourse, don't train, but, just like in boxing, if you're really doing this, you train." Morones continued, "You don't go in to get your ass kicked. You have the skills and everyone can tell during the warm-up who's got the edge. It's your conditioning, your response, your improv ability that bring out the good elements. Don't just show me you can read. If you're a contender, I'll find out."

Best Way To Get Seen by Him

Showcases. Yes, even with no agent and no union affiliation, you can get in front of him. "I like those afternoon showcases. I am always surprised by the quality I find. In ten to 12 scenes, I'll see one or two people who stand out. For that alone, I get so excited." Okay, but does he cast from showcases? "Absolutely! I've cast from CBS Comedy on the Lot, TVI's screening process yields good performers, and Gloria Gifford's Rubiat Ride on Melrose. Those are some phenomenal showcases," he summarized.

What about theatre? "At Universal, I covered a lot of little theatre. I would seek out a performer and see his performances," he said. So, even before Morones tracked actors by seeing three to seven movies per week, he was tracking them in local theatre, years ago. Lately, however, he doesn't have the time to attend quite as much theatre in Los Angeles. Still, he does go, on occasion.

His Opinion on Alternative Submission Methods

"I wish I could be a man of the new millennium," Morones joked. In his opinion, Internet browsing of headshots and resumés is too slow to be worthwhile. "Maybe with DSL connections, it's getting better, but right now it's slow," he said. "It's taking 20 minutes to half an hour online to look for people. I can make one phone call and get 2000 photos."

Morones' recommendation for money well spent? "Get in the *Academy Players Directory*." This is a task that requires membership in a minimum of one union, representation by a manager or agent, and $75 a year. "It's worth it," Morones indicated.

Trends He Has Observed in the Casting Process

"Young and younger," Morones summarized. "Once, a leading man was in his mid- to late 20s. Then, offbeat casting became popular, with off-center, interesting people in major roles. Now, it's youth." As for whether or not this trend yields greater talent, Morones said, "It's healthy any time competition comes from a bigger arena."

Most Gratifying Part of His Job

"When I see that I was right. When I take a risk on an actor and he delivers."

JENNY O'HAVER, CCDA, DEBBIE SAVITT-SALNERS, & MIMI CALLARD

Jenny O'Haver is the owner of O'Haver + Company, a group of three casting directors (O'Haver, Debbie Savitt-Salners, and Mimi Callard) specializing in commercials. While all three have worked on theatrical projects, their focus as a group is commercial casting. In 2002, O'Haver + Company announced the creation of a Spanish Language Division, specializing in the casting of commercials for Spanish-speaking markets. Callard heads up this division, but all three casting directors cast bilingual projects (including spots for Gallo Wine, Pontiac, and Coca-Cola).

With a goal of doing more groundbreaking casting and session-delivery via the Internet, O'Haver + Company is on the leading edge of commercial casting. The trio finds, more and more, they are casting real people in commercials, a trend they find very satisfying.

First Casting Job

For O'Haver, that was in 1989, assisting Barbara Claman on the feature *Defending Your Life*. Savitt-Salners joined that project in 1990. "I was temping," said O'Haver. "Barbara had been looking for months for a man who [director] Albert Brooks referred to as a 'Dark Clark.' This was basically an African-American Clark Gable. I was a little intimidated, but I told Barbara, 'Uh, I know I guy.'" Brooks hired O'Haver's friend Leonard O. Turner for the role. "Turns out I saved the day. Albert was so pleased. From that point on, Barbara loved me."

Savitt-Salners had been interning with Vicki Rosenberg. "We were working on *Who's the Boss*," she recalled. Her first job with O'Haver was "*Equal Justice*, the 13-part Thomas Carter series. "This is the first time we've worked together since then," O'Haver explained. "I was looking for something flexible," Savitt-Salners clarified. Their existing trust level made working together an easy choice.

Callard's first commercial casting job was for McDonald's in 1985. "I was an agent, and I wanted to give more, so I went into casting. I began working as an assistant to Dennis Gallegos, which was wonderful. I worked with him for seven years. He taught me everything," Callard recalled.

Coolest Casting Gig

Spots for the American Cancer Society, for which O'Haver + Company found women enduring chemotherapy. "The best part was these real women were coming in," Callard interjected. "These cancer survivors were coming in and sharing the whole thing they'd experienced. It was amazing." O'Haver chimed in, "These women were so giving, so open, so beautiful. The actors auditioning to play image consultants to these real women were so moved during the casting session. So were we."

Their New Spanish Language Division

"I speak Spanish, and I had been doing some Spanish language stuff off and on. I really wanted to flex those muscles," O'Haver began. "I had a good handle on the Spanish language market, I knew the actors." O'Haver brought in Callard late in 2001. Callard's extensive experience in commercial casting with Tepper-Gallegos made her an easy choice to head up the Spanish language division of O'Haver + Company. "She just worked out so brilliantly with us. We knew she'd be great to head it up. We want to make this experience as fulfilling as possible to everyone who works with us," O'Haver insisted.

Key Things They Look for in an Actor

Savitt-Salners quickly responded, "Professionalism. Preparedness for the role."

Callard clarified, "Many times we're very busy, each of us is doing something different. I may be running a session and also running the camera, and we need actors to come in, know where the camera is, and do their job. Don't come in behind me; don't bring bags and bags in with you. You only need your keys and your picture and leave those right by the door. Otherwise, you're distracted and so are we."

Savitt-Salners continued, "Have a quick entrance and exit."

"Actors will want to stay as long as possible, and that's not helping anyone," Callard said.

"I look for actors to be professional," O'Haver insisted. "That means, being on time, being in character, knowing your lines, and having a good attitude," she listed.

Pet Peeves

Callard volunteered a big pet peeve, "There are ten people in front of you and you come in saying, 'I've got to go. Could I go in ahead of you?' Everyone has to go. Don't be rude."

Savitt-Salners dislikes the practice of dressing off base for the role. "Treat the audition like a job interview. Come in dressed well and prepared and on time," she requested.

Another consideration, according to Savitt-Salners, is the actor's headshot. "When actors don't look like their picture, it is a waste of their time. They're wondering why they're not getting booked and it's not because of talent, but because they don't look like their headshot, once they come in. We're saying, 'We wanted *this* girl in the picture. Who are you?'"

Callard added, "It's horrifying. Just look natural. The simpler the better. The client knows how to make you up. They get ideas when you're in the room."

"Fill out your size card," Savitt-Salners pleaded. "Actors will come in and fill out the size card, leaving off their numbers. We need your cell, your pager, your home number, all of it," she listed.

"We'll get headshots with no resumés attached," Callard added. "Or if there's a resumé, there will be no contact information on it. At least put your phone number on the back of your photo. In fact, print your resumé on your photo. It can't get lost that way, and it saves trees," Callard concluded.

Advice for Actors

"Treat your career like a business," O'Haver advised. "You, the actor, are the product. Your abilities need to be honed and kept fresh. Your headshots are your promotional material and should be kept up to date," she said. O'Haver further advised that actors have their most updated contact information on their resumés. "Make yourself easy to reach with a cell phone that is charged, a pager, a message center you check often," O'Haver continued.

"Try to find out as much information before the audition as you can. If you can get your hands on a script, or at least the sides, do so early. Ask questions of your agent or the casting director," Savitt-Salners said.

Callard suggested total honesty. "Especially with our Spanish projects, the clients are in the room at callbacks. If you say you speak Spanish and you only took it in high school, we've got a problem. That's of no use to us. It's gotten to the point where I'll explain the session needs in Spanish to see if the actors know what I'm saying."

Many times the problem is that the agent has submitted the actor because the actor's last name is Hispanic. "Agents will say, 'Yeah, Hernandez, she speaks Spanish,' and throw the headshot in the mix. It goes the other way too," Callard continued. "If your name is very Anglo and you're bilingual, you may be missing out on roles in Spanish. Make sure we know you're bilingual."

Specific to commercial casting is the need to consider the product you are trying to sell. "Don't come in depressed. That's not the way to sell anything," Savitt-Salners advised. "You're trying to tell everyone how wonderful this product is, or how happy you are to use this. Don't come in hung over or with no sleep," she added.

Callard agreed, "We want someone who can sell a product, and that requires that you are in top form. Be healthy-looking if you're selling something healthy."

O'Haver + Company recommends commercial classes. "It's important to know the basics for commercials. Get into a good cold read class," Callard recommended.

"We'll cast things using all improvised sessions," Savitt-Salners added. "Improv is pretty important because some commercials have no dialog.

Callard concurred, "You need to be able to respond immediately. We had a director ask an actor about herself and that actor just stammered and lost focus. The director said, 'Well... next.' That was her chance! Be ready for that," she insisted. "Be ready to play along."

Best Way To Get Seen by Them

Send your headshot and resumé. "Make it a simple, nice picture that looks like you," Callard insisted. "If you have something interesting or unique about you, put that in your cover letter.

We're looking for real people with skills," Savitt-Salners added.

The trio insisted that they see every submission. "Postcards are a great way for us to discover new faces," Callard admitted.

Along with your contact information, make sure you note your language skills on your submission. "We had a project where I was desperately looking for a Vietnamese actor who spoke Spanish," Callard recalled.

"We'll look for actors who speak Spanish even without an agent or union affiliation," Savitt-Salners added.

O'Haver + Company generally does not attend theatre or workshops unless they are casting something theatrical, and they do not accept unsolicited demo reels whatsoever. "We don't have the time to look at them," Savitt-Salners said.

Their Opinion on Alternative Submission Methods

"We're very technically advanced," Savitt-Salners said.

"Our sessions are very high tech," Callard agreed.

"I'd like to see more agents submitting online," O'Haver said. "Being able to prep from a computer gives us more freedom to work from anywhere and it's much less garbage to add to the environment. We do accept online submissions," she insisted. "I'd like to get into the habit of incorporating online submissions into our normal routine even more than we already do. Going through stacks of pictures is a hard habit to break," O'Haver admitted.

"There have always been companies trying to revolutionize the casting process," Savitt-Salners said. "It's not going to happen. Even though we love electronic submissions and we can see an actor's picture and credits on a computer screen, we like the physical element of headshots."

"They're just fast to flip through," Callard concluded.

Most Gratifying Part of Their Job

"I love people. All people. Actors are so wonderful. I love to spend that extra five minutes helping them be better in a scene and then have them get that job," Callard said.

"Providing employment for real people, knowing we're helping with that mound of bills, that's gratifying," Savitt-Salners explained.

O'Haver added, "Booking talent is my favorite part of the job. Isn't it everybody's? It's also fun to see our work on the air."

DONALD PAUL PEMRICK, CSA & DEAN FRONK, CSA

When I spent time with Donald Paul Pemrick for the
Talent Managers Association Symposium, Casting from A to
Z, I knew I wanted to meet the other half of the Pemrick Fronk
casting office.

    Pemrick spoke about sending postcards straight to the
trash bin, while commenting that his partner, Dean Fronk,
loved receiving postcards. Pemrick mentioned using technology
on a very minimal basis in his office, but I knew that he and
his partner had cast the hugely successful CD-ROM, Diablo 2.

    In an attempt to learn about their partnership, I visited
Pemrick and Fronk in their penthouse office in Sherman Oaks,
where their reputation for being actor-friendly shines through.

First Casting Job Together

    Fronk's first job with Pemrick was as casting assistant
for *Cyber Bandits*. "I came from Breakdowns. I covered all the
casting directors in the valley, which was Don's territory. He
really let me sit in and learn a lot about what he was doing.
He loves to talk."

Fronk continued, "He was doing *Cyber Bandits*, one of four films for IRS Media, and Donald offered me the job of assistant—or office PA, really—in his office."

"His rise to partner was fairly quick. I knew he was capable of doing it. Everything I threw onto him, he picked up on it. He could communicate really well and wasn't intimidated to stick up for who he thought was right for a role. He was running sessions within four months," Pemrick said of Fronk.

"When I came on with him, IRS was in the process of expanding. Don was so busy doing six MOWs for Showtime, four sci-fis for Columbia TriStar, and the Miramax film *Children of the Corn*. He had to have somebody else running the sessions. In seven months, we were doing *Crosscut*," Fronk recalled of his first casting director credit.

"I had a similar situation in becoming a casting director. I was working with Marc Schwartz in the 1980s and he had me go help with a pilot at Universal. We had been doing co-casting on *Three's Company* and Marc's request that I go do a pilot led to my staff position at Universal," Pemrick explained.

Coolest Casting Gig

"*One False Move*," Pemrick volunteered without hesitation. [Producer] Jesse Beaton and [director] Carl Franklin allowed me to be as creative in casting as they were in what they did," he explained.

"That was one of my favorite movies in college," Fronk chimed in. "It's one of the best independent films you can see."

Pemrick continued his list, "Family films are also fun to cast. Kids are so unpredictable. We just did five family movies last year and that's just a different kind of casting. Kids are fun."

"My favorite [casting gig] was *House of 1000 Corpses*. It's the Rob Zombie film we cast. [Zombie] let us find the most creative people we could, focusing on the look and acting ability, not what they'd done," Fronk explained. "It'll be a cult classic, with this eclectic cast."

Another favorite for Fronk was 2000's number-one selling entertainment CD-ROM, *Diablo 2*. "Even though it was voices we were casting, we wanted actors to bring the characters to life," he recalled. "I'm a video game nut, so, for me, it was a great experience."

Key Things They Look for in an Actor

"I personally want you off book. This is so my director can work with you. Ninety percent of the time, we don't prescreen. I want you at performance level because when you read for me, the director is there," Pemrick began.

"A sense of professionalism," said Fronk. "Actors need to know how to conduct themselves from the moment they get off the elevator. That time in the lobby and during their read, they should be 100% professional."

"Keep a sense of humor," Pemrick added. "If you don't like what you're doing, leave. Do something else. Don't bring a negative attitude in here."

"If you're nervous," Fronk continued, "everybody senses it. There's a level of poise that comes with confidence in your ability. If you're nervous, it affects your read." As for what an actor should do with that nervous energy, Fronk advised, "Use that flow of energy to hit your mark, but not so that we pick up on the fact that it's your nerves driving you."

Pemrick interjected, "Being in the room longer does not mean you are more likely to get the job. Don't assume if someone ahead of you is in here with us for a few more minutes than you are that you need to ask questions to get to stay longer. The length of time you're in the room really has nothing to do with how well you've done."

Pet Peeves

"Bring your photo. Always," Fronk requested. "Even if your agent has sent one, bring another. A client may take the one your agent sent, and if, after everyone is gone, we're looking through the headshots and yours isn't there, we're not going to spend a lot of time tracking another one down. It's Marketing 101. Have photos with you."

Fronk continued, "Treat the audition like a job. You wouldn't show up late to your job or unprepared to do your job. Be professional."

"At every opportunity, you should be 100% together." Pemrick detailed, "We book our appointments three or four days in advance. Get those sides and know the tone of the film. We try to make the entire script available to our actors, so that the actors have the most information possible by the time they audition. With television, it is your duty to watch the show you'll be reading for. Know whether it's two-camera, three-camera, live audience, filmed. This is all part of your job," he listed. "You should watch two episodes of every show. I do. It's good to know what kind of show it is, the tone of it. Research us."

Pemrick quickly added, "Always have pictures with you. Never come in saying, 'I thought my agent would send you one.'"

Advice for Actors

Pemrick began, "Do everything in your power to get as much theatre and student film as possible before getting in SAG. Then put all of your efforts and energy into getting SAG vouchers. SAG-eligible means I can hire you, but you'd better be able to pay your money to SAG before the shoot begins. Be up front. Be honest."

Fronk advised actors to have a good attitude. "Confidence comes from the versatility of your training. Make choices, follow your intuition, and make sure that your intuition is founded in training," he summarized.

Fronk continued, "Build a strong network of support around you. This should be friends, directors, writers, other actors—whoever—so that you can bounce things off of one another. It's a creative industry, but the business end is about generating dollars. It's not all by-the-book, so you'd better have a great support system and sense of humor or you'll go crazy here."

"Diversify," Pemrick added. "Doing that has kept me sane." Pemrick has written two television pilots, three films, and worked as director of a theatre company. "I've worn these other hats and that gives me a sense of perspective on the business. There's no normal promotional ladder in this business. Remember that work begets work. We have cast musicals, consulted on student films, all sorts of things. You never know!" he insisted. "If you like the material, never say no. You never know what little gem you may be working on."

Their Opinion on Alternative Submission Methods

According to Pemrick, "Any self-promotion is self-promotion." However, he suggested that, if your credits on IMDB are accurate, that may be enough, in terms of online accessibility. "Through that, we can find your representation, and that's enough. I still write lists on yellow legal pads by hand. I don't like computers. I don't like email. I think it's a way of separating people."

Fronk chimed in, advising that actors should, "Learn it now. It's gaining strength [as a method of casting]. Be ready."

Best Way To Get Seen by Them

"Let us see your tape," Pemrick instructed. Demo reels, according to Pemrick Fronk Casting, should only have an actor montage at the *end* of the tape, if at all. "We'll put our feet up and watch a bunch of them at a time. Send a self-addressed, stamped envelope to get the tape back. We don't want to throw them out. Don't send a scene from acting class, or a performance at your sister's bat mitzvah. Include three to four scenes and tell me what show I'm about to see. Also, include some credits, especially the directors' names," Pemrick suggested. "If you've worked with someone I know, I'd like to ask them about your work."

"It's a very small town," Fronk added. "We know those indie directors. And, if you want, send over a work-in-progress and let us tell your manager or agent how to help you make it a better reel."

Fronk further indicated that persistence is the best way to be seen. "If you're in a play," he explained, "*hound* us. We get five or six offers a day to see shows. If you're persistent enough about your show, we will give you a chance."

What about unsolicited mailings or drop-offs? "Be vague. Put the film name on the envelope, but not the role. The film we're casting is public information, but we'll know you're getting pirated Breakdowns if you also know the roles. In our office, we open the envelopes in the order received. All headshots are looked at," insisted Pemrick. "Personalize your submission a little bit, though. We read it all. Let me know that you've seen on cable something we cast and tell me what you thought of it. There's never a time we're not casting *something*, so just go ahead and send [your headshot and resumé]."

As for casting director workshops, Pemrick was very opinionated. "I absolutely go [to casting director workshops]. I have no qualms about it. I hire a lot from workshops. And from generals. We have an open door policy. Bring by your headshot and resumé. If we're here, we'll say hello," he reemphasized.

Trends They Have Observed in the Casting Process

"Reality TV is a trend," insisted Pemrick. "It's just like *Dynasty* and *Dallas* and how no actor could get away with not having a glamorous headshot. Reality television really hasn't impacted casting for us."

"A trend in casting sessions, I've noticed, is that there is much more filming of sessions," Fronk added. "Actors need to learn how to do on-camera auditions. We're sending tapes to producers now, rather than having actors in repeatedly for sessions. So, don't assume that, just because you're doing a read in front of a camera, no producer will see it. Don't get bummed out that the director isn't in the room. In fact, *more* people will see your audition when it's taped."

Pemrick agreed, "Prereads don't really exist anymore, for us. Be ready by knowing what colors to wear on camera. Have the mindset that you're going to be on camera, even if you haven't been told that, coming in for the audition."

Their Opinion on Diversity in Casting

Pemrick began, "Writers, please eliminate physical descriptions to parts. Set decorators can make changes. Cinematographers can change lenses. We're locked into a character type. A script is not a finished product. Lift those limitations and let us put the cast together. I can't wait until I see in the stage directions, 'Good actor enters room.' Until that's in the script, diversity will be an issue."

What has Pemrick/Fronk Casting done to move this issue forward? "Once, I did breakdowns with just character occupations. For the role of the janitor, I only got submissions of African-Americans. For the truck driver, I got white males, heavy, 35-50. It disturbed me that those limitations exist in the mindset of the actors' representation," Pemrick lamented.

Their Greatest Casting Challenge

Pemrick recalled, "Casting *Annie*. One mother brought her son to audition for the role of Annie and I told her that Annie was a little girl. She said, 'He can be a girl!' It was awful.

What They Would Change About the Casting Process

Fronk would make the process more informative for the actor. "I'd like the whole environment to be more actor-friendly," he said. "We try to meet you in the lobby and tell you what's been going on in the room over the course of the day.

We want you to have as much information as possible. If we're up front, it puts you at ease and gives you more information so that you can do a better job. And the better you do, the better we look," Fronk concluded.

"I still want to keep people meeting people. It's essential that the director and actor meet one another, face-to-face. We bring you in because we want to hire you. Casting a role in one day is our goal," Pemrick said.

Most Gratifying Part of Their Job

"When an actor nails an audition," Fronk said. "It gives me chills. We look at each other and say, '*that* was it!' when the actor walks out the door. There's nothing as cool as when someone really gets it."

"That's a rush," Pemrick added. "I love it when we have brought in eight actresses for a role and they were dynamite and did their homework and the director can't decide between three of them. I know we did a good job then."

LINDA PHILLIPS-PALO, CSA

When I interviewed Linda Phillips-Palo, she had just wrapped the pilot presentation of And Justice for Y'all. *Along with her husband [director Paul Palo] and Marty Breneman, Phillips-Palo produced this project. "It's basically Bubba's Arbitration Court," she explained. "Our two leads, Bubba and Babe the bailiff, are two actors I cast in* The Rainmaker. *The law is not accessible to the common person, so Bubba hears disputes, and whatever Bubba says goes. It really deals with the last vestiges of southern culture. If a blues singer stops by during a court hearing, he'll do a song for us. Bubba quotes the bible and we serve a buffet dinner, so that encourages people to come on by. We dispense ribs and justice," she summarized."*

The pilot was shot in Memphis, an "adopted hometown" for Phillips-Palo. "When I did The Rainmaker *[in Memphis], I stayed at the Peabody Hotel and I met everybody. I'd go into the film commission office and the blues clubs and just around town, asking who's the most colorful attorney in town?"*

Clearly, Artios Award-winner [in 2000 for The Virgin Suicides*] Phillips-Palo does not shy away from offbeat projects. In fact, she seeks them out.*

First Casting Job

"I was acting in Buffalo, and I was also teaching an acting class at the University of Buffalo, where I was getting my graduate degree. When I would see movies, I was attracted to any casting director who really used faces. I would always kind of make a note of that, but not being in Los Angeles, I didn't even know that job would ever exist for me. By the time I'd reached my early-30s, I realized that I'd been really responsible, but I hadn't done anything full-tilt-boogie yet in my life. I told my husband that I needed to go to California to work in movies and he was less than thrilled," Phillips-Palo recalled.

Phillips-Palo started out in San Francisco, registering at a temp agency called Star Personnel. "Los Angeles was just too huge for me to start out, but I figured, Star... Hollywood... close enough," Phillips-Palo joked. "I was over-educated and under-office-skilled, so, I figured that was it. One day I got a call from that temp agency saying, 'Please. Are you available today? Francis Coppola's office just called and they're looking for a secretary with a Master's degree.' I found out later that they had used Star Personnel for the same reason I had: Star... Hollywood... that's it. I started out coordinating apprentices and helping Gio Coppola get ready for his GED."

After the bulk of the studio moved to Los Angeles, Phillips-Palo received another fateful call. "Jennifer Shull called up to San Francisco and asked, 'Have you ever done an open call?' I said, 'Sure!' The minute I hung up the phone, I was like, 'What the hell is an open call?' What I learned was, if you put up a good front with a good smile and look like you know what you're doing, and then seriously turn around and learn what you need to learn, you'll be okay. You can't do one without the other, though. You have to be willing to learn the work," Phillips-Palo insisted.

"I ended up moving down here and Jennifer started me at a reception job first, which was part of the deal. We had to work our way up to casting, and that was how we made our relationships with agents, how we developed respect by saving one another's butts. I came in and said, 'I'm going to be the best receptionist of my ability.' And that's what I did. Then I started getting my promotions and I was in casting," Phillips-Palo recalled.

Recent Non-Traditional Casting

Shetan, the Young Black Stallion, for Buena Vista. "We had a website and went around the country to try and find a girl who was middle-eastern, who spoke Arabic, who rode a horse like the wind, and who was beautiful enough to be blown up on an IMAX screen. We went to pony clubs and equestrian centers worldwide," Phillips-Palo recalled. How did they find their lead? "This ten-year-old kid was surfing the Internet in Texas and found our site. He knew his friend would be right for the role. Bianna Tamimi sent in a tape and she was perfect," she said.

Another cool gig was one that Phillips-Palo co-produced: *Hostile*. "It's a feature about an Austrian town that bred Lipizzaner horses during WWII. As the Allies closed in, Adolf Hitler ordered them slaughtered. The German officer refused to do so and he turned himself over to the Americans and the officer he surrendered to was Dale Robertson, who later became a star in Hollywood in the 1950s," she explained. "The things I look for are not the most common things," Phillips-Palo added. "Some are mainstream, but I do look for projects outside."

Key Things She Looks for in an Actor

"I love focus, discipline, and actors who are just in love with what they're doing. These people have this joy for what they're doing. They come in and do their thing and the director and producer look at me and say, 'Thank you.' It is such a joy. It makes me so proud," she expressed. Of course, Phillips-Palo understands that actors have good days and bad days.

"If you've hit a bad patch, I recommend that you pull back until you can get yourself nurtured. The worst thing that can happen is for you to come in, after I've talked you up as a fun person, filled with joy, and you're so down. It's hard to explain away a scattered performance. I have to make sure that the actor has everything together before I bring them in again," she explained.

But performance isn't the only thing Phillips-Palo looks for. "As a casting director, I'm listening for any disruption. Actors have to be nice to my assistants. We have monitors out there for that, and if an actor comes in picking on someone, we'll make a note of that. We have to be aware of that because it'll happen on the set. We look at coping skills before casting someone. You don't have to be perfect, but have common sense," she advised.

Advice for Actors

"One thing I always recommend is a good haircut. A good haircut makes you feel like you're taking care of business. It also says something about your self-esteem. Being an actor is so much about self-esteem and so much of the time your self-esteem is getting battered. You have to be able to have internal tools to secure yourself. Now, actors are meant to be kooky, so I'm not trying to dictate their life. I just feel that certain things like drugs and alcohol deflect focus. They put a layer between you and what you want to get accomplished. They also dull ambition. Actors need balance," she clarified.

To that end, Phillips-Palo teaches a seven-week course at AIA called "Mastering the Actor Within," based on the Julia Cameron book *The Artist's Way*. "It is so emotional and involves so much work on the part of the actor. They have 98 pages of homework before they even get to the first class. I'm basically teaching an expanded version of the master's-level class I taught at the university," she explained. "If you're going to be an actor, be happy having chosen that."

Best Way To Get Seen by Her

"Let me count the ways! I watch a lot of television. I make a lot of notes on junior characters, people who deliver one-liners. If there is one scene that sticks out from the rest, after you've forgotten the rest of the movie, and that scene is yours, you've been noticed by me, for sure. That's the reason that Matt Damon was so prominent in *The Rainmaker*. I had seen his work in *Courage Under Fire*, and that was a film where he worked on basic character, putting everything into that part. A lot of producers, directors, and casting directors really took notice of that fully-developed role. It was easy to take a scene from *Courage Under Fire* and show Francis that Matt could really do *The Rainmaker*," Phillips-Palo related.

"Another really good way to get seen by me is to have excellent training credits, an interesting face, and write me a letter—not 'Dear Casting Director' or 'To Whom it may Concern'—but mention that you've seen films I've cast and noticed that I always use people of your type. Tell me where I can see your work. Offer to send your tape. I'll ask to see it if I'm interested. I discourage phone calls. Don't take the risk that you'll get on that bad list of actors who call a busy casting director," Phillips-Palo insisted. "Now, don't get discouraged if you don't hear from me right away, after you've sent a letter. It could be two years or more before I call you. So, if your phone number keeps changing, you'd better keep me updated, or else you've missed your chance."

"Be listed at SAG and in the *Academy Players Directory*. It's one of the biggest bargains in town. We use the *Academy Players Directory* all the time. All casting directors do. Actors can't use the excuse of not having an agent, because you can get yourself into the *Academy Players Directory*. You can do many things that don't cost an arm and a leg to improve your chances of getting seen by me," she insisted. "Postcards are good. Remind me where we met or tell me when I can catch you on a show. I attend theatre and a lot of showcases when schools are graduating. Choose wisely when deciding where you want to showcase your talent. Go see the showcase. Audit it. What is the cost? What is the caliber of the actors? Do they get a lot of casting directors to come out? It's better to not be seen than to be seen in a bad play where the casting director has wasted her time, has traveled, is there after a long day at work. We want to be entertained."

Phillips-Palo's take on cold reading workshops? "Use your best judgment when choosing where to spend your money. Some actor workshops provide valuable information and are worth the money. If I, as an actor, sat there and wondered, 'Where is my money going? I'm not getting anything out of this,' I would never go back and I would tell everyone I knew not to go there," she insisted.

Most Gratifying Part of Her Job

"I like getting up in the morning. Everything is gratifying about my job. I like to see actors when they start. Later, when they have these careers, and you can see the people who helped along the way, it's wonderful. I'm just happy at any given time. I'm so happy to see actors walk into my office."

ROBI REED-HUMES

Robi Reed-Humes has cast such films as The Best Man, Soul Food, Love Jones, *most of Spike Lee's movies, and the critically acclaimed* Don King: Only in America. *When I say Reed-Humes began casting as a child, I don't mean that she got her first film credit at that time. Instead, she discovered that she was born to be a casting director: she has an instinct for seeing the right actor in each role.*

Road to This Position

Reed-Humes knew that what she loved doing was called "casting" at the age of 15. "I thought I was gifted with an eye for talent. When I was much younger, when I read books, I would imagine certain actors in the roles. When I found out there was a title for the position, I knew I wanted to do that," she recalled.

Reed-Humes knew two people who made important introductions for her: Production coordinator Patt McCurdy and producer Peter Long. "They got me together with Reuben Cannon as an intern and then with Ellen Chenoweth, whom I assisted on *Sweet Dreams*, after college in 1984." After assisting Chenoweth, Reed-Humes spent two years working with Michael McLean and Diane Dimeo. It was there that she met Spike Lee. "He came out for the Los Angeles Film Festival with *She's Got to Have It*," Reed-Humes remembered. "On the same day we met, I introduced him to Ruth Carter who has done all of his costume design, and Otis Sallid who has choreographed his movies. It was a fateful night." Reed-Humes was an assistant at that time, then cast a project for PBS Wonderworks before joining Michelle Farberman as an associate at Kushner Locke. "We did a half-hour show for HBO called *1st & 10*," Reed-Humes explained. "Then," she continued, "Spike called me and asked me to cast *School Daze*."

Coolest Casting Gig

"I really had a great time on *Gridlock'd*, one of Tupac [Shakur]'s last films," Reed-Humes recalled, noting that she got to be as creative as she could be. She also remembers *Malcolm X* fondly, along with *Do the Right Thing*. In fact, Reed-Humes is still approached to speak on panels about that one. Most recently, she spoke at a Q&A session held by Los Angeles Film Critics.

Additionally, "The Academy of Motion Picture Arts and Sciences does this film school for high school kids and they showed *Do the Right Thing* to these kids who'd never seen it before. I went and spoke to these kids who were too young to have seen the film. They were in awe. They wrote papers on it," Reed-Humes explained.

Key Things She Looks for in an Actor

Preparation. "Preparation is so important. It's almost inexcusable not to be prepared these days. The material is available through so many outlets now," Reed-Humes insisted.

"I look for experience... sometimes," Reed-Humes added. Sometimes experience isn't as important as a good rap, which was the case for *Carmen Brown: A Hip-Hopera*, a film she cast for MTV.

Her Favorite Casting Tale

Reed-Humes brought Lucy Liu in for the Thandie Newton role in *Gridlock'd*, and cast her in a role with no lines. "We found a way to give her two lines on the set and that was a breakthrough job for her. That was very cool," Reed-Humes recalled.

Pet Peeves

Violating the parameters. "I don't think actors need to call me. I mean, you can call me and tell me you're back in town if you've been in New York for three months, but make the message or conversation short and sweet. Eight messages are not necessary," Reed-Humes said.

Unpreparedness. "When an actor is in an audition, especially at a callback, to say, 'I just got the material,' is not professional. Even if that's the case, make it work," she commented. Also, if you're going to ask to do the read again, do so before getting too far into the material. "People will knock on the door, come back in the room, and ask to do it again," Reed-Humes revealed. "Yes! People do this!"

Advice for Actors

"Update your photo and resumé as often as you can. It's your calling card. Have it be the best that you can be," she advised. "Also, look like your photo when you come in to meet me. That is really important," she said.

Be ready for anything. "Always keep your skills as sharp as they can be. Take workshops, and if you can't afford [high-end ones], go to LACC or Santa Monica City College or something like that," Reed-Humes suggested. "Be honed in your skills."

Best Way To Get Seen by Her

Depends on the project. "My associates cover theatre," she explained. "Showcases are good." As for submissions, Reed-Humes explained, "I give many people opportunities. It's not always the person with the A-list agent that gets into my office. Sometimes I'm going through pictures and there's just something about [an actor] that grabs my attention, so I'll bring them in. What is five minutes out of my day when it could change someone's life?" Reed-Humes asked. "I've been blessed to be in this position. It's my job to give that time," she insisted.

Her Opinion on Alternate Submission Methods

"Online submissions are the wave of the future. I've made myself aware of what's out there by staying in the office late to learn the computer," Reed-Humes revealed. Her awareness of the possibilities the Internet provides has led her to consider launching her own website. "It will be helpful for pilot season. It's an online database of diverse talent accessible to talent buyers throughout the world. This database, along with online submission methods, will never take the place of what we do," Reed-Humes explained. "It's a tool so that, as casting directors, we can cast our net as wide as possible and get the best talent, wherever they may be."

Her Operating System

"I write everything down. I learned a long time ago that you can't rely on your brain. You'll forget! I have files, my Rolodex, lots of folders. I keep an 'Actor to Remember' file so I can keep people who I can't use now, but maybe can later," Reed-Humes detailed. "I hold generals when there's time."

Trends She Has Observed in the Casting Process

"No trends, just talent."

What She Would Change About the Casting Process

In network television, she'd do screen tests for pilots. "You come in with sides in hand, or maybe memorized, with a room full of people who can change your life. You may or may not be having a good day. I worked with [writer-producer-director] Ed Weinberger on a couple of projects and we did screen tests for a day, edited it down, and took those in to network. That's a much more positive experience. I've been in the room where [actors have] been great five times, then this time, they blow it. That's nerve-wracking," Reed-Humes explained. "It's an expensive option, but it's worth it in the long run. You see actors at their best."

Highlight of Her Week

"Going home to my kids. That's fun."

Most Gratifying Part of Her Job

"This is why I've done it for so long: getting to be instrumental in helping someone achieve their goal, their dream. That is what it is for me. And I owe it all to God."

MARNIE SAITTA

Marnie Saitta is the casting director for CBS's The Young
and the Restless, *now in its 30ʰ year of production.*

*Saitta knows that an important part of her job is the
ability to assess the actor's needs, in terms of the amount of
direction or interaction they require in order to provide a strong
read. Saitta explained, "I am only as good as the actors I cast.
I wish that more actors would know that. Casting directors
are at the mercy of the actors we bring in. Actors are my body
of work: a representation of me. When an actor comes in and
feels nervous, I want to say, 'Hey, you're doing me a favor,
coming in here and making good choices. You're inspiring me.'"*

First Casting Job

This one. Saitta began working with *The Young and
the Restless* as an intern during her last year of college. "I had
studied acting in college. Actually, I studied acting most of my
life," Saitta said. "Casting was a way that I could still work
with actors without acting. I love acting, but I don't like people
looking at me," she revealed.

I loved the show and when my internship was ending,
they asked me if I'd be interested in working for the show. Of
course I said yes. I knew I wanted to be the casting director for
Y&R even though I wasn't interning in the casting department.

Saitta worked as an intern while Jill Newton was at CBS. "She was everything I could ever want to be as a casting director. She was inspirational and only influenced my decision to go into casting even more," Saitta recalled. She also worked with Meryl O'Loughlin. "I worked in her department and she brought me up through the ranks and showed me the ropes."

Key Things She Looks for in a Soap Opera Actor

"Acting is acting. A soap is no different than any other medium. I look for an actor who breathes truth into the material. All acting is in pursuit of the truth. That is magic to me. That's what I'm looking for: not a specific look or a specific type of person. I let the actor dictate that to me," Saitta explained. She finds that the actors she least expects, in terms of looks, will provide the most dynamic choices. "They'll bring [the role] to life in a way I wouldn't have thought of without having seen their performance," she said.

"If anything, daytime acting is more challenging in that the stories don't have a beginning, a middle, and an end. You're creating the day-to-day reality and so many times you have to generate your own back-story. You may not know where the character comes from or where the character is going. You are making choices based on the scripts that are coming in every day. It parallels life so much sometimes. Extremes of any emotion are sometimes the easiest part of acting, and you're not always doing that in soaps," Saitta continued. "You'll sometimes have to regurgitate information for viewers who may have missed a show and you have to find a way to do that very naturally. Your rehearsal time is virtually none and there is no luxury of multiple takes." Saitta underscored the importance of the amount of material covered in soap operas. *The Young and the Restless* is on hiatus only three weeks per year (one week in May and two in December).

How She Casts Contract Players

"We issue Breakdowns using the writers' description. That description is usually pretty broad. We receive anywhere from 2000 to 4000 photos per role. I sort through them, and if I have three weeks to cast, I'll see 400 or 500 people. If I only have a week and a half to cast, I'll still try to see 300. I'll bring eight of those people to producers and then three of them will screen test. Depending on the what the producers want to see, sometimes all eight will screen test, sometimes none do, if the producers make a decision right there in the room," Saitta detailed.

It is important for Saitta to bring in actors who can handle the rigors of the soap opera shooting schedule. "Our contract players are on set two to three times a week on average, but sometimes every day. I try to make actors as comfortable as possible. I admire what they're doing, and when they're comfortable, we get better work from the actors. In the end, that's what we all want. We're all reaching for the same goal."

Pet Peeves

While she mentioned the usual peeves such as actor unpreparedness, tardiness, and unprofessionalism, Saitta indicated a peeve of much larger scope: bias against soap opera acting. "It's an uneducated opinion from people who have no idea of the caliber of talent that works behind and in front of the camera at every aspect of the show; how utterly challenging it is. It makes me upset. I don't think daytime gets the respect that it deserves. An agent will call me and say, 'I have an actor who is so green and hasn't done much but she has a great look, she'll be great for daytime.' This is not a place where someone can do seven or eight takes for one scene. Daytime has been seen as a stepping-stone for so long, but that is changing. I can tell from the level of people who are submitting, from those who are open to doing daytime, the opinion is changing.

People are realizing that this is a very respectable, challenging medium."

Best Way To Get Seen by Her

If you don't have an agent, get in a big play. "Do as much local theatre as you can. Send a postcard and tell me you're in something, even if I haven't met you. I do tend to see a play with a larger cast," Saitta clarified, noting that she hopes to see many actors at once, when attending plays. So, while a one-person show is a fantastic showcase of your work, it is not what will draw Saitta to the theatre.

Saitta mentioned that she also accepts unsolicited submissions. "Any time I have downtime, I do try to hold generals, but if I kept all of the submissions I receive, my files would fill four rooms," she explained, noting that her cupboards are filled with the headshots of those actors she has seen and knows she wants to hire. "I do look at every piece of mail, though. If you submit a headshot as a general submission, I will see it, but I don't know that that is the best way to get seen by me," Saitta insisted. However, Saitta requested that actors not send demo tapes.

Her Opinion on Alternative Submission Methods

Simply put, Internet casting has not become a factor at *The Young and the Restless*. "We're not linked like that here," she admitted.

Her Biggest Casting Challenge

Recasts. "Especially when the role was originated by the person you're recasting, it's tough. We need to stay true to the essence of the character that was created, and in a lot of cases, that means staying true to the first actor who played that role. It's very limiting. Viewers are loyal to the actor who originated the role," Saitta clarified. "I try to make the transition easy on the actor taking over the role and on the viewer. We try to stay within the vision of the role, but those are usually incredibly big shoes to fill."

What She Would Change About the Casting Process

"There's not that much that I would change about it, really," Saitta happily revealed. "We don't put actors through unnecessary hardship here. We keep the number of times the actor comes in for a role down to a maximum of three; me, the producer, and the screen test," she listed. "I like how it goes down here. I have to be aware that I am always casting to the executive producer's and head writer's tastes, not necessarily my taste. I've been very fortunate, in that, most of the time, that will mesh. What we all agree on, at *Y&R*, is that we never sacrifice ability for looks. That makes me proud."

Most Gratifying Part of Her Job

"Knowing I've put the right actor in their perfect job." Saitta hesitated, then added, "I love getting to work with actors every day. I like being a part of their process. It's great to feel that I'm positively influencing that artistic endeavor, assisting in the artist's journey. I admire actors. I enjoy meeting them and watching them create magic."

BRIEN SCOTT

Brien Scott is a former child actor-turned-casting director. Scott, whose casting credits include Night Visitors, Full Moon in August, *and* Holding onto Holden, *brings a sense of "been there, done that" to his sessions, having a pretty good idea of how the actor facing him feels.*

What Made You Decide to Become a Casting Director?

Scott began, "I started acting at age 11 in New York. I did commercials, episodic television, and films. I went to the Professional Children's School in New York and went to college for film. *Highway to Heaven* was a major influence on me. It really changed my direction, getting to work with Michael Landon and being shown so much of what was going on, besides the acting," he said, of the man who taught him to look beyond the on-camera business.

Pet Peeves

Actors who forget that casting directors are people, just like they are. "We all have good and bad days."

Another peeve, for Scott, "Actors who change something from their audition when they come in for the callback. If it worked the first time, don't change it. Come in wearing the same clothes and do the same thing you did at the first audition."

Advice for Actors

For this, Scott had very simple advice. "Be yourself. There is only one you!"

KEVIN SCOTT, CSA

*"There was no time to be nervous. I just had to act,"
said Kevin Scott about his October 2001 acceptance speech at
the Casting Society of America's Artios Awards. For the second
year in a row, he and John Levey, along with then-Executive
Barbara Miller shared in the Outstanding Achievement in
Dramatic Casting [Episodic 2001, Pilot 2000] for* The West
Wing.

 *Scott had gone outside with a colleague during the
dinner break and was alerted by someone else that he'd just
won an award. "I don't know where my glass of wine went, but
suddenly I was running in. I kicked a woman in the process—
and I still haven't heard who that was—I ran up on stage with
my hands waving in the air, yelling, 'I'm here!'" Scott recalled.*

 Scott is most definitely here. *After two seasons casting*
The West Wing *with Levey, and working together on* ER *prior
to that, Scott has an eye for assembling an ensemble. As a
2001 Emmy winner [for Outstanding Casting for a Drama
Series, along with Levey and Miller], he'll continue to have
plenty of opportunities to perfect his acceptance speech, from
the look of his track record.*

First Casting Job

A music video for rap artist Too Short. "I went to school in the Bay Area and worked on 'Short but Funky' with Tony Lee. He and Robi Reed-Humes sort of ushered me into casting after I finished school." After that first partnership, Scott continued working on projects with Reed-Humes and Lee, including Michael Jackson's "Remember the Time" music video.

Road to This Position

Several years after moving to Los Angeles, Scott went on to assist Chemin Bernard at Warner Bros. Television on the pilot *Tall Hopes*. "I worked at the old Warner Bros. spot with John Levey, Andrea Cohen, Marcia Ross, and Marion Dougherty. Lorimar took over the old Warner Bros. and absorbed Levey. He and I got along well so about a month later, I came with him to the new Warner Bros. I assisted him for three years before Barbara Miller made me a casting director," Scott chronicled.

Coolest Casting Gig

The West Wing. "It had to do primarily with the writing," Scott said. "How often does one get to work with someone who creates such incredible material? I couldn't wait to get the script sometimes."

Key Things He Looks for in an Actor

"A comfort level with themselves," Scott said. "They need to feel comfortable in their own skin."

Scott further explained, "There's a certain depth to people that comes across in their pictures. I look at the picture and resumé thinking, 'Do I want to get to know this person better?'"

Pet Peeves

Self-doubt. "Actors set themselves up for failure," he said. "They'll come in the room and talk about how they just got the material, in essence making an excuse for the job they're about to do." Scott attributes this behavior to a lacking sense of self and a desire to indicate that they can do better. "There are all of these excuses. I'm sure we all do it somehow. I'm a tennis player, and I've had it said to me, 'I haven't hit in weeks.' This is an old tactic used by some to, in effect, lessen the trauma of their potential failure," Scott revealed.

Advice for Actors

Quite simply, for Scott, the advice is, "Get the material ahead of time. Study it. Make a choice. Come in here and do it."
And always, "Practice your craft, whether it be in class, theatre, or something as simple as a staged reading of a work-in-progress. The point is: practice your craft," he insisted.

His Opinion on Alternative Submission Methods

"Internet casting is a great idea, in that it cuts down on paperwork, but it's hard, for me at this point, to make the transition. Some of us are trying. For now, though, it's safer the old way. We don't know if everyone is linked yet and we don't want to miss anything. Soon, I think all the agents and casting directors will be linked up to [online casting services] and we'll see a change," Scott concluded. "I could see it getting to the point where I will see your picture, click on it, and see a demo reel without having to wait for it to arrive in my office. It's gonna be the way to go. I can't wait to have it all at the click of a mouse."

What about theatre? "Here in Los Angeles, I don't go that often. I'd like to go see more. I used to do workshops," Scott revealed. "It's a touchy situation for lots of casting directors," he said. "My first year as a casting director was my last year doing workshops. The majority of workshops I did when I was an assistant."

What were they like? "People would constantly ask how to get on *ER* and I would specifically say to them, 'I'm not here for *ER*. I'm here because I won't always be an assistant. You should be here because you believe in me as a potential casting director and that when I become a casting director, I might remember you.' Sure enough, there are people I've brought in since I've become a casting director. I think actors should take these workshops to learn something, not to get a job, as many casting directors are very good teachers," Scott summarized.

Best Way To Get Seen by Him

Through your agent. "We have relationships with agents. We know certain agents' tastes which, over time, we learn to respect and trust," Scott explained.

What about unsolicited headshots? "I open everything," he continued. "I like postcards—if I've met you—and you're catching me up on something. Send me a postcard if you've changed agents since I last saw you, you're doing a new play, you've booked a job on another show or film. It's nice to be kept abreast of the progression of an actor's career."

His Biggest Casting Challenge

"The last episode I did of *The West Wing*. We were looking for [President Bartlett] at about 17 and Mrs. Landingham at about 22. That was not easy. It wasn't just about a look, but a quality that each actor has," Scott revealed. "I wanted to hire actors that would make you say, 'Wow! That is Kathryn Joosten at 22. That is Martin Sheen as a teenager.'"

Best Casting Discovery

"Dulé Hill. Hands down. I'm proud that he was put on the map through his part on *The West Wing*."

And a rediscovery, of sorts: Rob Lowe. "His agent wanted him to come and audition. I don't think all of us were on the same page when we were working on that role. We finally agreed, 'Let's give it a shot.' His was one of the most amazing readings I've ever been witness to," Scott explained. "In my mind, there was nobody else who was right for it. He had *it*. There was no comparison."

It is...? "Most of the times we don't know. *It* comes into the room and we go, 'That's it!'"

Highlight of His Week

"Seeing the final product," Scott summarized. "Seeing how an episode finally turned out and knowing I had some part in that."

Most Gratifying Part of His Job

"Meeting new people. I studied Veterinary Medicine at UC Davis, thinking I liked animals so much, and then I realized what I liked was meeting all of these people who brought their pets in. I'm a people person."

FRANCENE SELKIRK, CCDA

You may have heard that commercial casting director Francene Selkirk was once an actor, but would you have known that she was Francene the Teenage Queen on Rip Taylor's $1.98 Beauty Contest? Aside from having performed humiliating acts on television, Selkirk knows the actor's life and she brings that ability to commiserate to her sessions.

Selkirk, whose ad campaigns include Coca-Cola, Lexus, and Nintendo, has one major note of direction: make sure you read the signs posted in the lobby of Zydeco Studios. Selkirk posts important instructions that will only help you in your audition process.

What Makes a Former Actor a Good Casting Director?

"Casting is a fast and furious activity. You can't be lazy, you have to listen, and every single day is different. These are things that go with the acting profession as well. I'm kind to actors. As an actress, I didn't know who the casting director was. I found the audition to be a cold, scary situation. I will tell actors what to do in a callback situation based on what I've heard from the inside of the process," she explained.

Francene Selkirk, CCDA–327

Road to This Position

"I went to the High School of Performing Arts and toured with various theatre groups. I played the ukulele for Rip Taylor's—and I would love to get a copy of my appearances on—*$1.98 Beauty Contest*, if anyone reading this knows how I could do that. With that show it didn't matter what you looked like or anything, you just had to have fun," she recalled fondly.

"Over ten years ago, I was still acting and I did some work as a line producer for commercials. It wasn't as creative as I wanted to be, but on the set, I would clarify to actors, in Actor Talk, what the director meant when he was asking for something in their performance. Seeing that, David Wild, of Wild Scientific, asked if I would do some real people casting for him in Los Angeles. It was like an 'I could've had a V8' moment, as if everything I'd been doing until then led me to this job," Selkirk explained.

Pet Peeves

Actors who aren't prepared for their opportunity. "I think actors should take a class before they audition. It's good to know how you look on camera. But also, so many actors show up and don't know to sign in, or don't pay attention to protocol in the waiting room. They'll just walk right into my office! Pay attention to how the audition session works. Also, make sure your resumé is stapled to your picture. I want to see your credits! It's so important, even for commercials, for me to see your resumé."

Advice for Actors

"Remember that the scene begins before the audition begins. Enter and leave the scene with your choices intact. Stay in character for a beat. Give us a moment to go there with you. Then get out of that room! It's unprofessional to do your schtick. Sometimes a client will ask for a joke or something, but unless you're asked to do more, just say thank you and leave," Selkirk advised.

Her Opinion on Alternative Submission Methods

"I'm all for it! At first, I didn't think I wanted to sit in front of a computer all day, and I do still love to look at pictures by hand, but I think the online services are great for me to use to find someone specific."

Other methods Selkirk uses to cast commercials? "I open every envelope, I attend theatre always—even the smallest theatres—in fact, I'll look at tapes of shows when I can't make it to the performance. So, anything that gets you in front of me is good."

Most Gratifying Part of Her Job

"Booking the talent. In some very small way, it's like I'm giving back. It's not like going to church or anything, but it's giving something back, to book someone."

JULIE SELZER, CSA

In 1997, producer Robert Halmi's production of Truman Capote's In Cold Blood, the CBS miniseries, won a CSA Artios Award. Julie Selzer (who won the Artios along with then-partner Patrick Rush and location casting director Lynne Carrow) is proud of that accomplishment. Halmi was so pleased with Selzer's work that when he produced the 2000 miniseries Jason and the Argonauts for NBC, Selzer was, again, his casting director.

Selzer, a former actor, has also cast the feature films Heathers, Amazon Women on the Moon, Bad Girls, *and* RoboCop, *just to list a few. Recently, she and current partner Lauris Freeman have done an MOW for TNT, after having partnered up for* Brokedown Palace *in 1999. On partnership, Selzer comments, "I like having a partner. It's how I was trained. It makes casting more fun."*

First Casting Job

"I think it was *Grease 2* in 1980," Selzer calculated. "I knew all the young kids in town from drama festivals because I was acting and doing waiver theatre. I was a Theatre and Journalism major at Cal State, Northridge. I started working as an assistant to Sally Dennison, who later became my partner. We had to do the singers, the dancers, the actors," Selzer recalled of her work on *Grease 2*. As for leaving acting behind, she commented, "I found that I liked working behind the scenes better. I fell into it naturally. I had a good eye. I knew where the actors were coming from. I could speak their language, having been one." One of the best aspects of being a young actor-turned-casting director? "The ability, at a very young age, to have a room full of men take me seriously. That was really empowering," Selzer said.

Road to This Position

Selzer was an assistant until the age of 23, at which time she began casting films on her own, in addition to casting for Catalina Productions Theatre. "I partnered up with Sally in 1984. We were both up for the same job at Paramount and decided to go in as a united front. It worked out well because I was young and knew the young talent and she had been in the business a long time. It was a great fit. We were together through 1992." Then Selzer partnered with Patrick Rush, her former assistant.

Her Biggest Project

"Keeping up with Molly," Selzer's ten-year-old daughter. Does she have aspirations for the business? "I'm afraid so. Her dad's a director; her mom's a casting director. And while we do have her in basketball and playing drums, she does want to act. She did, however, say no to doing extra work on *ER* because she didn't want to get covered in blood. She thought that was pretty icky," Selzer joked.

Coolest Casting Gig

"With the exception of one film that I quit, I've loved every movie I've ever done. I've found actors and formed relationships on every project. I always have a really good time working with [director] Jonathan Kaplan [Selzer's former husband]. *The Accused* meant a lot to us because of Jodi

[Foster] getting the Oscar. And I had a great time on *RoboCop* too. That was back in the days when we got to do the location casting too. It was a collaborative effort all the way around. Casting really is putting a family together. A lot of times, the question is, 'Do we want to have this person in this family?' Actors need to understand that," Selzer added.

Her Favorite Casting Tale

"My first picture [*Grease 2*]. We found Michelle Pfeiffer for that. She came in with her then-husband, Peter Horton. She was literally waiting to pick him up. We saw her face and started grabbing things for her to read," Selzer recalled. Pfeiffer had not come in to audition at all. "There's an important lesson in this, for actors," Selzer began. "You might not get the first movie you read for with me, but maybe the fourth or fifth. I have a whole stable of actors that I just keep bringing in and in and in. Eventually, it'll hit. And you never know when. I still work from old-fashioned notebooks to keep up with who I've seen. As for Michelle, she just had a look. We'd seen everyone in town and hadn't found *it*. We were looking for something special and she had it. So, you never know," Selzer summarized.

Key Things She Looks for in an Actor

"I look for talent. I look for confidence. I also look for if the actor is having a bad day or not. I am the queen of understanding that some actors just don't audition well or have an off day. The casting director and the actor both know if the actor is having a bad day. The hard thing, in a callback situation, is to convince the producer or director to see someone again when they're the ones who are now under the gun. But if you've really got a legitimate shot and you just blew an audition, I'll bring you back in. If you don't really have a shot, I won't bring you back because it could actually hurt you," Selzer explained. "A good casting director is worth her weight in gold. Trust us. We've been in the room all day. We can give you clues and advice based on what's going on in that room."

Pet Peeves

"Someone who is unprepared, for whatever reason, and then who tries to act, once in the room, like it's the casting director's or their assistant's or the agent's fault. We're all adults. Be honest. Otherwise, it makes me look bad too. My job is to help you, and if you do a good job, even if you're not right for that role, directors will remember you for other projects. I did *RoboCop* with Paul Verhoeven, and a lot of actors we weren't able to use he ended up using in *Total Recall* and *Basic Instinct*.

Another peeve, for Selzer, is a bad attitude. "Any kind of negative attitude, leave it outside. I understand if you're in the moment in a scene and need to have something going on in you, but there's no excuse otherwise. You're not going to be allowed to be that way on a set," she concluded.

Advice for Actors

"Be prepared, obviously. Have the lines as memorized as you can. Some actors need the security blanket of holding onto those sides, and that's fine, but have a good handle on the material. Auditions have different tones, whether they're feature film or television auditions. It's hard to know that, until you've had the experience."

Selzer continued, "Read the room as if you're at a dinner party. Follow the leader. If it's a casting director you're comfortable with, let them segue into everything. If you get into the room and realize you know the writers, follow them. I'm real careful with this: some actors like to come into the room and do the material with no chitchat. I really try to steer it that way. Sometimes you can't help it if the director wants it to go another way, but I understand that. I get that. So, I try to let the actor take the space. It's your time. It's your space.

Whether it's five minutes or 50, if you're not ready, take a minute. People will only respect you for it. Just say, 'Can I have a minute?'"

Best Way To Get Seen by Her

"Through an agent, obviously. Another way is by being in a show around town that's getting raves. It's hard to get seen if you're a complete unknown unless you're in a really great show. As far as mailings go, or postcards, for me, if it's a current project, and it's a quick little, 'Hey. Remember me? I'm on *Law & Order* tonight,' that helps me more than, 'Here I am. Let me meet you.' Unsolicited photos for me are very job-specific. I find, if I'm doing a search for a big project, part of the process is uncovering every stone, putting out Breakdowns, getting the word out, 'Come one. Come all,' especially when we're looking for young talent."

Her Opinion on Alternate Submission Methods

"I don't use [online casting services], personally. [Internet casting] won't have an impact for me. Now, a network or television casting director might find it essential, but for me, an excellent photo is the best use of your money, ever. A good photo never goes out of style, as long as you still look like it. That kind of consistency is helpful, actually," Selzer added.

Trends She Has Observed in the Casting Process

"Everything is quicker and we don't have as much time in the process. I'm sorry about that. Time gives everyone a chance to know one another better. It used to be a little looser, where there would be a lot of time spent in auditions. Everyone uses video now. Everyone now wants first auditions taped. I don't like doing that. I only like to use the videotape for callbacks. It takes away from what you're there to do, in that first audition, to tape it. I'm a big believer in the rehearsal process. In theatre, in films, and in life, and I don't like having to put that down on tape. We don't have the luxury of *not* taping first auditions, though, if that's what the director wants," Selzer lamented.

Her Biggest Casting Challenge

"In general, just convincing some director or producer that I'm right, that the person I know is capable is right for the role. The big challenge is hanging in there and fighting for who you want. It's not just the casting director getting the director to agree. It's then getting the studio to go along with it. The power of the casting director really fluctuates from project to project. Some projects are just more of a collaborative effort, where I can say, 'Trust me on this one.'" An example of this, for Selzer, came with casting Jodi Foster in *The Accused*. "Paramount didn't want to see her that way," Selzer recalled. "She had been at school and out of the limelight, and I just had to keep saying, 'Test her. Test her.' It's about finding someone who has the right energy for the part, and that means every job is a challenge. It's about the chemistry."

Most Gratifying Part of Her Job

"Getting actors work. Discovering new talent. It's always fun being there in the beginning, and being able to say, 'I got so-and-so her SAG card.' That's great."

MARGERY SIMKIN, CSA

Margery Simkin is a casting director with a broad range of credits such as Brazil, Living Out Loud, Top Gun, Field of Dreams, Bowfinger, *and* Little Shop of Horrors. *The variety in her work is what she loves the most, but this busy CSA member seems to have quite a passion for the craft of casting itself.*

First Casting Job

"The first thing I ever cast was *Ladies and Gentlemen, Introducing the Fabulous Stains*. I had worked on *Fame* and *The Wanderers*, but that was my first casting director credit," Simkin recalled.

Coolest Casting Gig

As is common, for casting directors, she has a soft spot in her heart for whatever project she has just cast. "The last one I've done is always my favorite," she said. "*Erin Brockovich* was great because there were so many wonderful small roles. Even if the characters were just in one scene, they were really good parts, and I got to use a lot of people I'd wanted to use for a long time."

"*Bowfinger* was also great because I got to use a whole different group of people than I was familiar with," she added.

Advice for Actors

"Be sure acting is what you really want to do. For me, over the years, I've seen that it's a combination of talent and determination [that makes a successful actor]. You have to really be able to hang in there and appreciate the fact that there is value in working. I think that people don't want to take smaller [roles or roles in smaller projects] because they think they're not impressive enough. I think doing good work is always good to do," Simkin advised.

Best Way To Get Seen by Her

Agency representation is at the top of Simkin's list. "The best way is representational, but I saw somebody today from submissions. When I'm working on a project, I look through every picture that comes through my office. If someone's right, I'll meet that actor. I can't meet everybody, that's the problem. I think that's where the frustration comes in, for casting directors. We don't want to miss anyone."

Her Opinion on Alternative Submission Methods

"The problem for me with online submission methods is that I don't keep a permanent office. I'm wherever the project is, which means I move every couple of months. So, for me, in its current form, [Internet casting] hasn't yet proven to be that valuable," Simkin explained.

Most Gratifying Part of Her Job

"I'm grateful to have variety in my work. It's just fun. It's good to work on good material, no matter what the genre is."

MARY JO SLATER, CSA

I'd bet that Mary Jo Slater remembers the name of everyone she meets. Considering she's logged over 30 years of casting, that's an impressive task. From Broadway to features to MTV, Slater has cast hundreds of projects (such as Babylon 5, The Contender, *and* Ace Ventura: Pet Detective*), and she's not stopping there.*

With her tiny dog curled up in her lap, Slater and I discussed the usual Casting Qs *material, plus runaway production, while soap operas aired on a muted TV nearby in the temporary office space next to the production office for MTV's* Undressed.

First Casting Job

Neil Simon's *Chapter Two* on Broadway. Slater was working as an agent but wanted to get into producing, so she took a job as a receptionist in a producer's office. "I was a rotten receptionist. The producer said, 'I'm firing you, but I'm giving you a job casting *Chapter Two*,'" Slater recalled.

Coolest Casting Gig

The feature *12 Angry Men*. "I felt like I was in a world of extraordinary human beings," Slater remembered fondly.

Key Things She Looks for in an Actor

Three qualities top Slater's list: charisma, depth, and education. "If you attended Yale, ACT, North Carolina School of the Arts, NYU, Carnegie Tech, I know you can act. I know you have certain credentials that help to hone your abilities. Usually you can tell the difference in someone who's had a college training experience and someone who's just come in from class here," said Slater.

Her Favorite Audition Tale

"When I was very young, I was casting *Hair* on Broadway—the revival—and Treat Williams and Peter Gallagher came in and I had to tell them to drop their drawers," Slater laughed. She saw it as a strange, controlling experience that just happened to be a part of the job. "The requirements were very specific," Slater shared with another laugh.

Pet Peeves

Slater doesn't want to see actors who are unprepared or who will apologize for their audition. "Come in, do your five minutes, you own those five minutes, and say thank you and get up and leave. That's your time. The part is yours during that process. You don't come in *trying* to get the part, you *have* the part," Slater advised. "I think acting is instinctual. You either can or you can't. I don't think it's something that can be trained in. You can learn a craft, but it's the level that's instinctual. It's a gift," Slater indicated. So, while training is essential, an actor must have that gift if they're to impress her.

Advice for Actors

Slater provided a non-traditional piece of advice for those who want to be in this business. "Marry into it. That's the truth! Give birth to it. Look at the kids who are famous and who their parents are. Nepotism does pay off. That's the reality of it," Slater—who is actor Christian Slater's mother—admitted.

She attended the American Academy of Dramatic Arts and graduated with Danny DeVito and Clevon Little, who introduced her to her first husband, Christian's father. "He was an actor. So, I know how hard it is to be a kid, starting out, and wondering where you go from here. So, take my advice: marry an actor. That's a way to be in the business to start out with. That's how I wound up here!"

Slater knows that it takes something very special to be an actor. "You have to have something very unique. I knew I wasn't one of those 'special' types. I just didn't have the chutzpah to stick it out. I certainly respect those that do. I have great admiration for the people that hang in there. It's an unbelievable task. I couldn't have done it."

Her Thoughts on Runaway Production

While Slater felt the commercial strike was a "horrific situation for everyone in this industry," she wants to see runaway production addressed. "Everyone who's reading this article, do they realize that their work is going to Canada? My first co-producer feature shot in Canada, and I had very mixed emotions about that. They said, 'Look, to shoot it here is $18 million. To shoot it there is $12 million.' I'm now working on something that's shooting here and I'm like, 'Oh, my God, I get to cast everything!' It's so rare," Slater lamented. When she cast *ThirtySomething* and other shows at MGM, the shows were cast and shot locally. By 1994, when she returned to MGM, each pilot went to Canada. "All that work, for a kid getting started, getting an opportunity to do a day player role, is not here for these kids. We have to do something to change it. If I become a successful producer, I'm praying that I could have the weight to move production back," said Slater. "But, if you want to package a film these days, sit at the bar in the

Sutton Place Hotel in Toronto or Vancouver. Every actor you ever dreamed of meeting is sitting there, and that's a shame."

Best Way To Get Seen by Her

Slater doesn't have time to do generals, but she loves meeting new people. "If there's a role and your agent is a good agent, he'll pick up the phone and say, 'Meet this person.'"

"One person shows, Off-Broadway theatre, I do that. I see everything in New York. I have an apartment there, so I'm back and forth all the time. I cast in both places. I really want to expand that," Slater revealed.

She really enjoyed working with MTV. "That was an opportunity to see the new crop of kids. I had a ball with Roland Joffee's *Undressed*. I loved the kids because kids are so unjaded, so excited to be there. I would go on the set and hear, 'Oh, I loved it!'" For *Undressed*, Slater looked at every headshot that came in. "Everyone who's 20, was in to see me! And I got job offers because people wanted to know where I found all these hot young kids," Slater revealed. "We cast kids from open calls who'd never done anything. I call it embryo casting! They're so fresh and so new, I feel like I'm giving birth to most of them. It's so much fun. It's a whole different level from having done the classics like *Inherit the Wind* and *12 Angry Men* to doing *Undressed*. Talk about eclectic! I feel like the queen of eclectic casting," Slater shared.

Her Opinion on Alternative Submission Methods

While Slater joked that she lives in the 12th century, she does intend on taking a course in computer use, just to catch up. She wants to take advantage of technology by have casting sessions in Los Angeles that folks in remote locations can see live, in real time, via webcam.

Her Operating System

"I use *The Film Actors Guide* a lot because it has everyone that's ever been in a film and their credits. I go to *ScreenWorld* when I have to make lists." Beth Blanks, her casting associate, and Steve Brooksbank, her partner, are computer-savvy, according to Slater. "I am the brawn, they are the brains."

Highlight of Her Week

Slater loves attending film festivals. At the time of our interview, Slater had just attended the Big Bear Film Festival. "It was charming. It was very provincial and quaint. I want to help out with this festival. It's so good for young filmmakers. You don't have to be somebody in order to get in there. There are student projects and it's a wonderful venue for the up-and-coming filmmaker," Slater said. She enjoys seeing people go for it. "You have to take your life in your own hands. You have to control your destiny. There's just too much competition. You can't expect someone else to do it for you. You've got to find your own road."

Most Gratifying Part of Her Job

"Being proud of what's on the screen. That a lot of my fighting for what I believe in was worth it. Sometimes I lose the fight, but when I don't, I'm very happy with the outcome. I have a good life. I love what I do. Life's too short not to."

STEPHEN SNYDER

Stephen Snyder refers to himself as a pit bull. He is tough and opinionated, not afraid to offend anyone. His work on Unshackled, Unconditional Love, First Watch, *and countless network promos, music videos, film, and commercials has provided thousands of hours of contact with actors. He has seen it all... and has a lot to say about it.*

Key Things He Looks for in an Actor

Preparedness. "We have no time to do two to three weeks of prereads. We'll take you directly to the director. Come in prepared. The script is everywhere we can make it available, and you should at least read the entire breakdown to learn relationships," he advised.

Another element of being prepared is having extra headshots and resumés when you read for him. "It's a marketing tool, it's a tax write-off, it's your job." He added, as an afterthought—but an important one—"Show up. Actors don't show up sometimes."

"And be good to my assistants. That's very important."

Advice for Actors

"Go to every audition you get offered. It's a numbers game, and the more times you show up, the more opportunities you have. If you can't make it, *call.* I remember the names of the people who don't show up," he insisted.

Further advice from Snyder included developing an attitude that makes you hirable. "We casting directors help with the psycho factor. Sometimes the producer tries to pick between actor A and actor B and will ask, 'Who's less of a psycho?' We know the answer, so don't be a high-maintenance actor."

One last item he mentioned involves being on the same page with your rep. "Let your agent know up front if there are limits, like you won't do soaps or music videos."

His Opinion on Casting Director Workshops

"I do workshops. For me, they're a great opportunity to visit with 20 actors in two to four hours. I'm no good at the general [interview]. I'd rather see you *work.* Workshops let you establish a relationship in a no-pressure environment. You're not paying to audition. We don't do it for the money. We do it because we have passion for what we do. Just make sure you're at a level to show the goods before you do workshops," Snyder qualified.

Best Way To Get Seen by Him

Submissions. "Every submission gets opened, but I need you to tell me why you're sending it. Are you looking for a general? Inviting me to a play? You'd better enclose a cover letter letting me know what's what." Snyder added, "I love postcards. Include your agent information and a little resumé on the back. Let us know you're out there."

Snyder also regularly attends theatre. "You should be in a theatre company, doing improv, sketch comedy. Work out constantly. You should love acting and love the process of acting. Now, if you have a theatre-heavy resumé, here's a tip: if you've done 80 plays, say that, but then *list* only your top ten on the resumé."

His Opinion on Alternative Submission Methods

"I'm as old as a dinosaur, and I access IMDB or *Academy Players Directory* online or other online services. A demo reel on CD is fine. Send me a link to your headshot and resumé in an email. Have your bio and reel on your website, but I don't want to have to take a test to get on your website. Make it easy for me. The best part of the Internet is that you can update everything constantly. Don't say your agent should update us. Your agent gets 10%, you get 90%. You do the updates."

There is one element of technology that Snyder strongly recommends for actors. "Use Actor Access. This is a free service from Breakdown Services that allows me to share breakdowns directly with the actor."

His Biggest Casting Challenge

Simply stated, Snyder summarized, "Finding good material, and finding scripts with some budget."

What He Would Change About the Casting Process

Snyder would have a casting director union, which, of course, the CSA is working toward creating. "Actors have it better than we do. Casting directors don't even have a union. We have a society. We have luncheons. I love the CSA, but our dental plan is: brush three times a day," he joked.

MARK TESCHNER, CSA

Mark Teschner is a former actor. His main piece of advice on choosing a career in acting? "Do it because you have to act. Do it because you love acting. That's the only reason to do it. Don't do it for fame, for money. Those are things you have no control over and they either happen or they don't. If you act for the craft, the art, you always have that with you. That's the only reason to be an actor."

From his office in the General Hospital building on the ABC Television Center lot, Teschner and I discussed the volume of work that exists for a soap opera casting director, the new daytime Emmy for casting (Teschner was nominated for the award in 2002), and what it takes to show up on his radar screen.

First Casting Job

Teschner began as a casting assistant in New York 20 years ago. "My first desk was two saw-horses and a wooden plank. We were in a one-room casting office, with as few frills as possible. I came on to do one small job [for casting director Elissa Myers] and we became partners. It took one day for me to go from actor to casting director. Two years of acting in New York had drained me, and casting seemed like the logical leap. I could get agents on the phone who wouldn't talk to me before. Acting feels like another lifetime for me," Teschner said.

As is typical with this industry, one job led to another for Teschner. "Eventually, I left my partnership to go to ABC full-time to cast [the New York-based soap opera] *Loving*. It was supposed to be a six-month job and I ended up doing it for four-and-a-half years," Teschner recalled.

"I love the pace, the feel, the sensibility of daytime. It feels electric," he explained. Teschner has been with *General Hospital* for almost 13 years. The Manhattan native now considers Los Angeles his home, from which he casts *Port Charles* as well.

Coolest Casting Gig

"*General Hospital*. I get to work on a show that has such a broad canvas to cast for. There's no one thing that we're looking for. We cast so many actors a year that I get to meet hundreds and hundreds of actors. It's very exciting. *General Hospital* is a prestigious show. I'm working with the show that I grew up watching. Here it is, the show I grew up with as a kid, and I've cast one-third of its 10,000 episodes," he calculated proudly.

Key Things He Looks for in an Actor

Truth. "I look for an actor with a strong inner life. Those actors find a way of making the material come to life in a way that feels unique to them. There's a sense that the material speaks to them and that they are the actor that was meant to play that role. That's all it really is," Teschner summarized.

Pet Peeves

Actors who do not look like they do in their headshots. "The picture should not be how they'd *like* to look, just how they are at their best. It's very frustrating when an actor walks into the room and I look at their picture and I can't connect the actor to the picture. It says to me that the actor doesn't know who they are. Sometimes an actor will give a wonderful reading, not be right for the role, but I'll be hesitant to save the picture because I feel I won't be able to remember the actor because they don't look like their picture. For every audition that they get based on a misleading picture, they're losing out on the audition that they would've gotten as themselves," Teschner insisted.

Teschner added to his peeves list, "Unprepared actors. Actors need to make strong choices and bring that role to life in a short period of time. You'd better make your time with me count."

Advice for Actors

"Love acting. The money, the fame, these are not tangible elements. It's the craft. Remember, there's a lot of down time, so you'd better love what you do, not the rewards. Hang in there. Do not take rejection personally. It's often not about talent, but about who's 'more right' for the role. Just let it go and trust that you have something unique and when it's your turn, it's your turn."

"Make a strong choice with the material so that you really connect with it. If you play it safe, there's nothing at stake, and you have no commitment. If the actor cannot commit to the material, I cannot commit to the actor. If I see something in an actor, I can always make an adjustment. I want to go along with the actor. I want to go with their energy. The minute they walk in the room, the actor comes in with an energy. An actor needs to come in with confidence," he said, noting that confidence is not the same thing as being cocky or arrogant.

"If you're nervous, you can't let that get in the way of the work," Teschner continued, noting that a nervous audition makes him nervous about hiring that actor.

Teschner continued to list a few things that have a tendency to get in an actor's way. "Do not give your power away. When an actor tries to please me, that actor will not get the job. When an actor comes in to do good work, that's what I'll remember. Talent and dignity are the only two things an actor really brings into the room. There are so many factors that go into the mix as to why an actor doesn't get the part."

After going through the 1500 submissions he receives per contract role, Teschner brings in 200 to 300 actors to audition. "That doesn't mean that other actors [who didn't book the job] didn't leave their mark. Trust the work will stay with me. An actor's skill is what they bring into the room and the legacy they leave behind. You have to trust that if you do a good job, that will stay with me. And if I don't cast you for this role, there may be something else. Don't try to be anyone else. While you're busy trying to be someone else, you could miss out on the role that you would get as yourself."

Best Way To Get Seen by Him

Being submitted by your agent or manager for a specific role he is casting. "I get 350 unsolicited headshots per week. I do open every piece of mail I get. I look at them all, and if someone is right for something I'm casting or something innately interesting jumps out at me, and I want to meet that actor, I will put that picture aside."

"It is possible to get seen by me without an agent or manager, but it is hard to build a career without an agent or manager who knows what's being cast, who has access based on relationships that they've built over a number of years. It's not enough to send your photo out. You have to be in the middle of it," Teschner advised.

How does Teschner advise actors to be in the middle of it? Theatre. "I think theatre is a great opportunity to see actors doing what they are supposed to be doing. One of my favorite things is to go to the theatre, see an actor in a play, and then hire them for a job. There's something very pure about that. Actors need to act. Actors need to get out there and create an opportunity to be seen. Remember that everyone was non-union at some time. Everyone had no agent at some time. Do theatre and get seen," he advised.

Note that Teschner prefers to attend theatre performances that will allow him to see as many actors as possible. "It just makes sense for me. I will go anywhere where there's something that draws me. I'll go to a night of one acts or big-cast plays so that I can see a lot of actors in one evening," he said.

To get Teschner to attend your show, send him a flyer. "It's really difficult to get through to me on the phone. Send a flyer, which is a great marketing tool. Make it look like there has been some investment in this production. Treat it like a business in terms of the marketing of it and the craft of it. Know that every other production is competing for the casting director's attention as well," he insisted.

His Opinion on Alternative Submission Methods

"Some people use Internet casting. I try to be aware of what's out there, but I do casting the old-fashioned way. I like to have the photo in my hand and look at it, process it. We have all of the technical capabilities but those services aren't at their full potential. Plus, I'm just set in my ways," Teschner said, indicating a stack of headshots and resumés.

His Biggest Casting Challenge

Teschner explained that every role is a challenge to cast. "We're looking for that combination of talent, charisma, and sex appeal. We're looking for someone the viewers will want to watch every day and go on a journey with."

Teschner shared the joy he felt in a recast he did for the role of Lucky Spencer. "Jonathan Jackson had won two Emmys for playing that role. I brought in Jacob Young to continue the role and when he won the Emmy this year, it made me think that I did a good job of selecting an actor who could continue the sensibility of what was so popular about the character but not be a clone."

What He Would Change About the Casting Process

Timing. "We're shooting 254 episodes a year. I'll see 35 to 40 actors a day when we're busy. The realities of the time constraints make it very difficult to see every actor that I'd like to see when I'm casting three and four roles at a time."

Most Gratifying Part of His Job

"Once we finally get the part cast, being able to watch [the actor] on the screen. Seeing the meshing of the right actor in the right role, the right timing... you just know you've really hit pay dirt."

DELICIA TURNER

Delicia Turner admits that she hasn't been casting long enough to be jaded about it. "I love actors and I love to give honest feedback. Maybe that will change," she said. But for now, Turner likes to echo the sentiments of San Diego Rep's artistic director, Sam Woodhouse. "He may have been quoting someone else, but he says to an actor, after an audition, 'You did great. Now it's time for us to do our mumbo jumbo.' That's what we do."

Turner mentioned some incentive for Los Angeles actors to head south. "We pay housing and travel and, hey, San Diego is gorgeous," she laughed, adding, "My job is to make sure that the art is in good hands when I leave it. I am interested in fostering the next generation of artist." In her rise through the ranks at San Diego Rep, Turner is doing just that.

First Casting Job

The one she now holds. Turner started out as Associate Casting Director for San Diego Rep in 2001. "I'm currently transitioning into the Casting Director position," she said. The first show she cast was the very successful *I Love You, You're Perfect, Now Change.*

Turner came from a general theatre background. "I was doing stage management and directing here at the Rep," she recalled. "They needed a casting associate. I said, 'I can probably do that,' and began filling that need."

Coolest Casting Gig

Recent hit *Love, Janis*. "This was a big project. The show was running Off-Broadway already. The director, Randal Myler, is fabulous. It was so nice, working with him and also Janis Joplin's brother. Sam Andrew, an original member of Big Brother and the Holding Company (Joplin's original band), was involved. The musical auditions were just amazing. It was wonderful to hear all this great music all day every day. The atmosphere was cool. Everyone was so generous and complimentary. Even those who weren't cast were generously treated and complimented by Randal. It was a good time. I loved seeing the people auditioning getting to participate in a jam session," Turner recalled.

Key Things She Looks for in an Actor

Personality. "I want to know who the actor is. I get to that by seeing how relaxed they are when they introduce themselves. Are they a ball of nerves or are they warm?"

Something that assists Turner in her assessment of an actor's personality is her background as a theatre director. "I look at the kind of choices they make in their audition," she said. While Turner admitted that the skills involved in presenting a monologue differ wildly from the skills of performing an entire play, she explained that she can size up an actor's personality in the first 30 seconds of the audition. "It's about choices, discipline, preparation. I could be wrong in my assessment, but it's a starting point for me getting to know who this person is."

Turner also looks for training, but finds a confidence level with auditioning to be even more telling of an actor's skills. "The more auditions you have, the better you are. Auditioning is a skill you need as an actor. It's important to know what auditioning feels like so that you are not so dependent on getting the part. Auditioning regularly lets you know what it feels like when you nail it. It also helps with rejection because you learn that you sometimes don't get the part because of matching."

Matching, according to Turner, is about the entire cast and its composition, rather than about the performance of the actor himself. "It happens all the time," she said. "It's one of the biggest challenges about casting. The director will have an idea of what he wants to put together. Sometimes that's a shared view with the casting director, but sometimes it's not. I might bring to the table, after screening hundreds, five actors I think are perfect. If none of them matches with the idea of the leading man the director has in mind, we'll start again. It's completely subjective."

Pet Peeves

"Some casting directors don't mind, but I hate it when an actor has to start over more than once," she said. "I expect some nerves, of course, but I love it when an actor has confidence, knowing they're going to nail the audition. Starting over and over is just the actor letting his nerves get in the way of the performance."

Turner continued, "I have a lot of admiration for actors. It's brave work to stand in front of people and say, 'Let me show you this and I hope you like it.' So, since it's brave work, be brave."

Advice for Actors

"I really want the actor to be good. I think, if you keep that in mind, you will do better work. Know that I'm not sitting there thinking I'm going to see 20 bad people in a row and hope for one of them to be good. As the actor, you should think of your audition as doing me a favor. I try and tell my actor friends, 'Look, if you're good, you're making my job easier.'"

Turner hopes that, holding that information in mind, the actor will be more relaxed during his audition.

"So often, talent is only one part of what goes into casting an actor. It's not a small part, mind you, but there are so many other elements. Actors need to know that. All you can do is have a great audition."

Best Way To Get Seen by Her

"We generally put ads in *Back Stage West* and put notices on our website [www.SanDiegoRep.com] when we're casting. When we cast for the entire season, we do Breakdowns for agents as well," she detailed. Turner conceded that many excellent actors do not have agency representation, and explained that it is because of this that she uses other methods to bring actors in. "We publicize in the trades so that actors in Los Angeles and San Diego can learn for themselves what we have going on."

As for seeing actors when not holding seasonal auditions, Turner encouraged submissions. "When actors send their headshots and resumés, I do go through them. I'll put together a list of people I want to see and then meet them. Most of the people I see will be on a per-show situation, but sometimes an actor is passing through town and wants me to see his work. If I have time, I will always see actors."

One detail to note, when submitting your headshot and resumé for a specific show, is that Turner scrutinizes your resumé for work that is similar to the show she is casting. "We were casting the musical *Working* and received resumés with no musical theatre listed. I'm not just going to take your word for it that you did a musical. I want to see that in your credits," she said.

Another note about submissions: "I don't have time to read all of the shit actors sometimes attach to a headshot and resumé, like reviews and stuff." When asked about postcards, Turner was quick to say, "I like a full headshot and resumé. A postcard won't cut it."

Her Opinion on Alternative Submission Methods

"I wish! I don't know if [online casting] will ever be so much of a force in casting. We'd have to print it all out. There's so much to flipping through the headshots," Turner said, adding that she will see actors on tape when they cannot attend an audition for a specific role.

What She Would Change About the Casting Process

"Spiritually, if I could change the way actors view auditioning, that would be something. I've seen actors do really good initial auditions and then blow it at the callback because there's more at stake. I call those actors and go, 'What are you doing?!? Come in. Relax. This is your part to get,'" she insisted.

Turner acknowledged that making calls to actors after auditions may be a case of extending herself too much, but mentioned that doing so is a big part of what she enjoys about casting.

Most Gratifying Part of Her Job

"I love it when casting an unknown talented actor—someone who maybe doesn't have an agent or who is not in the union—and they're just perfect for it. No offense to movie stars—I understand that having a name is a box office draw—but I love it when that unknown kid is just great. That is why I will call [the actor] and say, 'They love you. What I want you to do is be more relaxed and do what you know how to do.'"

KATY WALLIN, CSA

Katy Wallin, founder of Katy & Co. Casting, Mystic Arts Pictures, and AIA Actors Studios is proud to wear many hats. In addition to casting projects ranging from Trumpet of the Swan *to* BASEketball *to* Sweet Valley High, *Wallin cast and produced the feature film* Finder's Fee, *which won Best Picture at the Seattle International Film Festival as well as Best Screenplay at Method Fest. She also serves on the board of CSA.*

None of these successes, however, compares with the joy Wallin exudes when talking about the love of her life, the baby boy sleeping in the next room.

First Casting Job

Assistant to Cathy Henderson. "We did a movie called *I Don't Buy Kisses Anymore* starring Jason Alexander and Nia Peeples," Wallin recalled. "Cathy loves actors. I learned so much from her. Cathy inspired me to pursue a career in casting," Wallin exclaimed.

Before that casting job, however, Wallin pounded the pavement, looking for any job in the business. "I moved here, and went door-to-door with my resumé. I was here from Oregon, straight out of college," she explained. An executive overheard Wallin being treated rudely by a receptionist at the end of an ego-bruising day. Right then, she was hired to replace that woman. "After three weeks, I was promoted to the talent department for a TV show at CBS, where I worked on a show for six months. I put in 80 hours a week, made almost no money, and loved every minute of it. At the end of the season, they came in and said, 'Okay, we're now on hiatus.' And I said, 'Okay, what does that mean?' And they said, 'Clean out your desk.' So I started my own company," Wallin summarized.

"At 22 I was so naive. I had absolutely no fear," Wallin explained. In her 14 years in the business, Wallin has cast hundreds of commercials and music videos, 500 hours of network television, and 65 movies.

Coolest Casting Gig

Producing and casting Jeff Probst's *Finder's Fee.* "This was an incredible opportunity," Wallin said of assembling her cast of Erik Palladino, James Earl Jones, Matthew Lillard, Ryan Reynolds, Dash Mihok, Carly Pope, and Robert Forster. "It was the most challenging, most rewarding experience. It was an independent [film], so it was not about the money. It was a passion project. All of these actors were so dedicated to this project," Wallin revealed.

"We spent two years casting it and the actors had genuine chemistry," Wallin shared. "I always do a chemistry callback. It's essential to a good movie."

Key Things She Looks for in an Actor

"A solid sense of one's self. An actor who genuinely is positive and feels good about who they are really stands out in a casting room," Wallin explained. "There's this unique and magical charisma that, when an actor has it, lights up the entire room. They may not even be right for the role, but there is something so special that often we'll hire them, and they're nothing like what we put out in the breakdown."

Another key thing: Professionalism. "You have to treat an audition like a job. Go in prepared. Be professional. Take that audition seriously." Wallin added, "If you're given the opportunity to read the script, read the script."

Pet Peeves

Props. "I have been burned by a fire-eater, hit in the head with numchucks, had a gun put to my head, knives put to my throat, and have been kissed in a casting session," Wallin revealed.

Her favorite tale of inappropriate audition behavior? "An actor was auditioning for a role in a film I was casting. He was so into the scene that he head-butted a hole in the wall of the studio. I just sat there, looking at this hole in the wall, questioning what it is that I do for a living. He was fine, despite his headache, and he came back the next day with plaster and paint to fix the hole in the wall." So, the use of props isn't Wallin's only pet peeve.

Advice for Actors

Realize how much you've accomplished, just getting to an audition. Wallin advised, "Reward yourself for an audition. Don't beat yourself up for not getting a job. As an actor, the journey is what it's all about. Actors have to love and appreciate that process. Embrace the journey."

"This is a business. Acting is a profession. You need to put a strategic marketing plan in place for yourself. Remember this, above all: you have a unique asset. You are president and CEO of your company, and you have to know how can you best market yourself in this competitive industry and maintain peace and tranquility. You have to have an overall, well-balanced game plan," Wallin insisted.

Wallin also advised that you find a mentor and create a support group. "You must have emotional, mental, and spiritual stability. Find that stability and balance, whatever that means to you. Don't put everything into acting. Have a whole world so that you can survive the emotional roller coaster that is this business."

Her Favorite Audition Tale

Wallin was working with Trey Parker on the feature film *Orgazmo*. "At auditions, Trey was great. He was so open and receptive. He asked actors a yes or no question, 'Can you fake an orgasm?' One actor he asked proceeded to fake one. For ten minutes. I was embarrassed for the camera operator, the reader. An employee here had an ear to the door, trying to figure out what was going on. Trey thought it was great. He loved it. The actor was brave and he did a great job but he didn't get the part," Wallin concluded with a laugh.

Her Opinion on Alternative Submission Methods

"I'm sure [Internet casting] works for some casting directors. I'm still a little old fashioned in that I love opening envelopes, laying out the headshots, and matching people up."

Best Way To Get Seen by Her

Postcards. Wallin elaborated, "I love postcards. I love when actors talk about the work they're doing so I can look for them on TV or in a film."

Wallin advised that an actor use postcards as an ongoing marketing tool. "Let me know you're working. Let me know you're doing plays. That's your advertising. Make sure you have a small advertising budget together and use it or else we don't know what you're doing. I've hired a lot of people from postcards. Don't send just one. Every time you're doing something, send one," she said, "just to keep the industry apprised of your career."

And theatre? "Since I had my baby, I don't go to theatre as much as I used to, but you should still get yourself out there. Meet people, gain valuable advice, let people see your work."

Her Opinion on Casting Director Workshops

Wallin founded AIA Actors Studio. "When I opened my companies, I recognized that the key to this industry was developing and building relationships. As a casting director, I needed to get to know producers, directors, and most importantly, actors. I wanted to provide a warm, nurturing place where people could educate themselves and meet with the various industry professionals. I recognized quite quickly that we were able to bridge the gap between those in front of the camera and those behind it."

Wallin continued, "We provide an environment where people can be creative, where they can educate themselves, and where they can meet these entertainment professionals. We believe acting is a process and a journey. Part of that process is studying, working on your craft, networking, and marketing yourself. AIA is a resource center that can help you put a strategic marketing plan together and give you resources and information. We're bringing 14 years of our relationships to you. We provide a platform and an environment where we can bring the industry together."

"A few people have asked if it's a conflict of interest, being a CSA casting director, a producer, and owning AIA. I have never felt that anything I am doing is a conflict! In fact, all of my companies share a common goal, and that is to provide an environment where entertainment professionals can come together to achieve their artistic, creative, and business goals. Yes, I founded AIA. Emily Yost, whose background is education, runs the day-to-day operation of the company along with a staff of highly qualified entertainment professionals."

Bottom line on paying to meet casting directors? "An actor, at least at AIA, is not paying to meet a casting director and audition for a specific role. Actors come here to learn perspective on the business, build powerful relationships with industry professionals, and perform for those casting directors. This is a business and an actor has overhead. Every other business has workshops and seminars to help [people] strengthen their chosen craft and give them the knowledge they need to succeed. AIA meets those needs for actors, casting directors, and other industry professionals," Wallin summarized.

Highlight of Her Week

"Being able to bring my baby to work. It is one of the reasons that I opened my own business. He's the love of my life, next to my husband. I talked about this business being a human roller coaster ride. When any day is down, he's my instant gratification."

Most Gratifying Part of Her Job

"It's incredibly creative. I love the challenges that have been presented to me. I turn every obstacle into an opportunity. I love meeting actors and seeing people succeed. That's exciting. I love seeing people's hard work pay off."

APRIL WEBSTER, CSA

April Webster, who has cast everything from Knight
Rider *to* CSI *and from* Meat Loaf: To Hell and Back *to* Eight
Legged Freaks *casts with the eye of a director—a theatre
director. She views her staff as a team, a crew. "We have a
history, our own language," she said. This team allows Webster
to access the massive database of actors she keeps in mind.*

*"When you've been in casting this long, you do remember
everyone, but sometimes you begin to think you need a new
hard drive," Webster joked, of the metaphorical server space in
her brain. With all the gadgets in use on* Alias, *Webster could
hook up an auxiliary system that is as stylish and diverse as
the cast.*

First Casting Job

Webster started out as a theatre director and stage
manager in 1978. "I was working at the Mark Taper Forum
as an assistant to Gordon Hunt and Frank Bayer. I'd come
from the Public [Theatre] in New York, and had only cast
projects I was directing. I was asked if I could cover the phones
in the casting office at the Taper and then worked for a year
as an assistant. After that, I went back to New York and assisted
Gordon Davidson on *Children of a Lesser God*," Webster
recalled.

Road to This Position

"I came back to Los Angeles, called around, and got some work casting independent films and television," Webster continued. Her work on *Shoot the Moon* with Linda Phillips-Palo at Zoetrope started what she calls, "the magical years." She went from film to television. "I never did just one kind of show. I worked on *Night Court* and *The Nanny* but I also did a lot of action shows at Universal and Paramount and the mini *Grand Avenue* for HBO," she said.

Coolest Casting Gig

Grand Avenue. "I'm very big into diversity casting and the mainstreaming of nontraditional types. We were booking Native American actors and [then-partner] David Bloch went to Santa Rosa to hold an open call," Webster explained. "I felt, with this project, that a service had been done—and I say that with no hubris," she qualified. "This was nice because it was modern, and not the typical period piece for which these actors would usually be sought out. Those were tough roles, and Sheila Tousey, A Martinez, they did great work."

Coolest at another level is *Alias*. "*Alias* is great! I'm having more fun casting this than any episodic I've ever done." Webster tips her hat to Megan McConnell and Janet Gilmore for leaving, "such a legacy," in their original casting for the series. "We're getting to use wonderful actors to fill these amazing roles. As a theatre person, I love these roles!"

Key Things She Looks for in an Actor

On a practical level, Webster looks for training. "If I see ACT or Juilliard on a resumé, I know that these actors will come in with the craft behind them. I look at who they've studied with and also at their theatre background," she summarized. "But, you never know where you'll find talent.

Sometimes someone with very little training can have something special going on."

Another key thing Webster looks for is an interest in the world. "It's hard to find here, as opposed to New York, where there is more opportunity to go to museums or to travel. I want to see an interest in more than just the role you're auditioning for. That creates something special and shows part of who you are in the role. You bring yourself into the role. That is what is unique to you."

"In Los Angeles, we have this self-perpetuating myth," Webster continued. "We make stars out of people and then ask them to come up with the goods afterwards. It's really an unfair way to do it. Granted, some have a natural ability, but we make it very tough on actors, when we make them stars before they've been trained."

Advice for Actors

Find your center. "Know how to use your instrument. Let me hear your voice. An actor can stop her energy three inches from her face and that is easily correctable. It's about learning how to come in here and take the space," Webster said, of her staff and their offices. "We try to make this a safe space for the actor. It's a service that I can give so that the actor feels that he or she has the right to try something out. It's not altruistic. I want you to do your best work because that makes my job go smoothly."

"Do your own prep work," she continued. "If you know the lobby is not the right place for you, go out into the hall and breathe. Do jumping jacks. Know what you need and don't negate those feelings, just because you may have different prep work than another actor. It's how you bring your humanity into the room. It's what makes you unique. Value that," she advised.

"The hardest thing is to stay present. That's a hard process. There's whispering, there's note-taking. Keep your focus. Connect to your reader. Remember who you are, not who they want you to be. Have integrity and fill the room with your energy. Take the space. Know you're a contribution to the project. The right thing will happen. Know that casting directors are nervous at those meetings too. Be clear on your technique and focus on the task. It's not about getting the job."

Webster sees acting as the art of listening. "It's a practice, like meditation. I look for actors who listen—both in the scene and in general. It's essential for an actor to surrender. You must be fully aware and present in that moment, not thinking about the result [of your audition]. *We* don't know what's going to happen. There are infinite possibilities."

"The disease of perfectionism can kill you. Obsession and workaholism are valued here and they can really damage your soul. Every experience you have had adds up to what you are, and that is *not* just like the 17 people that may look like you in the waiting room," Webster said. And how does an actor remove focus from perfectionism? "I find that breathing helps," she concluded.

Pet Peeves

"In auditions, I don't need to hear what your whole day was. This is especially the case in producer sessions," Webster revealed. "Get the material ahead of time and come in prepared. Come in. Do your job."

Webster indicated a pet peeve specific to pilot season. "We get busy. I will add a casting director to our office for pilot season. The stakes are very high. Actors become overwhelmed and their priorities are skewed out of line." How can an actor combat that necessary evil? "Be fully prepared. Your agent can help by not scheduling 12 appointments in one day. Don't be so attached to the outcome that you are depleted and your energy is gone, and you're not present for your auditions. That just adds tension," Webster concluded.

Best Way To Get Seen by Her

"Keep me apprised of your appearances," Webster requested, asking that actors not make phone calls to the office. "We are always glad to get postcards. They are a good, inexpensive way to get seen. Use them to let me know when I can see you in something. We save postcards and we do cast from them."

Webster regularly attends theatre. "I try to see as much theatre as I can, because I still direct and want to see what is being done out there. There is hard-core theatre here," Webster commented on Los Angeles theatre, having come from New York. "Actors have to work harder to make [Los Angeles] a theatre town because of the time commitment in getting to and from the theatre for rehearsals—you can't just hop the subway a few stops like in New York—but there is excellent work going on here." Specifically, Webster mentioned enjoying the Pacific Resident Theatre, the Odyssey, and the old Met.

Webster strongly discourages unsolicited demo reels. "You're just throwing away your money. Your best calling card is your photo."

Her Opinion on Alternative Submission Methods

"We are using [the Internet] much more than ever," Webster insisted. "I use The Link and the *Academy Players Directory*—especially the books," she said. Webster indicated that her relationships with agents and managers are still the most reliable resource in casting.

Her Biggest Casting Challenge

"Each project has its own challenge," Webster said, noting specifically the challenge posed in filling the role of Gabriel in *The Patriot*. "[The actor] had to play Mel Gibson's son, and Heath [Ledger] was very Mel-like. It was a very important role and we looked at every young actor in Los

Angeles, New York, and Chicago. Heath has that Australian self-confidence that Mel seems to have as well," Webster commented. "It was a real opportunity to put together a palate of actors. I didn't take any other work at that time because I was so focused on *The Patriot*. With casting all the roles, it was exciting to work with that caliber of actors, to meet them and read across the table from them."

Highlight of Her Week

"I love directing. And I do that every day to some extent, in sessions. Watching the process is a blast. The industry can be so fear-based," Webster added. "If I can, through my own inward journey, not come from a place of fear, I can hold a space for actors to come in here and do their best work."

Most Gratifying Part of Her Job

"Finding somebody new—or someone who has been around—and matching them to the right role. I enjoy that moment of, 'Yeah! All right!' It's not about kudos for doing a great job, it's about having the opportunity to work at this level of casting."

DEBRA ZANE, CSA

Is it possible to have never seen a film cast by Debra Zane? Doubtful. With films like Ocean's 11, Traffic, Stuart Little, American Beauty, Pleasantville, Wag the Dog, *and* Men In Black *to her credit, Zane has populated cinematic worlds supported by millions in box office dollars. When Kevin Spacey thanked Zane in his Oscar acceptance speech for his role in* American Beauty, *he made fans out of the casting community, including—of course—Zane herself.*

From her modest offices in Miracle Mile, Zane and I discussed the lack of a Best Casting Oscar, the pending renovations to her office ("When we can be elsewhere for a couple of weeks"), and the elements that make casting a gratifying job, Oscar or no Oscar.

First Casting Job

Assistant to David Rubin on *The War of the Roses* for 20th Century Fox. "Danny DeVito directed it. I'd worked on the film *Men Don't Leave* that Paul Brickman directed. David was the casting director and I was a PA for the last month of preproduction. That's where I met David. After *Men Don't Leave*, he hired me to be his assistant," Zane said.

"I always thought that I could do [casting]. I loved actors, and that's all I really knew of it—was actors and their different roles. As a child I was aware of the casting director's place in the credits of a film. I knew she put actors in different roles," Zane explained.

Coolest Casting Gig

Zane thought about this question for quite some time prior to answering. "The most fun? For a long time, that was *Get Shorty*, which I also did with David [Rubin]. That was so much fun. Every day was a blast. [The film] is so good," Zane recalled. "What project am I the proudest of? There are two: *American Beauty* and *Traffic*," she listed.

Key Things She Looks for in an Actor

That depends on the role. "I make it very role-specific, in terms of what I look for," Zane explained. "Am I looking for a bartender? Am I looking for the president of the Rotary Club? I'm going to need the most appropriate qualities for that character. I heard myself say on the phone today to an agent, 'Yeah, of course, she could play the part, but [she's] not exactly what I'm looking for. [The actor] needs to be more like [this].' I need to believe [an actor] the most in that role. I need to believe that the actor could *live* as that other person," Zane concluded.

Pet Peeves

Unpreparedness. "You can never be too prepared," she said. And when Zane's office calls you in, you will have time to prepare. "To be not prepared—that really bugs me. We give people [appointments] days in advance. Today is Friday and we're booking appointments for Wednesday. You don't really have an excuse, even if you have three appointments in one day. With us, you've had time to go through the material a little bit," Zane summarized. "Honestly—and I think Cuba Gooding, Jr., said this—your job, as an actor, is to come in and do well at auditions," she reported.

Advice for Actors

"Stay on top of the business. *Read* the trades and know who's who and what's going on. Don't expect that your agent will always have you in mind [while looking at the Breakdowns]. If you're aware of projects going on, you can call [your agent] and say, 'I hear so-and-so is casting this project. Can you get me an audition? Can I get a script?' You can even send the casting director a note. You have to help yourself." Zane stressed that telephone calls are frowned upon. "Actors need to contact us by mail," she insisted.

Best Way To Get Seen by Her

"I know there are many actors in this town who will tell you that they have been in this office and have been hired by sending a postcard or sending a picture and a resumé in the mail," Zane assured. "No agent, no nothing."

What About Theatre?

"I have to admit, I attend very little theatre these days because I have a new baby, but Erin [Toner], my assistant, does go to showcases that I think look interesting and she will tell me who she thought might be interesting [to bring in]."

Trends She Has Observed in the Casting Process

Internationalization. "It's a global marketplace, as we all know, but I've noticed a lot more international actors in movies, and they're more and more accepted in leading roles, which is really nice, I think," Zane asserted.

Her Biggest Casting Challenge

"Chris Cooper's role in *American Beauty* was hard to cast," Zane recalled, thoughtfully. "It's hard to explain, but it was so delicate, and we knew we didn't want to signal things by casting it a certain way. But I knew when I read the script that that role would be the tough one [to cast]. Sometimes you can tell right away which roles will be hard [to cast]," she noted.

"Kids are hard. When kids have a big part and you have to do searches, you're looking at as many six-year-olds as you can find, and then you see a child in the mall and you ask the mom, 'Can I talk to you for a moment?' it's just a funny situation."

Her Opinion on Alternative Submission Methods

Zane's office does not use any online casting services. "We still pop a tape in the VCR here. We do it all day long. We're big TV/VCR people." That does not mean that Zane wants your unsolicited demo reel. "An unsolicited tape is a little tricky, especially if it's not sent for a specific role. We're so busy looking at tapes we've requested and then editing together tapes of actors to send to directors and producers, there's just no time to look at an unsolicited demo. It's not a top priority," Zane shared.

A goal for Zane's office is to begin editing sessions onto discs. "We're big tape-makers right now, but later this year, we'll be doing editing on the computer and sending out our sessions on DVD."

What She Would Change About the Casting Process

Zane considered this concept carefully before answering. "It's a *very* awkward process, and yet a very necessary process. It's imperfect, but it is what it is," Zane expressed. "I'm tempted to say that I'd like more actors to be more willing to audition. But we're working with directors now whom actors are thrilled to read for. They are happy to do it, eager to do it. Luckily, we've got that enthusiasm now."

Highlight of Her Week

"We like auditions. I bet there are too many casting directors who don't enjoy sessions. We love them. We *really* love them! We're always happy to see the actors, we always thank them for coming, we have a good time, we always wish we had more props for them to play with and could set the stage and rehearse it more," Zane concluded with a laugh.

Most Gratifying Part of Her Job

"We're happy whenever a decision gets made," Zane said with a broad smile. "That, and when we go to the movie and say, 'Gee. Look at that,' when it exceeds our expectations."

GARY ZUCKERBROD, CSA

When Gary Zuckerbrod was named president of the Casting Society of America, he went to the top of my "Interview Wish List" of casting directors. Little did I know, when scheduling our interview, that it would take place on the day the California Labor Board issued a cease and desist order on paid casting director workshops. Amidst of the buzz over casting the Larry Gelbart pilot for ABC (which Zuckerbrod described as a gritty social-political satire from the creator of M*A*S*II*), Zuckerbrod—whose credits include* Pulp Fiction *and* Without a Trace—*maintained his focus on upcoming producer sessions and pushing forward his agenda for a stronger CSA.*

First Casting Job

Zuckerbrod interned for Bonnie Timmerman in New York. "I was applying to Columbia University for an MB/MFA in the arts," Zuckerbrod recalled. He connected with Timmerman while she was casting the Phoenix Repertory Company. "I was curious about theatre management. I ended up working for Bonnie for three years."

Road to This Position

"I was a freelance casting assistant in New York and was hired by Bob Weiner for *To Live and Die in L.A.* They were searching for the leads in New York." After his initial job of three weeks on the project ended, Zuckerbrod was asked to continue on in Los Angeles for another three weeks. "That turned into five months," he laughed. "The day I was leaving, Bob was offered the new *Twilight Zone* series, so he asked me to stay for three weeks, help set up his office, get him an associate. A week later they made me his partner." Within two months, Weiner left the project and Zuckerbrod cast *Twilight Zone* for two years.

Key Things He Looks for in an Actor

"Preparedness is probably what I look for the most. And that's very difficult in pilot season, so I give actors a lot of slack and tell my directors and producers that they too have to give actors a lot of slack. Actors are going out on 14 auditions in a day and really don't have the time to prepare or get the chance to make choices. It's an unfair system and we all have to be accepting of that," Zuckerbrod said of the crunch everyone feels at pilot season. "While having that understanding and giving the benefit of the doubt, actors do have to come in prepared. I make scripts available to everybody, including dayplayers, if they'd like to have them. You should have understanding of what you're going in for. To me there's no difference between an audition and a job interview. I would never walk into a job interview without first doing some research. That's part of your job," he summarized.

Pet Peeves

Zuckerbrod has only one. "I usually find most actors I read to be incredibly professional. The only pet peeve I have is really if you aren't prepared. You should understand that, if you choose to walk in and audition for a project, you should have some knowledge of what you're walking in for. I find that most do. Most are very respectful."

Advice for Actors

"Understand that this is a craft that requires upkeep," Zuckerbrod advised. The type of upkeep he recommends: "I strongly encourage studying, doing theatre, honing your skills. As far as auditioning goes, auditioning is as much a technique as anything else. Often times it has very little to do with what you may actually do on a set. Unfortunately, you have to learn that skill too and be good at it. The only way to learn that skill is through experience. I know that's a catch-22, but that's the way it goes." How did Zuckerbrod suggest an actor get experience auditioning, if having a hard time getting called into offices? "Absolutely do student films and thesis projects. Any time you walk in front of a casting director or producer, no matter what level, you're still learning a valuable lesson."

His Goals for the CSA

Going union. "The biggest goal is leading the CSA, and leading casting directors who are not in the CSA, toward unionization. We're working very hard and that is moving rapidly and well-paced at this point." The overarching goal on Zuckerbrod's mind is "creat[ing] a greater unity among casting directors." How? "I think we're doing that strictly by getting the world out that we're trying to unionize and that we're trying to better our professional lives. We are the only major entity on a film that does not get pension and welfare, that does not have the protection of a union." Zuckerbrod had mentioned pacing, so I asked about a timeline for seeing CSA go union. "I honestly think that will change in 2002." I asked Zuckerbrod whether he sees the casting director union as an alliance with a union that is already in existence. His calculatedly brief answer was, "Yes, I do."

His Opinion on Casting Director Workshops

"I think that the California labor board has made an egregious error. As far as I know, from reading their letter, the coverage in *Variety* and *Back Stage West*, and talking with lawyers that represent some of the casting director workshops, the labor board has only been talking with one casting director who has one opinion and one point of view. They've never bothered to or have not responded to other casting directors who have a different point of view and have a better standing in this industry. I think to make a judgment call like that without at least contacting the only governing body, which is the CSA, is negligent."

What next? "I welcome them to contact me to get a different point of view and a point of view of a body that has a greater standing in the casting industry. The casting director leading this movement is a CSA member and we appreciate his passion, but he had not done this in any official capacity with the CSA," Zuckerbrod disclosed. On whether paid casting director cold reading workshops should be investigated, Zuckerbrod commented, "It absolutely needs to be looked at but CSA is not the place this will be examined. The CSA encourages its members to participate in only those showcases that members feel are legitimate and to discourage casting directors and their employees from participating in ones that aren't up to par. Many casting directors feel that these are valuable venues for actors to learn about their craft. I don't know any casting director who looks as this as a way to get payment for an audition. I will guarantee you that none of the casting directors in the CSA feel that way. Many of these showcases are very legitimate and give an actor experience and exposure that they normally would not get. And I don't mean exposure to casting directors; I mean exposure to a process. They are legitimate businesses and they should not have been shut down in this manner, not without very serious consideration and a great exploration. I'm shocked that they would handle this in such a poor manner. This is not the way to effect change," Zuckerbrod concluded.

Best Way To Get Seen by Him

Through an agent or manager. "I attend a lot of theatre back east. I attend some here, but I go back to New York five to seven times a year." Zuckerbrod generally does not open unsolicited submissions. "When you're working freelance, it's almost impossible. I have three weeks to cast a pilot with seven series regulars. There's no way to open envelopes. I have no luxury of time. So, I have to rely on the relationships I have with agents and managers."

His Opinion on Alternative Submission Methods

"It would be great, if an actor is with an agent and this agent says that an actor's demo reel is online. I can easily access it and would gladly do so," he said.

Trends He Has Observed in the Casting Process

"Fortunately, there is a major emphasis on diversity, which is wonderful to see. Something happened to me last year where I brought an actor in who was black for a role that wasn't written black. There was something about the essence of that actor that I knew worked for the part. The producers said, 'Gee, he was really good.' I said, 'Yeah, so what's the problem?' They said, 'Well, we never saw it that way.' We ended up hiring him because he was right for the job. I'm hoping that that will continue and that we'll start reflecting population of the United States in what we're seeing on television," Zuckerbrod explained.

A further trend Zuckerbrod noted was one of youth-before-experience. "There was this period during the early '90s, when there was such an emphasis on young actors that many were unpolished or untrained. While they might have been very talented, they really didn't have a craft. I think that's really changed. I'm so impressed with the level of young actors. And I'm also so impressed that producers want quality and not just youth."

What He Would Change About the Casting Process

"In essence, a lot of it works very well. If there's one thing that really needs to be changed in the process of casting is this concept of everybody casting a pilot at the same time," Zuckerbrod opined. Does mid-season work and non-network programming even out the timing throughout the year? "Cable tends to cast at the same time as the networks! There's just more people casting all at once. It really does no one a service. I don't know what the fix is, but somebody should look at how to fix this," Zuckerbrod admitted.

Most Gratifying Part of His Job

"The most part of any casting director's job is when we can fulfill the vision of a director, a writer, a producer, a studio, a network—all those people—and still feel that our vision is there."

THERE IS NO OSCAR FOR BEST CASTING

I can only imagine the level of frustration felt by professionals who have populated the worlds for Oscar-nominated and Oscar Award-winning films again and again only to be *not* thanked during the acceptance speech, *not* mentioned in interviews, sometimes even *not* invited to wrap parties. I only write about casting directors and I find myself increasingly dissatisfied with the Academy of Motion Picture Arts and Science's official word on the topic (that word, by the way, is "NO"). I recently spoke with a few long-time lobbyists of the Best Casting Oscar about their attempts to persuade the Academy, their thoughts on the likelihood of a Best Casting Oscar in the future, and how they continue to stay gratified by a job that is often forgotten.

"I have been fighting this battle for over 20 years," said Mike Fenton, former president of the CSA and one of the casting directors on the front line of the battle to win AMPAS recognition. "They have no interest in creating one and they don't have a valid argument. The one they use, though, is that casting is a collaborative effort about which the director makes the final decision."

"We agree that the director makes the final decision on casting," said Jane Jenkins, who, along with partner Janet

Hirshenson, has cast *Harry Potter and the Sorcerer's Stone*, along with most of Ron Howard's features, including the Oscar-winning *A Beautiful Mind.* "The director also makes the final decision on costumes and on makeup and on shots. It *is* a collaborative medium and that goes for all areas of filmmaking. The Academy feels there is no clear delineation for a casting award, but what we do is contribute to the fabric film. We embroider that fabric so that we don't end up with kettle cloth. We bring in the 100 people that Mel Gibson has to speak to over the course of the film. That's what we cast!"

Debra Zane, who cast multiple award-winning *Traffic*, explained, "I think people are not really aware of what casting directors *do*. They'll assume the star was the producer's idea. When we have something with a very big cast, I'll be asked, 'Who did you cast?' I'll say, 'Uh... all of them.' They think directors cast films. We provide a list of actors that the director may not even know exist. We've created that list with specific intentions. Yes, sometimes there are stars attached to the project before it gets to me, but that may be just one role of hundreds."

In December 2000 former casting director David Rubin and Mike Fenton together presented their case for a new category to the membership group of AMPAS. "The jaws of the people in the room dropped. It was an amazing presentation. David is one of the brightest people in this business and this presentation was perfect," Fenton recalled. "Three days later, there was a blurb in *Variety* that we'd been turned down. They hadn't even let *us* know! That's how we found out we'd been turned down. I called [the Academy] and wasn't put through. I got a letter by messenger the next day. The letter said that we had perhaps the most intelligent approach to the situation they'd ever been exposed to, however, they have no interest in ever giving an Academy Award to the casting directors. Ever."

Zane recalls, "I've gotten phone calls from the costume designers on films saying, 'Thanks. This cast is so great on-set.' The crew will call and thank me. I have to accept those calls as my recognition," she said.

"If I hear, 'You should [have gotten] an Academy Award for *A Beautiful Mind*,' one more time, I may scream," Jenkins joked. "People are actively involved in ignoring the contribution a casting director makes to a picture. We've signed petitions; we've started letter-writing campaigns. When directors we've worked with write the Academy, we're told, 'Of course they would write something on your behalf. They're the people you've worked with.' What a slap in the face!"

Jenkins recalled the letter director John Schlesinger wrote on behalf of Marion Dougherty about casting Jon Voight in *Midnight Cowboy*. "It's a well-known fact that her insistence is what made his career," Jenkins said. Some actors will acknowledge the contribution of the casting director, such as Kevin Spacey's mention of Debra Zane in his *American Beauty* acceptance speech. "He got gold stars for that," Jenkins said.

One way the Casting Society of America attempts to combat the lack of praise casting directors receive for their efforts is with the creation of the Artios award.

"Artios" is a Greek word meaning "perfectly fitted." The Casting Society of America has held its Artios Awards each year since 1985, under the direction of co-chairs Jane Jenkins and Alice Cassidy. "The fact that it has become such a big event and so successful is really personally satisfying for me," Jenkins said. "I'm just happy that we pull it off every year."

At 2000's Artios Awards, mistress of ceremonies Mo Gaffney said, "I love casting directors. They are the ones who get the Breakdown that says, 'beautiful 20-year-old woman,' and decide, 'Okay, she's a neurologist. The has to at *least* be 25.'" Gaffney continued to joke about the job that is casting, saying, "It all resembles that 'pick me, pick me,' feeling from the playground as a child."

Another actor present at that night's awards was William Petersen, whose hit show *CSI* was proving its merit with critics and fans alike. "Ironic, isn't it? I'm here in a room full of people who could hire me for their next projects and Les Moonves has made me completely unavailable," Petersen said, prior to introducing Moonves to the crowd. "You folks, no matter what my agents tell me, are the reason my colleagues and I get jobs. For your difficult and insightful work on our behalf, I thank you."

President of CBS Moonves took the stage next, joking, "I can't believe, as a former actor, I'm standing in front of 400 casting directors and I don't have a monologue prepared. For all of you who did not hire me, I want to thank you for guiding me in a different direction with my creative juices." His take on the craft of casting? "Marriage of the written word to the right actor is what casting is. This group doesn't get nearly enough recognition or credit for the creation of successful programs, films, and plays. For every big deal that's closed—or little one—I guarantee you there was a casting director talking to the agent, lunching with the manager, and researching previous work to gain a greater understanding of what material would be suitable. Please keep up the good work, casting directors. It is your tireless effort, your distinctive casting choices, and your passion that help make this the greatest business in the world."

To the casting director, the task of casting is one of balance, requiring an eye for talent, an understanding of the material, an ability to negotiate, and a passion for seeing a character description as more than just words on a page. "It's really exciting to be acknowledged for your contribution. We participate in fighting for people who go on to be enormously successful," Jenkins explained.

"I long ago gave up the feeling that every actor I gave a shot to owed me anything. I know what I did. Actors go from being names on a list to being millionaires. It's nice to watch that process," Jenkins admitted. "Look, audiences don't go to see a film that's been cast by me. That's not the hook that brings them in. I know that."

In Zane's opinion, it is the director that must shine a light on the importance of the role of the casting director. "SAG even awards Best Ensemble Cast," she noted. "It's embarrassing that casting directors aren't credited for that. People don't know that it'll be between two actors and the director and I will talk forever about why it should be this actor and not that one. The adjectives I have to come up with in order to describe each actor, no one knows what that's like!" Zane added, "And they can't know. It's absolutely classified, what goes on in those conversations, and it has to be that way."

Fenton admitted that there is no chance he will be the recipient of some future Best Casting Oscar. "All of my best work is behind me," said the man who cast *ET*, *Raiders of the Lost Ark*, *Norma Rae*, and *Chinatown*. "They don't hire casting directors over 45 years old to cast big projects. I'll never get an Oscar. But to think that the Academy won't even say, 'Hey, for your *body* of work, *thank you*,' that is truly insulting. I've even said to the Academy, 'We'll take an award on the steps of UCLA's Royce Hall at midnight!' We don't need to be in their telecast. We just want the recognition. And if the casting directors of motion pictures stayed home from work for *one week*, the Academy *might* realize their contribution to the process."

When recently pressed for an answer to the question, "Why is there no Best Casting Oscar?" the AMPAS refused to comment. "I don't know that it's going to happen in the lifetime of my career," Jenkins said.

She noted, however, that her job is part of "a collaborative embarrassment of riches," adding, "When we recently did a cast read-thru, the writer came to me and said, 'Thank you for the good people.' I responded, 'Thank you for the good words.'" Let's hope the Academy learns the value of the casting director's contribution so that verbal praise isn't the only reward these collaborators receive.

HOW TO BECOME A CASTING DIRECTOR

I asked a few casting directors to explain the process of becoming a casting director. Well, there is no one way in, but I made sure to get plenty of advice from theatre, film, television, and commercial casting directors, in an attempt to round out the range of experiences they had, in becoming casting directors.

Participating Casting Directors

Julie Ashton, films, television
Judy Belshé, commercials, films
Terry Berland, CCDA, commercials
Billy DaMota, CSA, commercials, films, television
Sarah Halley Finn, CSA, films
Dean Fronk, CSA, films
Jeff Gerrard, CCDA, commercials
Jan Glazer, CSA, films
Peter Golden, CSA, Senior VP of Talent & Casting, CBS Entertainment
Elisa Goodman, CSA, films, MOWs, television, former actor
Randi Hiller, CSA, films
Stuart Howard, CSA theatre
Gary Marsh, Breakdown Services

Mark Paladini, CSA, films, television
Linda Phillips-Palo, CSA, films, MOWs
Cathy Reinking, films, television
Marnie Saitta, CBS Television, former actor
Brien Scott, films, former actor
Stephen Snyder, films, MOWs, music videos, commercials
Mark Teschner, CSA, ABC Television, former actor

Getting Started

The best route in, though not necessarily the only route in, is through an internship. The time spent as an intern is valuable and exhausting, according to most casting directors. Belshé earned $30 in her first year as an intern. "There is no better training you can get," she insisted.

"The hardest part is getting that first job as an assistant," Glazer admitted.

A former actor, Goodman recalled observing other actors in her classes. "I remember thinking, 'This one will never work,' and 'This one is interesting.'" Goodman started auditioning for Equity Waiver plays in Los Angeles and felt frustration over the lack of organization during the audition process. "I wrote a letter to [several theatres] and offered my services as a casting director. They jumped at the opportunity," she explained.

Several casting directors likened the experience of interning in a casting office as going to casting college. "They don't teach this in schools," Finn exclaimed. She continued to explain the importance of the internship period. "People would look at that time and think, 'Oh, I'm not getting paid.' Well, you're also not paying to get a Master's Degree in what you want to do. Maybe someday there will be a course in how to become a casting director and they'll cover how to do a commercial, how to handle pilot season, how to cast a film, how to release a breakdown, how to run a session, how to negotiate a deal. But, until then, the way to learn is to get a job as an intern. There is so much to learn just listening to the process while sitting on the floor going through pictures."

Interns and assistants generally answer phones, open and sort submissions, sign in actors at sessions, provide sides, answer questions, run cameras during sessions, and run errands. More than that, interns learn. "It really is graduate school," explained Reinking of the internship period. "I really wanted to do it. I gave up a high-paying job to do it. You know after one week if you're cut out for casting."

Snyder recalled, during his three months as an intern, opening envelopes at first, and eventually running the camera during sessions and working on deals. "It was a very quick rise through the ranks, which is really unusual," he said.

Saitta explained that an entry-level position in a casting office allows an aspiring casting director to get respect for the casting process. "When you deal with actors coming in, agents on the phone, and the day-to-day work, you learn very fast," she said.

"You learn first-hand how a specific office operates while you familiarize yourself with agencies, actors' names, different types of scripts, and—most importantly—how to deal with heavy phone and submission loads," explained Fronk of the intern position.

"When someone is looking for a job as a casting assistant, they should send their resumé to both CSA and Breakdown Services," said Paladini.

In fact, Marsh confirmed that Breakdown Services will gladly accept resumés from prospective casting assistants via e-mail in Microsoft Word format. "We put the resumé out there. It's not a fee service. We're just helping casting directors who need assistants as well as helping assistants who need casting directors to know they exist," Marsh explained.

Ashton recommended a more proactive approach. "You have to go for it. Call casting directors and ask, 'Can I take you to lunch?' It's a competitive field and you need to be able to aggressively pursue it," she said.

"Apply everywhere you would be proud to work. Devote as many hours per week as possible. Inevitably, the interns who spend 30-40 hours per week with us come out with the most knowledge," Howard explained.

Goodman recommended the internship program offered by the Television Academy. "They screen applicants about why they would want to [intern]."

"Find a casting director whose work you respect, send your resumé, and try to get in the door," Golden instructed. "The tricky part is finding a casting director who is generous enough to let you grow as you learn more. You need to spend time in sessions, talk with producers. A good mentor will know when this is appropriate."

"I think the time you spend as an assistant and an associate is incredibly important," said Hiller. "You need to have such a database of actors who you can rely on. That database takes a long time to assemble and then you still don't connect until you've met each actor and you know their work."

Required Skills

❖ promptness
❖ great attitude
❖ stamina
❖ willingness to serve
❖ commitment
❖ trainability
❖ calm demeanor
❖ ability to multitask
❖ tendency to be both left- and right-brained
❖ intuitiveness
❖ openness
❖ good handwriting
❖ passion for sessions
❖ willingness to work long hours (12 or more a day)
❖ willingness to attend theatre and screenings after work
❖ excellent memory

- ❖ patience for the grunt work
- ❖ ability to handle very heavy phones
- ❖ confidence
- ❖ good sense of humor
- ❖ organizational skills
- ❖ great taste
- ❖ negotiating skills
- ❖ ability to leave your ego at the door
- ❖ love for reading stacks of scripts
- ❖ people skills
- ❖ ability to think clearly in chaotic situations
- ❖ motivation
- ❖ ability to develop relationships in the industry
- ❖ enthusiasm
- ❖ vision
- ❖ creativity
- ❖ love for actors
- ❖ great eyes and ears for what is going on
- ❖ respect for the process
- ❖ team spirit
- ❖ strong opinions
- ❖ love for coffee ("Coffee is the only constant," said DaMota.)

Moving Up

The title of Associate Casting Director is one that comes with more experience and responsibility than an assistant has, but without the full responsibility of the project's main casting director. "Some people give away that credit pretty freely," explained Hiller. "I never got it very freely. When I was an associate, I was negotiating deals and holding sessions with the director on my own."

Associates sometimes work on their own projects under the supervision of the casting director, according to Goodman. "They may make baby deals (Scale + 10%), preread actors, make lists, check quotes, speak with producers and directors, sit in on the sessions, read with actors, and scout for specific roles (especially children)," she detailed.

Reinking's training as a theatre director aided her rise to associate. "It took me a couple of years. You need to find somebody who is willing to give you a big break. It's so great to have someone who believes in you." Reinking continues to cast USC thesis projects while on hiatus. "November to April, we're really busy. Otherwise, I'm out of a job. If you work in television, you have to have something else going on."

There is a long apprenticeship period to becoming a casting director, according to Teschner. "You have to learn good acting. You have to develop the ability to look at a script and conceptualize who could play what role. It's a synthesis of talents," he said.

"My apprenticeship never really ended," said DaMota. "Even after I was promoted, I continued to soak up the casting process like a sponge."

"Do a good job, make sure your employer is aware that you are doing a good job, and make sure your employer knows you wish to go further in this field," listed Howard.

"The industry moves fast. An assistant can move on to bigger and better things all the time. If you are a level-headed individual who knows films, TV, and theatre, a busy casting office will grab you," explained Fronk.

Berland described elements specific to becoming a commercial casting director. "You have to learn all the elements—choosing talent, setting up sessions, protecting a client from fines and overages beyond their budget. You are only as good as your last job, and you have to come up with fresh new ideas for your clients," she said.

According to Golden, a future casting director moves up through the ranks by seeing everything. "Watch one episode of every show, attend as much theatre as you can—Broadway, London, waiver theatre in Los Angeles, see every movie. You must get to know actors and their work," Golden insisted.

Belshé described the most "honorable way" to move up: "don't take the connections of the person that took a chance on you and trained you."

"A good casting director has a well-defined personal list of favorite actors and their credits and abilities. Your list becomes vital to you as a casting individual," said Phillips-Palo.

Saitta suggested taking an acting class. "Casting directors should study acting, get up in front of people, know what it is that actors are going through. It helps casting directors to be in tune with what the actors need to do and helps us speak their language," she explained.

Being a Casting Director

An average day at the beginning of a feature film, according to Goodman entails phone calls, prereads, opening mail, putting actors on tape, setting up sessions. "During downtime it would be cleaning, throwing out old headshots, date-stamping headshots to save, alphabetizing headshots so that we can find them in a hurry," she listed.

Pay, of course, is a touchy subject. The rate of pay for casting directors is not standardized, but I did the best I could to get an idea of a range of pay for the profession. Assistants earn $400-$650 per week. Associates earn $700-$1000 per week depending on how much responsibility they have. Casting directors earn anywhere from $2500-$80,000 to cast a feature film (and pay rate is sometimes calculated as a percentage of the budget for hiring actors). Theatre casting directors receive a fee to cast the play and a weekly salary for the run of the show (in case there are additional casting needs). Commercial casting directors earn $500-$1000 per day of casting. No one I spoke with in television casting would go on record with a salary amount.

When I asked casting directors about CSA, the Casting Society of America, I was met with vastly different opinions on the benefits and importance of membership. "On my card, it says CDWTA [Casting Director, Writer, Teacher, Actress]. I was a casting director before there was a CSA. I provide myself freedom and my own medical insurance [CSA provides no medical insurance or pension plan for its members] and it's two more initials than the CSA," quipped Belshé

"Besides the free Academy Players Directory and the terrific staff, CSA provides casting directors the opportunity to make a difference for the community of casting directors," explained Paladini.

Teschner added, "CSA is moving toward unionization. Meanwhile, it's a supportive body. It's nice to encourage what it is to be a casting director."

Gerrard, as president of the Commercial Casting Directors Association, wants to see a move toward unionization as well. "CCDA membership is open to all commercial casting directors with a minimum of two years casting for their own company with 80% of their income coming through commercial casting," he detailed. CSA membership also requires two years' experience, plus letters of recommendation and sole screen credit.

"We have no benefits whatsoever," explained Howard. "Unless you work for an employer who pays your insurance, who offers a profit sharing or a retirement plan, you're on your own."

Casting is NOT for you if...

❖ you don't like people.
❖ you don't like redoing things.
❖ you expect a regular paycheck.
❖ you mind being unemployed.
❖ you hope to hang out with celebrities.
❖ you are an actor with even 1% desire to remain an actor.
❖ you are not willing to pay your dues.
❖ you are on a power trip.
❖ you don't watch TV, see movies, or attend theatre.
❖ you desire the spotlight.
❖ you have a tendency to bite off more than you can chew.

❖ you expect weekends off.
❖ you believe you'll have a better chance at getting roles as an actor.
❖ you second-guess your choices.

The Rewards of Casting

As a former actor, Snyder summed up the joy of casting in terms of the actor's experience. "Instead of doing one individual role per project as a performer who creates and explores the role, a casting director gets to help breathe life into 12-50 characters per project," he mused.

"Casting has everything to do with meeting and knowing and accepting people. It's all about communication," said Scott.

"I have a sample reel just like an actor has a demo reel," revealed Gerrard. "We go out there the same exact way an actor goes out there. And when things are slow, there is always paperwork to file with the guild and the ad agencies. And with independent films, the job continues months after it's in the can sometimes."

"Remember, if you're doing your job well, someone else will shine. It can't be all about you," Golden said.

"What's so wonderful about casting," began Finn, "is that it combines so many elements of our industry: acting, directing, budgeting, negotiating, managing, all the business parts of it."

"The rewards are emotional," insisted Teschner. "The reason we all do this is because we enjoy the feeling that we found someone that the world now enjoys in the role."

A NOTE ABOUT CASTING DIRECTOR WORKSHOPS

When I was a non-union, unrepresented actor, I knew the only way I would get seen by certain casting directors was to do a one-night workshop with them. Was it an effective use of my resources as an actor? Hard to tell. So much of the work you do as an actor is building on relationships in the long-term that it is almost impossible to draw direct correlations between events and outcomes.

I looked at it this way: I'm going to spend a certain amount of money on being an actor each month. Sometimes, that money went toward new headshots. Sometimes, toward improv workshops. Sometimes it went toward membership fees for theatre companies. Sometimes postage. Sometimes getting my reel edited. And sometimes toward workshops. I could never say that *one* of those elements was more valuable than another, because it all made up the total cost of being an actor.

Now, did I learn anything from the workshops I attended? Sure. Sometimes I learned a lot. Sometimes I learned next-to-nothing. But learning isn't really what a one-night workshop is about. Don't get me wrong. Some casting directors are amazing instructors. I have learned quite a bit from some casting directors in ongoing workshop environments.

There are some casting directors I have interviewed whom I would love to see teaching a class. They have so much to share with the working actors in Los Angeles and New York. But, in the current environment, they won't tread the workshop path (and I can't say that I blame them). There are also many casting directors I have interviewed who feel very strongly that an actor should not pay to be seen, ever. They, in fact, will not see people who have paid to meet their own associates, despite the fact that their associates claim, during the workshops, that they have the power to bring actors in. And then, I have interviewed casting directors who see workshops as a great opportunity to see 20-30 actors at one pop, without the phones ringing or any distractions, and they say they readily bring actors in from their workshop files.

Doing casting director workshops is really a personal choice. Get informed and then make your choice. Good luck, whatever you decide!

ABOUT THE AUTHOR

Bonnie Gillespie, originally from Atlanta, Georgia, holds a Master's degree in Journalism from the University of Georgia. Her thesis, *Broadcasting in the Elementary Schools*, is an ethnographic study of live television news broadcasts developed and produced entirely by students. Bonnie has worked as Instructional Technology Coordinator for Athens Academy and developed extensive staff enrichment courses in the integration of media and technology in education. As Graduate Advisor to WUOG, 90.5fm, Bonnie was named College Radio Advisor of the Year, 1997, by the National Association of College Broadcasters.

Bonnie's pursuit of acting brought her to Los Angeles, where she soon began working as a freelance writer for several publications. Recent freelance clients include the Sundance Institute, Roxbury Publishing Company, Hey Anita, Reel Noir and several online publications, including ExtraPadding.com, the home of her humor column, *Don't Get Me Started*. Bonnie has retired from acting, preferring instead to write and teach about the craft of casting and the business of acting. She works as a personal consultant to actors and is a frequent guest speaker at several acting studios in Los Angeles.

Her column, *Casting Qs*, appears weekly in *Back Stage West* and she dispenses advice at ActorsBone.com, ActorPoint.com, and BackStage.com's Career Chat. Bonnie lives in the Hollywood Hills with her fiancé and two cats.

INDEX OF NAMES

Why have I included such a comprehensive index of names? Well, for one thing, an actor needs to know names. It's part of the business of acting. Also, I thought you might find it interesting to track which casting directors have worked together, which named certain people as mentors, and which told great stories about actors they have cast. Perhaps you'll remember a story, but not who said it. Well, look here for the name you recall, and then you can find the story again. Let the tales inspire you!

ONLINE RESOURCES

http://corona.bc.ca/films/MainFramed.html
 Film information, news and gossip
http://flickeringimage.com
 Film, TV, radio, graphic, web design, and film editing
http://forums.delphiforums.com/proactors
 Free professional actors resource discussion forum
http://hometown.aol.com/lapaladini/
 Casting director Mark Paladini
http://ibdb.com
 Internet Broadway Database
http://idotvads.com
 Free discussion forum for commercial actors
http://paaw.com
 Performing Arts and Artists Worldwide directory
http://us.imdb.com/
 Internet Movie Database
http://www.acadpd.org/
 Academy Players Directory
http://www.actingworldbooks.org
 Excellent resource for agency guides
http://www.actorpoint.com
 Resources and forums for actors
http://www.actorsbone.com/
 Free actor discussion forums courtesy of Paul Molinaro
http://www.actorsequity.org
 AEA

http://www.actorservices.com
    Services for actors
http://www.actorsfund.org
    The Actors' Fund of America
http://www.aftra.org/
    AFTRA
http://www.agentassociation.com/
    Association of Talent Agents
http://www.americantheaterweb.com
    Nationwide theatre locator
http://www.askplay.org/
    ASK Theatre Projects
http://www.backstage.com/
    Back Stage and Back Stage West
http://www.breakdownservices.com/
    Breakdown Services
http://www.breakdownservices.com/access/awindex.htm
    Actor Access Breakdowns
http://www.cafeshops.com
    Put your mug on a mug!
http://www.canadianactor.com
    Canadian Actor Online
http://www.cashmancommercials.com
    Jingle singer booker Marc Cashman
http://www.castboy.com
    Casting director Billy DaMota
http://www.castingsociety.com/
    Casting Society of America
http://www.chezjim.com/writing/monologues.html
    Original monologues
http://www.cmeg.com
    Casting director Marki Costello
http://www.dailycelebrations.com
    Inspirational quotes
http://www.donotpay.org
    Do Not Pay (for casting director auditions)

http://www.eidc.com
    Where things are filming in Los Angeles
http://www.erinfiedler.com
    Photographer Erin Fiedler
http://www.filmcamp.com
    Digital Media Education Center
http://www.grooveaddicts.com
    Jingle singer booker Dain Blair
http://www.holdonlog.com
    Excellent organizational system for actors
http://www.hollywoodreporter.com/
    The Hollywood Reporter
http://www.kalmenson.com
    Casting directors Cathy and Harvey Kalmenson
http://www.katywallin.com
    Casting director Katy Wallin
http://www.laawc.com
    Los Angeles Actors Workshop Coalition
http://www.laweekly.com/
    LA Weekly includes theatre reviews
http://www.learningannex.com
    Offers courses in entertainment studies
http://www.liencowancasting.com
    Casting directors Michael Lien and Dan Cowan
http://www.martincasting.com
    Casting director Melissa Martin
http://www.michaeldonovancasting.com/
    Casting director Michael Donovan
http://www.ohaver.net
    Casting director Jenny O'Haver
http://www.pfcast.com
    Casting directors Donald Paul Pemrick and Dean Fronk
http://www.photographychick.com
    Photographer Deborah Vancelette
http://www.reproductions.com
    Litho and photo print reproductions
http://www.quickviewbeseen.com
    See-thru headshot mailers

http://www.reviewplays.com/
Theatre reviews
http://www.sag.org/
SAG
http://www.samuelfrench.com/
Samuel French bookstore
http://www.showbizkid.com
Casting director Judy Belshé
http://www.showfax.com
Source for audition sides
http://www.soapcity.com
Soap opera fansites, interviews, and discussion forums
http://www.stageagent.com
Nationwide audition information
http://www.stuart411.com
Casting director Stuart Stone
http://www.take1filmbooks.com
Take One! bookstore
http://www.talentmanagers.org/
Talent Managers Association
http://www.terryberlandcasting.com
Casting director Terry Berland
http://www.thecastlist.com
Fee-based database of actors
http://www.uclaextension.org/
Department of Entertainment Studies
http://www.variety.com/
Daily Variety
http://www.watchreels.com
Library of demo reels
http://www.whorepresents.com
Find out who represents whom
http://www.wolfesden.net/
Free actor discussion board courtesy of Sterling Wolfe

FORTHCOMING TITLES FROM BONNIE GILLESPIE

Self-Management for Actors:
Getting Down to (Show) Business

Summer 2003

Casting Calendar: An Actor's
Datebook and Action Log

Pilot Season 2004

Casting Qs Order Form

Online orders: visit http://cricketfeet.com/castingqs.

Postal orders: send this form with check or money order to

Cricket Feet Publishing
P.O. Box 1417
Hollywood, CA 90028

Please do not send cash.

We will send a copy of *Casting Qs: A Collection of Casting Director Interviews* as follows:
Name: _____
Address: _____
City: _____ State: _____ Zip: _____
Telephone: _____
Email Address: _____

Price: $21.95 per copy. Please call 323.871.1331 to arrange for bulk discounts to bookstores and educational facilities.

Sales tax: please add 8.25% tax for products shipped to California addresses.

Shipping: United States: $3 for first book, $2 for each additional book; International: $10 for first book, $4 for each additional book.

Payment (in U.S. dollars):
    Check   Money Order   (circle one)

Total Enclosed: _____

❑   Check here if you would like to be added to our mailing list for notification of future publications, speaking engagements, and other promotional activities.